PENGUIN BUSI

GROUND SCORCH

Arun Kumar is a well-known economist and the country's leading authority on the black economy. He has written, studied and lectured extensively on this subject for nearly four decades. He was educated at Delhi University, Jawaharlal Nehru University (JNU) and Princeton University. He taught economics at JNU for three decades and retired in 2015. Kumar's focus areas include public finance, development economics, public policy and macroeconomics. His work has been published widely in these areas, both in the popular press and academic journals. He is currently the Malcolm Adiseshiah Chair Professor at the Institute of Social Sciences, New Delhi.

GROUND SCORCHING TAX

Arun Kumar

BUSINESS

An imprint of Penguin Random House

PENGUIN BUSINESS

USA | Canada | UK | Ireland | Australia
New Zealand | India | South Africa | China

Penguin Business is part of the Penguin Random House group of companies
whose addresses can be found at global.penguinrandomhouse.com

Published by Penguin Random House India Pvt. Ltd
4th Floor, Capital Tower 1, MG Road,
Gurugram 122 002, Haryana, India

Penguin
Random House
India

First published in Portfolio by Penguin Random House India 2019
Published in Penguin Business 2023

Copyright © Arun Kumar 2019

ISBN 9780670091102

Typeset in Minion Pro by Manipal Digital Systems, Manipal
Printed at Replika Press Pvt. Ltd, India

www.penguin.co.in

To my sister, Rashmi Ravindra, and brother-in-law,
Koka Ravindra, who have always been a great support

CONTENTS

ABBREVIATIONS

ADB	Asian Development Bank
ADR	Association for Democratic Reform
B2B	Business to Business
BEPS	Base Erosion and Profit Shifting
BOP	Balance of Payment
CACP	Commission for Agricultural Costs and Prices
CBEC	Central Board of Excise and Customs
CBIC	Central Board of Indirect Taxes and Customs
CCT	Commissioner of Commercial Taxes
CD	Compact Disk
CENVAT	Central VAT
CFC	Chloro-fluoro-carbon
CGST	Central GST
CMIE	Centre for Monitoring Indian Economy
CPI	Consumer Price Index
CVD	Countervailing Duty
DTAA	Double Taxation Avoidance Agreements
DTC	Direct Tax Code
DTT	Direct Tax Turnover
ED	Enforcement Directorate
EPFO	Employees Provident Fund Organization
FD	Fiscal Deficit
FDI	Foreign Direct Investment
FERA	Foreign Exchange Regulation Act
FII	Foreign Institutional Investment
FRBM	Fiscal Responsibility and Budget Management
GATT	General Agreement on Tariffs and Trade
GDP	Gross Domestic Product

GoI	Government of India
GSPs	GST Suvidha Providers
GST	Goods and Services Tax
GSTC	GST Council
GSTIN	GST Identification Number for Businesses
GSTN	GST Network
GSTR-1	GST Form 1 to be submitted by the 10th of the month
GSTR-2	GST Form 2 to be validated by the 15th of the month
GSTR-3	GST Form 3 to be submitted by the 20th of the month
IDS	Income Declaration Scheme
IEBR	Internal and Extra Budgetary Resources
IGST	Integrated GST
IMF	International Monetary Fund
ITC	Input Tax Credit
JD(U)	Janata Dal (United)
LTFP	Long Term Fiscal Policy
MANVAT	Manufacturing Value Added Tax
MCI	Medical Council of India
MGNREGS	Mahatma Gandhi National Rural Employment Guarantee Scheme
MNC	Multi National Corporation/Company
MODVAT	Modified Value Added Tax
MRP	Maximum Retail Price
MRTP	Monopolies and Restrictive Trade Practices
MSME	Micro Small and Medium Enterprises
NAA	National Anti-Profiteering Authority
NDA	National Democratic Alliance
NEP	New Economic Policies
NIC	National Informatic Centre
NOIDA	New Okhla Industrial Development Authority
NPA	Non-Performing Assets
PAN	Permanent Account Number
PIT	Personal Income Tax
R&D	Research and Development
RBI	Reserve Bank of India

RCM	Reverse Charge Mechanism
RD	Revenue Deficit
RJD	Rashtriya Janata Dal
RNR	Revenue Neutral Rate
RTI	Right to Information
SAD	Special Additional Duty of Customs
SAKSHAM	IT project called for computerization
SAL	Structural Adjustment Loan
SAP	Simplified Assessment Procedure
SEZ	Special Economic Zone
SGST	State GST
SIT	Special Investigation Team
SPV	Special Purpose Vehicle
TIE	Tax Information Exchange
TIN	Tax Information Number
TINA	There Is No Alternative
TRANSIN	15 digit Unique ID for Transporters
TRIMs	Trade Related Investment Measures
TRIPS	Trade Related Intellectual Property Rights
UGC	University Grants Commission
UN	United Nations
UPA II	United Progressive Alliance II
UTGST	Union Territory GST
VAT	Value Added Tax
WB	World Bank
WPI	Wholesale Price Index
WTO	World Trade Organization

PREFACE

Implementation of Goods and Services Tax (GST) is one of the most important economic policy initiatives. Its proponents and the government have called it a new 'freedom' and a 'win-win' for all. I have termed it as a disaster for the unorganized sectors of the economy and, therefore, for the economy. Good or bad, it has administered a big shock to the economy whose consequences need to be understood by the wider public.

I have been writing on the subject since 1986 when Modified Value Added Tax (MODVAT) was introduced. The concern has been that the marginalized sections of the people will suffer due to the complexity of this tax and that will have adverse consequences for society. I have been greatly influenced by Gandhi's talisman of 'last person first'—when in doubt, think of the last person in society and figure out whether that policy will benefit her/him?

I switched from a PhD in physics to a PhD in economics in Jawaharlal Nehru University (JNU) in 1977. In between I did rural development for a while and observed the marginalization of the poor. That motivated me to study economics

At that time, I had no idea that I would specialize in Public Finance and Black Economy. I was thinking of energy crisis, India's macroeconomy, problems of Indian agriculture and inequality in India. As I progressed with the dissertation work, it became increasingly clear that government plays a crucial role in a modern day society and slowly I strayed into Public Finance. My own experience of real estate and stock markets led me to the understanding that the black economy has a critical role in the Indian economy. It also linked up to Public Finance.

When I joined National Institute of Public Finance and Policy (NIPFP) in 1982 after submitting my PhD dissertation, the Institute had just started a project on the black economy for Central Board of Direct Taxes (CBDT). I was recruited for the project. That set me firmly on the path to study Public Finance and Black Economy. Two years later, when I joined JNU this is the special paper I started teaching.

My Public Finance course was very different from the way it is taught in Indian universities. The autonomy then available to academics in JNU enabled me to teach it so differently. The course provided a unified view of the Indian economy by bringing together various sub-disciplines of economics and incorporating the impact of various government policies on the economy. The black economy was introduced in an organic way as an aspect of policy failure.

I am grateful to Professor Alan Blair who taught us Electrodynamics at Princeton University, USA, for showing how a good course can be taught. He brought together various strands of physics in one course. I learnt the value of interconnecting the different aspects of a discipline to develop a wider view of that subject.

Teaching the course differently, helped me to develop a new perspective on Public Finance and I found myself being a contrarian. This along with the study of the black economy made me question the data and the analysis given by the government in its various documents—budgets, economic surveys and reports. Based on my unique perspective, I produced alternative budgets and wrote for the alternative economic surveys presenting an alternative perspective.

My views on taxation differed from the mainstream views. While the economy was becoming more and more dependent on indirect taxes I was arguing in the 1980s for shifting towards collecting more of direct taxes. When MODVAT was introduced in 1986, I wrote why it was not such a good move for the Indian economy. I argued that the Indian economy is not mature enough to be able to handle Value Added Tax (VAT).

So, before GST became a reality, I wrote in 2015 why it is not so desirable for India. In 2005, when VAT was introduced for sales tax,

I wrote why it was difficult to implement in India and that we need to go for a much simpler tax.

I had predicted what the pitfalls of GST would be and I presented my analysis at various seminars. Many analysts at that time argued that there was no data to prove things either way. I had to argue that one can make theoretical predictions, otherwise what use is theory.

After my article on GST came out in the popular press, the Parliamentary committee called me to make a presentation. However, as these committees go, one makes a short presentation and to which, it appears, most members pay little attention. Before one starts talking, the chair makes clear that only a few minutes are available to make the presentation. This is too short a time to explain the pitfalls of a very complex tax like GST. So, the points I made about the macroeconomic contradictions in the various claims for GST and its deleterious impact on the unorganized sectors seems to have been missed by the committee members.

In July 2017, after the GST had been operationalized, I was again invited to make a presentation before about twenty members of Parliament. This time the meeting lasted an hour and a half with ample time to explain. The members of Parliament (MPs) understood the arguments but it was too late to change anything. However, over time, I find that the arguments I have been making are widely accepted.

This says something about policy making in the country. Contrary views are marginalized while the mainstream views are bulldozed through by the vested interests. They are in constant touch with the powers that be, both officially and socially. It is such a pity that discussions on GST went on for more than a decade but the main points on its adverse impact on the Indian economy were missed. Various governments that pushed for it went on a propaganda mode, calling it a 'win-win' for all sections of the population.

So, why do governments not do what they should, especially for the marginalized sections? The ruling elite uses an ideology which helps camouflage their real intentions. Their control of the media helps spread their message. After all, politics is all about serving narrow interests and not the wider national interest. In fact, their narrower interest is presented as the national interest. This reinforces Gandhi's view in 'Hind Swaraj' that political parties serve narrow interests.

A year and a half after the launch of GST, now its adverse effects, as predicted by me since 2015, are visible. It is important to move towards an alternative tax system and it is necessary to debate this and implement it sooner than later. Hopefully this book would help in this direction.

This book is written differently than other available material on GST, written by chartered accountants and lawyers. They go into the details of the various acts and rulings and how they apply in different situations. They analyse the legal complexities and the possible interpretations but not the structural aspects which lead to the complexity. The macro and the structural aspects are taken as given. As practitioners, they only analyse how to deal with the ever changing rules as a practical matter for their clients. This book presents the macro and the structural aspects which result in the complexities and infirmities. Thus, the book argues that the problems resulting from GST are not implementation issues alone but largely structural ones.

The book is written so as to be accessible to not only the experts but also the informed readers. Except for one place where there are formulae, there is no mathematics anywhere. Since the technical terms occur again and again and the reader may not remember them, a glossary of abbreviations is given in the beginning and technical terms are explained in several places. Thus, there is deliberate repetition so that the reader can read the text continuously without searching for the terms where they occur first. The attempt is to make each chapter complete and readable.

Whether or not the book brings clarity to a complex subject, will be decided by the readers—the ultimate arbiter.

8 November 2018   Arun Kumar

THE GROUND SCORCHING
TAX: INTRODUCTION

On 1 July 2017, the Goods and Services Tax (GST) became a reality in India. It was hailed by the government and most analysts as the biggest tax reform of independent India. A special session of Parliament was organized by the government, similar to the session on 14 August 1947 when India gained independence on the midnight of that day.

The GST was heralded as a new freedom for the nation. It was argued that the political significance of the move was that the nation was to be unified by the creation of a single market. The slogan given was 'One Nation One Tax', implying that until the introduction of the GST, India had not been functioning as one market, and therefore could not have been functioning as one nation.

From the day of its inception, severe problems beset the implementation of GST. Actually, even before 1 July 2017 dawned, businesses were apprehensive of the move into uncertain territory. Big businesses which were better prepared to deal with the new situation than the small businesses were nonetheless uneasy because they learnt of the new GST rates very late—in May and June 2017. They were also concerned as to how the new tax would play itself out and what would happen to the old stocks of goods that would be carried forward beyond 1 July. In June, many businesses offered large discounts on big ticket items like consumer durables to unload stocks. The public took advantage and went on a buying spree, believing that prices would rise after 1 July. Many companies stopped production in June so that they could off-load their stocks.

Proponents of GST suggest that it is a win-win for everyone in the nation. What are the benefits of GST? By bringing goods and services and all the indirect taxes on one platform there is supposed to be simplification for businesses, reduced paperwork and bureaucratic hassles and ensuing 'ease of doing business' which would improve efficiency. It is supposed to be good for the consumers since it is said that prices will decline. It is expected to benefit the government since it would lead to an increase in tax collection and would check the black economy. In effect, it is billed as the biggest tax reform in India and a game changer which could lead to an increase in GDP growth by 1–2 per cent.[1]

However, I had pointed out[2] in 2015 that these statements taken together were contradictory. It was pointed out that small businesses would not be able to cope with the new tax and would suffer a decline. Thus, even if the output of big businesses rose, overall, there would be a fall in output. Further, because GST is an indirect tax, if more tax is collected, it will lead to an increase in prices. If one single tax rate is implemented on all goods, the prices of basics would go up and that would feed into all other prices. Thus, if more tax is collected, prices would rise and output would fall rather than rise. The argument that the black economy would be checked by the introduction of GST was also discounted.

The post July 2017 developments bear out these criticisms of GST. Prices have risen, the economy slowed down, GST collection has not risen as expected and evasion of taxes continues; quite the opposite of what the proponents had suggested. Why this has happened needs to be understood. Are these problems transitional and will they disappear over time or are these inherent structural problems of the GST which are further exacerbated by India's complexity as a nation? To understand all this, one needs to take a wider view of GST. It is necessary to understand taxation, the role of government and of public finance, the nature of the black economy and the diversity of India. This book discusses these issues to help build a holistic understanding of GST.

---

[1]   NCAER (2009)
[2]   Kumar (2015)

Why Taxes—Understanding Government's Economic Role

Proponents suggest that GST would benefit everyone in the nation, hence desirable. What are the main features of GST? Also, why is a tax necessary? Is a tax beneficial to the public at large even if some feel it is a burden?

GST: Six Important Elements:

The GST is an indirect tax and has the following important features:

a. Combining together of indirect taxes like excise duty, sales tax and service tax. Seventeen taxes have been replaced by one[3] and this is to lead to ease of business.

b. GST will be calculated on 'value addition' and not the 'value of the good or service'. 'Value addition' is the value added to the raw materials and other things purchased by the producer. 'Value' refers to the price at which the item is sold, that is, the value added plus the cost of purchased inputs. This change in the way the tax is levied removes the 'cascading effect' of tax on tax and profit on tax and thereby lowers the tax burden on goods and services. When the tax is on the value of the good, the tax paid on the inputs purchased is again taxed and this is the 'cascading effect'.

c. Not only would the cascading effect of each of the taxes (excise, sales, services and so on) be removed but even that across these taxes would go. This would lower the effective tax rate leading to a fall in prices, if all else remains the same, and, to ease of doing business which could boost the rate of growth of the economy.

d. It is argued that greater tax collection may follow if the black economy is curtailed.

e. It is supposed to lead to economies of scale. Supply chains would be simplified and warehouses relocated resulting in efficiency for large scale suppliers.

---

[3] See Annexure 1.1

f.   Transportation would be easier because of elimination of tolls and introduction of the e-way bills. Movements of all goods would be tracked automatically.

Theoretically, the above elements refer to two important theoretical considerations. First, all indirect taxes have been brought together on one platform from the earlier separate ones so that there would be less paper work and fewer complications. GST is levied on 'supply'. The tax is no more on the act of producing or sales, etc. Second, all indirect taxes will be calculated as Value Added Tax (VAT) with input tax credit[4] available from one level of supply to the next in the chain of production and distribution. Thus, the cascading effect of one tax on to the other is eliminated.

Earlier while each tax was calculated as VAT, the input credit was not available across different taxes. For instance, a manufacturer A producing an item was liable to pay an excise duty on it. The person B supplying the inputs had to pay both excise duty and sales tax. A could deduct the excise duty paid on the inputs by B out of the excise duty she was required to pay but she could not deduct the sales tax that was paid on the inputs by B. So, there was a cascading effect of excise duty on sales tax paid by B. Under GST, a set-off is available for any tax paid on any of the inputs since all taxes paid on them are under GST and accounted for by computerization.

Kinds of Taxes: Direct and Indirect

GST is an indirect tax. Why are such taxes required? How do they impact the economy and society?

Broadly speaking there are two kinds of taxes—direct and indirect. Both ultimately fall upon the income of the citizens but as

---

4   Input tax credit (also referred to as 'set-off') means the producer gets the benefit of the tax paid at the previous stages of production. So, if the tax liability of A is Rs 100 and she purchased inputs from B who had paid Rs 50 tax on them then A's tax liability becomes Rs 50.

the name suggests, direct taxes fall on the income, at the point of earning, while indirect taxes fall on incomes through consumption of goods and services as and when that happens. Direct taxes cannot be postponed while the indirect taxes can be, by not consuming.

Indirect taxes fall on everyone's consumption whether rich or poor—everyone comes into its net. Since the rich consume a small part of their income, they pay a smaller per cent of their income as indirect tax. The poor consume almost their entire income so they pay a tax on every item of consumption and end up paying a higher per cent of their income as taxes. That is what is meant by a tax being regressive—those who earn more pay a lower rate of tax than those who earn less. Direct taxes typically fall more on the well-off sections and therefore, are usually progressive. It is because of these characteristics of the direct and indirect taxes that it is preferable to have more of direct than indirect taxes. But, India has had the opposite with more of indirect taxes than the direct taxes.[5]

Among all the indirect taxes levied, customs duty plays a different role than the other indirect taxes. It provides protection to the internal production from the cheap goods that other countries try to sell in the domestic market of the country. While at times the goods from abroad may be cheap due to use of better technology and greater productivity of workers, it is often the case that foreign goods are kept cheap by the sellers, to undercut local production in India. Customs duty has various components which help in preventing this from taking place. Thus, customs duty is treated differently from other indirect taxes and it is not included in the scheme of GST.

Direct tax collection as a per cent of the GDP is low in India. It is one of the lowest in the world. Thus, to meet its expenditures without creating a deficit in the budget, the government has been increasing its collections of indirect taxes. They have been the most important sources of revenue for the government to perform its functions.

---

[5] See Kumar (2013)

Indirect taxes are calculated in three different ways. Each has its pluses and minuses. Associated with indirect taxes is something called 'cascading effect'—it refers to levy of one tax after another and their accumulation. So, if iron ore is used to make pig iron and that is used to make steel then the tax on iron ore is again taxed when tax is levied on pig iron and so on. This is called 'tax on tax'. There is also 'profit on tax'. This makes the effective rate of tax higher.

One of the three methods of calculation[6] is called Value Added Tax (VAT). It is the most difficult of taxes to implement but it does not suffer from the cascading effects. Thus, the effective rate of indirect taxes is lowered. This happens since the tax on the earlier stages of production is not taxed. But, if the cascading effect is removed, then less of tax would be collected by the government unless the rate of VAT is raised.

This brings one to the concept of 'Revenue Neutral Rate' (RNR) of tax. Namely, it is that rate of tax which allows the government to collect the same amount of tax that it collected earlier. This is a most complex calculation and can be done in two different ways with different results. First, one can go for overall revenue neutrality with one rate of tax on all goods and services so the total tax collected remains unchanged. Secondly, the same amount of tax should be collected from each commodity and each service as in the earlier situation. In the former case one overall tax rate would apply to all goods while in the latter case, there would be different tax rates on each of the goods and services. In the latter case, the situation becomes not only complex but the cascading effect reappears. It disappears only if there is one tax rate on all goods and services. Clearly the government has a tough choice to make.

It was shown earlier[7] that with RNR rates of taxes, while the cascading effect is removed, the prices do not fall since the same

---

[6] In Chapter 1, it is explained that there are three methods of collection of indirect taxes—specific duty, ad valorem tax and Value Added Tax (VAT).

[7] Kumar (1986)

amount of indirect tax is collected. Further, it was shown[8] that there is an equivalence between the earlier tax regime and the VAT regime. Thus, it makes sense to shift from the earlier scheme of things to a more complicated VAT regime only if the government is willing to give up tax revenue and help reduce prices.

However, a crucial issue is whether businesses will pass on the benefit of lower taxes to the consumer or simply absorb it as an additional profit? To make businesses reduce prices, the government would have to be vigilant and use strict measures to ensure that this happens.

Expenditures and Revenues

Government needs revenue to finance its expenditures, hence the need for taxes. But are expenditures essential or can they be curtailed? Over time, in all countries, government expenditures have been rising since the governments have been required to perform a variety of tasks in modern day societies. This is a result of societies becoming more and more complex, recognition that some things are better done collectively and failure of the markets to deliver optimally.

The key task in a comparatively poor country like India has been promoting development to overcome deprivation. For a majority of the poor, market does not provide a solution whether it be in education, health, water, energy, rural development and so on. Further, the government has to provide for defence, money, public goods and so on. All this requires funds and good governance, which requires more finance.

Finance may be raised either via borrowing from those who save in the economy or from taxes or the returns on past investments by the government. Borrowings are not the government's own resources and it has to pay a return on them. So, it must try to earn a return on the money it borrows to meet the future obligations. If it does not

---

[8]   Kumar (2005a)

earn enough return to pay back the interest on the borrowing then it is in trouble since it would have to use the tax and non-tax resources to pay the interest and return the loan taken. If this continues for a while, it puts the finances of the government into a debt trap—namely, the borrowing and the interest to be paid on it keep on increasing from year to year. This squeezes the funds available for development and other essential tasks of the government.

The other two sources of revenue are its own resources and do not impose any future obligations of interest payment or repayment of capital. These funds can be used to finance administration and other current requirements of the government like subsidies and defence, which do not earn a return. After meeting these current requirements, if there is a surplus then that can be ploughed into development and government investments into building infrastructure required by the economy and the poor.

The gap between the government's expenditure and its own revenues is the deficit in the budget. This also plays an important role in the economy by boosting demand. If the economy is running well and capacity of industry is fully utilized then this will lead to inflation but if the economy has slacked, then this can help boost demand and lead to an improved functioning of the economy. Globally, in the period after 2007, such deficits helped economies weather the downturn due to the global financial crisis.

Expenditures, revenues and deficits are the issues studied together as 'Public Finance'. These impact all other aspects of the economy—both macro and micro. Thus, they are crucial to the understanding of the functioning of not only the economic role of the government but the way any modern day economy functions.[9]

Black Economy, Taxes and the Budget

All the elements of public finance are impacted by the black economy. Expenditures are higher than necessary since there is

---

[9]   Kumar (1988)

leakage of funds. For instance, in the case of road building, less tar and aggregate would be put than in the specifications. So, for a given expenditure, the country gets poorer quality roads. Further, since the quality is deficient, when the rains come the tarmac would get washed away and become potholed so that repairs would be required. Thus, additional expenditures are required and rather than building new roads, the funds are spent on maintenance. Potholed roads lead to more consumption of fuel and higher maintenance costs for vehicles which tend to breakdown more. All this results in waste of resources. As was famously said by a finance minister, 'expenditures do not lead to outcomes'.

Black economy implies that people do not reveal their true incomes and avoid paying the taxes due. This is true for both the direct and indirect taxes. Thus, the revenue collected is much less than what it could be. With the current estimate of black economy of 62 per cent of GDP,[10] at current rates of taxes, 40 per cent of this could have been collected as taxes. So, the budget could have had an additional 24 per cent of GDP as taxes while it collects only 16.5 per cent currently. Thus, there would be no shortage of resources for development.

The current fiscal deficit of 5 per cent of GDP would have become a surplus of 19 per cent of GDP. Thus, borrowing requirements of the government would become zero and the interest payment on borrowings would decline dramatically freeing tax resources for further expenditures on development. Indirect tax collection which is inflationary could be reduced to lower inflation. This would reduce the need for subsidy to the poor.

In brief, the black economy results in higher expenditures, lower revenues, higher deficits, higher borrowings, higher interest payments and lower levels of development. It is the biggest cause of policy failure in India resulting in the state's inability to achieve its goals in areas like education and health. The government gets discredited and there is demand for its retreat from the economy. So,

---

[10] Kumar (2016b)

tackling the black economy is crucial for accelerated development of the Indian economy.

It is argued that GST will help tackle the black economy by preventing double bookkeeping by businesses. It is also said that due to the massive computerization under GST, the human intervention would be reduced and that would also lower the opportunities for corruption. For a variety of reasons these best laid plans can fail and it remains to be seen how much of an impact GST would have on illegality that underlies the black income generation process.

Historical Evolution of GST and VAT in India

A justification for introducing GST in India has been that it is in operation in more than a hundred countries and it was first introduced in France in 1954. In other words, it is well known and understood. However, full GST has been in operation in six countries only. It is also said that wherever full GST has been introduced, there have been complications and prices have risen. This is not unexpected since GST is an indirect tax and they tend to be inflationary.

What is full or partial GST? It depends on the extent to which goods and services become a part of GST. If the entire set of goods and services are a part of the GST then it is a full GST otherwise it would be a partial GST. In a sense, a partial GST is only the introduction of VAT for calculation of the indirect taxes on some goods and services.

Reports on Indirect Tax Reform

India's experiment with the introduction of a 'GST like tax' began in the late 1970s. Jha Committee in 1978 suggested that Excise duty be levied as MANVAT.[11] But this could not be implemented

---

[11] GoI (1978)

due to various complications involved. LTFP in 1985[12] suggested MODVAT—which was introduced step by step as more commodities were brought under its purview. But research shows that tax collection was not robust.[13] CENVAT replaced it in 2002. For sales tax, VAT was introduced in the states and most of them came under it in 2005. Various earlier committees had suggested that this be done.

The Chelliah Committee suggested that service tax be introduced.[14] This was initiated in 1993 and slowly it expanded its base to include more and more services. The idea is that if goods are taxed when they are produced so should the services be taxed. This was also important because the services sector became the dominant sector after 1980 and its potential to yield taxes was high.

Thus, the country has had several indirect taxes. The difficulty faced was that the input credit was not available from one tax to the other so that there was a cascading effect. Also businesses had to deal with several agencies and that added to their paperwork. All this is sought to be taken care of under GST.

All the committees on indirect taxes mentioned above suggested a 'wider VAT' without calling it GST. In a meeting chaired by Atal Bihari Vajpayee in 1999, extension of VAT to sales tax was proposed. Action was taken to initiate the design of this tax. A Committee was set up under the chairpersonship of Ashim Dasgupta, then finance minister of West Bengal. This Committee was later asked to look into the implementation of GST.

So, the move towards GST was pursued by the NDA-I and then by the UPA-I. A GST Council consisting of the representatives of the states and the Centre was set up in 2016 to carry out the task of implementation of GST. The Thirteenth Finance Commission also set up a Committee[15] to look into the matter and later there was the

[12] GoI (1985)
[13] Singh (2006)
[14] GoI (1992)
[15] GoI (2009b)

Subramanian Committee[16] to decide on the rates of tax. So, work on the basic structure of GST started a long time ago.

A Constitutional amendment was carried out in 2016. There was much political wrangling over the GST and that delayed matters. All political parties played their part in delaying the implementation since they did not want the credit of introducing GST to go to the ruling dispensation. But none of them took up the real issues that are plaguing GST.

GST: The Larger Issues

Elements of GST

Prior to implementation of GST, there were many indirect taxes, like, excise tax, sales tax, service tax, Central sales tax, additional excise tax, Octroi, entertainment tax, cesses and so on. These are all absorbed in GST. So, in the pre GST regime, separate forms had to be filled up for each of the taxes and filed to different agencies. This multiplicity led to complications and additional costs. Now it is said that there is only one tax to deal with and less paper work to do. This is supposed to make for 'Ease of doing business' and, therefore, to increased efficiency.

GST is passed on to the final stage since the tax paid at the intermediate stages is given back as a credit. Thus, it is said that it is a 'destination' based tax. If the production and distribution chain goes through various states then the state where the final sale takes place collects the entire tax. States where the intermediate stages occurred will not get the tax that they got until now under the sales tax. India is very diverse with developed states (like Tamil Nadu and Maharashtra) that produce much more of the goods and services than the lesser developed states (like Bihar and Assam). The former are called the producing states and the latter the consuming states.

The producing states have been concerned that they would lose taxes to the consuming states. That is why there was opposition to

---

[16] GoI (2015b)

the implementation of GST from the former. The Centre assured compensation for any loss to bring these states on board. How this scheme works out remains to be seen.

However, if there is only one tax rate on all goods and services it could prove to be inflationary since all basic and essential goods would also get taxed and their prices would rise.[17] Hence the essentials were exempted and several tax rates kept under GST to distinguish between the luxury goods and the common items. This has complicated GST. Similarly the small and cottage sectors were given concessions and that has also added to the complications. Has all this made India's GST a half-way house?

Missing Macroeconomic Elements

It is argued in earlier articles[18] that all the fiscal policy (the ones on which government acts in a budget) variables work together via the national income identity. They together constitute the fiscal policy regime consisting of the indirect and direct taxes, subsidies, investments, interest payments and so on. In this framework, it was shown that with all other things being equal, if the indirect tax collections rise then there would be an increase in prices and a decline in the output in the economy, in other words, it is stagflationary. In contrast, the claim of the proponents of GST is that it would lead to higher collection of taxes, lower prices and higher level of output.

Macroeconomic analysis does not support such a claim. The proponents' argument is based on microeconomic analysis. They look at the three elements independently—namely, tax collection, prices and output. They believe that since all the goods and services will be under the net, more taxes would be collected. Independently, they believe that since input credit would be available, prices would fall. Finally, due to higher efficiency, output would rise. Each of these

---

[17] Kumar (2015)
[18] Kumar (1988) and Kumar (1999a)

results is based on not taking into account what happens to the other two variables, hence, incorrect.

Unorganized Sector and GST

There is a large unorganized sector in India which is made up of the micro and small scale units. It hardly ever keeps detailed accounts. That is why it is unable to calculate what is the value added in its production. Thus, it is not able to calculate how much VAT to pay. This was the difficulty due to which implementation of VAT could not be undertaken earlier and alternatives like MANVAT and MODVAT were considered. The idea that the entire production from the beginning to the end would come under VAT could not be implemented. Even now this difficulty persists.

The present scheme of GST accommodates this problem by exempting those with a turnover of less than Rs 20 lakh from registration under GST. Those with a turnover of between Rs 20 lakh and Rs 1.5 crore[19] are under a special dispensation called 'Composition Scheme'. They also are not required to do detailed accounting but they face severe limitations. They cannot do inter-state sales or get input credit or provide input credit to those who buy from them. In effect, they have been given concession but put at a disadvantage compared to the organized sector units that are registered and can provide input credit to those who purchase from them.

Due to these disadvantages, it is argued that the market for the unorganized sector units would shrink with GST. This would impact employment and demand in the economy. As output from the unorganized sector falls and is substituted by the organized sector raising its output, there would be less employment in the economy given that the organized sector employs far fewer people

---

[19] To begin with this limit was Rs 75 lakh. As difficulties for this segment mounted, the GST Council raised this limit to Rs 1 crore and then to Rs 1.5 crore. Earlier businesses under this scheme were required to file monthly returns but later this was changed to quarterly returns and the tax rate was fixed at 1 per cent.

for a given level of output than the unorganized sector does. A fall in employment would result in less demand in the economy, lower level of capacity utilization and less output as well as lower investment. Thus, at the macro level, GST is creating problems for growth, etc.

GST Design: Nuts and Bolts

Difficulties also arise at the micro level due to the implementation of a very complex tax. India is a highly differentiated country. A policy impacts the different segments differently. Some can cope with them but others cannot. So, GST has been ostensibly designed to take care of both the complexities of VAT and the difficulties likely to be encountered by the weaker sections. The design of GST needs to be understood to appreciate the complexities.

GST Has Three Components

GST is made up of three main components—a Central component (CGST), a states component (SGST) and an integrated tax (IGST) for inter-state movement. The rate of CGST and SGST is 50 per cent each of GST.

From one stage of production to the next, CGST paid in the previous stage of production is to be adjusted (input tax credit) against the CGST due at the current stage and similarly for SGST. CGST cannot be adjusted against SGST or the other way round. IGST is for inter-state movement of supplies. The Centre collects it, keeps 50 per cent of it and passes the rest to the state which is importing the supply. If the exporting state had collected any of the tax on that supply then it passes that also to the importing state. A rather complex arrangement.

Complex Tax Structure and Exempted Items

Some major items are exempt from GST. They are petroleum products, alcohol for human consumption, real estate and electricity.

The first two items are taxed heavily both by the states and the Centre. They did not wish to give up their hold on these taxes. This has complicated the tax structure and one can say that full GST has not been introduced in India as yet. While the government can bring petroleum products under GST when there is consensus on it, the case of alcohol is more complicated since it requires a constitutional amendment.

The other complication is that a large number of essential items are kept at zero rate of tax. The idea is that the items of common use by the poor should not be taxed otherwise they would be adversely impacted by GST. So, food items and many such items bear a zero rate of tax. This breaks the input tax credit chain and adds to the complications.

The finance minister made a distinction between items of common use and high end items, like luxury cars. He argued that they cannot be taxed at the same rate. The former had to be exempted or kept at a low rate of tax while the latter had to be taxed more heavily. Thus, GST has six different rates and a few special rates at present. This has complicated the GST structure and created problems in its implementation.

Further, one needs to take into account the fact that in the case of indirect taxes, the place where the tax is levied and where its impact is felt are different. So, the price of goods that pay no indirect tax also rises when basic and intermediate goods prices (like trucks and fuel) rise due to a higher tax on them. Thus, they also bear the burden of tax even though they are not taxed.

Impact of GST on the Economy

Since the implementation of GST, some trends in the economy have become apparent. While one can discount the teething troubles, the long term and structural problems cannot be ignored. These include

a. Impact on business activity and changes in the supply chain

b. Overall impact on economic activity taking the organized and the unorganized sectors both into account
c. Impact on prices and
d. Complexity of GST procedures.

Difficulties

Implementation has been a problem for businesses and the common people have had to face price increase. The obvious difficulties were not taken care of. Just like for demonetization, many changes were brought about in quick succession creating further confusion. For instance, it was too ambitious to think that every business would be equipped to file three returns every month and one annual return for supply to each state. In other words, thirty-seven returns are required for each state a company operates in. Further, the system of input credit and filing of returns had to be computerized and billions of entries every month are required to be coordinated/ matched. For this purpose, a GST Network (GSTN) has been set up but it has been running into problems.

It was suggested by analysts that implementation may be done in stages. But, the government argued that there is no option but to start and learn as one goes along. It was stated that GST was proposed in 2005 and its implementation should have started much earlier but due to lack of political consensus and objections by the states, it could not be implemented earlier. It was felt that enough thought and discussion had taken place and immediate implementation was needed.

As pointed out earlier, the unorganized sectors have faced difficulties due to the complexities in GST. It is supposed to benefit the large and medium scale producers and they have welcomed GST but it turns out that even they have found the implementation problematic. Difficulties have arisen because the implications of GST, as it was being designed, had not been thought through and problems in pricing, implementation of reverse charge and input credit were not anticipated.

The revenue neutral rate (RNR) turned out to be contentious and to get adequate revenue, it was pitched high which then proved to be inflationary. Thrice the GST Council has reduced rates on certain items. Some prices declined but on the whole prices rose. The e-way bill to keep track of movement of goods and check the black income generation turned out to be tricky and is unable to overcome the problem it was supposed to. Stoppage of trucks to check authenticity of the bill is still required. If checking is minimized it would lead to misclassification and if checking is routine, truck movement would slow down.

Fiscal Federalism Impacted

In the design, there was a harmonization of the tax rates for any good across all the states. That dents fiscal federalism. The power of the states to fix the tax rates has been given up, and this required a constitutional amendment, the 101st, was carried out in 2016. A GST Council was provided for under this amendment. It consists of all the finance ministers of the states and is headed by the Union finance minister. Its purpose is to take all policy decisions regarding functioning of GST. This council is a compromise and provides the fig leaf to argue that federalism is intact. The Empowered Committee set up to work out the design of GST was also to give a say to the states and sort out the differences among the states and with the Centre. The finance ministers of Opposition ruled states were appointed as the chair of this Committee.

The autonomy of the states and fiscal federalism are needed in a diverse country like India since different states have different needs. These can be fulfilled by raising and spending resources in different ways across different states. One size fits all is not good for the nation. GST runs counter to this requirement.

Fiscal federalism also implies autonomy to the third tier of India's federal structure, namely, the local bodies. They are entirely left out of the reckoning. This will have consequences for decentralization which is an important goal in a vast country like

India. It is supposed to bring about accountability of government and this could be a casualty. It would reinforce a top down approach which has been detrimental for India and is a reason for poor standard of civic amenities for the citizens.

GST, Black Income Generation and Digitization

In an earlier book on the black economy in India,[20] I had pointed out that black economy is the most important factor affecting Indian society. It impacts every aspect of the citizen's life. Its impact is political, social and economic. It sets back development of the country and aggravates poverty and inequality. It undermines policies of the government and leads to policy failure. This has undermined government intervention in the economy and led to the demand for the retreat of the state and dependence on the markets. It is also clear that the markets cannot cater to the needs of the poor since not only are they priced out but there is market failure in modern day economies. So, it is the poor who suffer the most due to the existence of a substantial black economy. Hence, there is an urgent need to tackle this menace which, like termites, hollows out the nation.

Various governments have taken steps to tackle the black economy in the last seventy years. Many committees and commissions have been set up to study the problem[21] and they have made many suggestions, of which hundreds have been implemented. In 2016, demonetization was announced with a big bang. It caused untold misery to the poor who never generated any black incomes while those generating black incomes and who had accumulated much black wealth went scot free; the problem did not get solved. The reason is that the underlying cause of the black economy's existence is not technical or economic but political.[22]

---

[20] Kumar (1999)

[21] Kumar (2017a)

[22] Kumar (1985a)

Proponents of GST have been suggesting that it would help tackle the black economy since data on all inputs and outputs in the entire chain of production and distribution would be computerized. As already argued, this is not entirely true for the Indian GST, in its current form of implementation, since there are various exemptions, and certain key commodities are kept out of its purview. Further, small and cottage sectors are not in its scope. More importantly, Indian businesses are adept at keeping two sets of accounts and they can continue to do so.

Finally, it is believed that digitization would help tackle the problem. It is argued that the informal sector would get formalized and come under the tax net. This is an incorrect understanding about the nature of the black economy in India. Most of the unorganized sector earns incomes that are way below the taxable limit. In India, taxation begins at a multiple of the per capita income and there is a vast disparity. Hence a vast majority of the people fall outside the tax net and an overwhelming majority of them are from the unorganized and informal sector. Thus, even if their incomes get revealed due to digitization, they will remain outside the tax net.

Key Features of Black Economy—Misunderstandings

Not only is there a misunderstanding that black incomes are generated in the informal sector, there are other misperceptions about the black economy. For instance, demonetization was premised on the notion that 'black means cash'.[23] So, it follows that if cash is squeezed out of the system, then the black economy would disappear at one stroke. Similarly, it has been argued that use of technology can solve the problem. It is assumed that the human element is incorrigible and if it is eliminated from transactions, the black economy would get eliminated.

This view of humans and of society that they can be run with technology is flawed since it is the human element that underlies

---

[23] Kumar (2017d)

illegality. There can be no perfect law since human ingenuity can find a way of circumventing any law.[24] Thus, the need is to reform the human element and technology cannot be a substitute for this. It cannot run society.

I have earlier discussed[25] many other misunderstandings about the black economy, like the assumption that black money is held abroad and that it can be easily tracked and brought back. Similarly, it is a mistake to believe that black money is generated in real estate. It has been shown[26] that black money is circulated via real estate but not generated there. Many also believe that if the markets are allowed to function then the black economy would decline. However, in the case of health and education as private sector has become more predominant, malpractices have increased dramatically.[27]

Black money is a stock while black incomes are a flow. It is the flow that leads to the increase in the stock of black wealth (including money). It is the flow that needs to be eliminated. Black incomes are largely generated by businesses by under and over invoicing costs and revenues.[28] These are not impacted by the various one shot measures that have been taken by the governments from time to time.[29] This process is likely to continue in spite of the implementation of GST. Further, the difficulties encountered by GST both because of design problems and implementation issues, are likely to result in further complexities that would enable the continuation of black income generation.

Thus, neither the implementation of GST nor digitization will help end the black economy given the political nature of the problem. It may only change form.[30]

---

[24] Kumar (2013)
[25] Kumar (2017a)
[26] Kumar (1999b)
[27] Kumar (2013)
[28] Kumar (2006a)
[29] Kumar (1999b)
[30] Kumar (2017a)

Social and Political Issues

GST as a tax not only has an economic impact but also social and political implications. These will be the result of the differential implications of the introduction of GST. As has been pointed out already, the organized sector will benefit at the expense of the unorganized sector and the well-off states will benefit at the expense of the lagging states. Thus, it will set into motion a process of greater marginalization. The computerization associated with GST will further marginalize the marginal. The wider impact on society needs to be understood.

The impact will not only be in the short run but also in the long run. The short run impact is both due to faulty implementation of a complex tax and the marginalization process set into motion. A part of the short run impact may be mitigated as the teething problems are overcome and the lacunae visible at the beginning taken care of by changes in the rules. The GST Council has been responding to the immediate problems that have arisen. For instance, the limit of the 'Composition Scheme' has been raised from Rs 75 lakh to Rs 1.5 crore, number of returns to be filed has been reduced, provisions for restaurants have been changed to simplify their accounts. Introduction of the e-way bill was delayed to 1 April 2018.

One of the short run disruptions was that the entire chain of distribution and production was adversely affected. Prices rose and demand fell which impacted production. The economy which was suffering after the shock of demonetization was administered another shock. Investment which had not yet recovered by July 2017, fell further.[31] This has long-term implications for growth.

The economy has got divided into two circles of growth. The organized sector has been growing at the expense of the unorganized sector. GST and digitization accelerate this process and that has political and social implications. The unorganized sector works with little capital and once it closes down even for a short time, it loses

---

[31] GoI Economic Survey (2018)

its entire capital and is unable to start production later on without capital infusion. This capital is often provided not by the formal banking system but by the informal credit markets which charge a high rate of interest. Thus, the costs of reviving the unorganized sectors is high and their incomes fall over long periods of time.

Introduction of GST has accentuated the long-term shift away from the small and cottage sectors which cannot provide the input credit and cannot do inter-state trade. This trend will only strengthen over time.

The marginalization of the unorganized sector leads to loss of employment since the organized sector offers little additional employment. It is going for increasing automation and has been experiencing 'jobless growth'.[32] Thus, the result will be growing disparity and a fall in aggregate demand.

The social implications will flow from this growing disparity and the decline in youth employment. The political aspects will also follow from this process of marginalization. Since the poorer states have a larger share of the unorganized sector, they will grow slower than the more prosperous states. This will aggravate inter-state disparities that have been rising over time.

The undermining of fiscal federalism which reduces the autonomy of the states to deal with their problems in their own way will further aggravate disparities. Tensions between the better off states and the poorer states are already rising in the context of the Finance Commission awards and they can only get worse over time as disparities rise.

GST's political message is based on the idea underlying 'one nation one tax'. It is as if the nation is being unified finally and it has not been a nation till now. This is a gross overstatement. Politically the nation has been unified since independence even though there have been separatist movements from time to time, in various parts of the country. At most, one could say GST is creating a single market.

---

[32] Kumar (2005a)

Goods and services were moving across state boundaries all the time. Yes, it may have faced impediments at the borders due to entry tax or Octroi but that did not mean that goods were not going across the nation unhindered. People were buying across states depending on where the tax rate was lower. Thus, one can only say that this slogan is just a hard-sell.

A crucial point that needs to be explored is how in a democracy can the interest of the vast majority of those employed in the unorganized sectors of the economy be ignored and GST implemented? Why didn't any of the political parties take up their cause? This can only be understood if one appreciates that there is a change in the consciousness of the public due to the policies of marketization that have been pursued since 1991.[33] While markets have always existed, even barter constitutes a market, it is marketization that is new. It implies the penetration of the market principles into social institutions.[34]

Marketization has meant the marginalization of the marginal and spread of individualism and consumerism in society. The interest of capital is pushed globally by all governments and the various global financial institutions. Due to unprecedented mobility of capital it is able to extract concessions from governments and push its interest. There is a basic shift in the people's thinking which weakens both the collective and democracy. In turn, these weaknesses have enabled GST to be enacted in India even though it is detrimental to the interest of a vast majority of people.

Conclusion

The question is, what is the alternative? Can GST be withdrawn and can one revert to the earlier flawed system? Clearly one cannot go back to the earlier system. A radical rethink is needed and that is discussed in the book. India cannot just copy what exists in some

---

[33] Kumar (1991)
[34] Kumar (2002a)

other nation and which may have been successful there. Something based on the Indian specificity is needed.

It has to be a simple tax which even the small and micro sector should be able to deal with or at least they should not be adversely impacted by it. The basic design of taxation needs to be changed and the balance between the direct and indirect taxes has to be altered.[35] In whatever is done, the economic, social and political impact needs to be taken into account. The long term cannot be ignored.

Outline of the Chapters

The book begins with an Introduction which raises the important questions in the context of GST introduced in India with a lot of fanfare but whose implementation left a lot to be desired. It left everyone confused. Chapter 1 presents the rationale for taxation in a modern day economy. Chapter 2 discusses how resources are raised and spent by the government. This is all in the budget. The chapter presents the linkage of taxation with fiscal policies and their macroeconomic impact. This constitutes the background to the discussion of GST.

Chapter 3 presents the historical evolution of GST in India and its characteristics in a few other countries. The latter is important since one of the justifications given for GST in India is that it now exists in more than 160 countries. Chapter 4 then goes on to discuss the macroeconomic impact of the introduction of GST. This is like looking at GST from above. This is what has been missing in the available analysis of GST and was largely ignored by policy makers who formulated GST. Chapter 5 looks at the GST from the point of view of its nitty-gritty—that is, its design and the micro view. Chapter 6 presents the components of GST and deals with its impact on the economy from the micro stand point. It then discusses the

---

[35] See (Little, 1951)

difficulties being faced by the economy due to the implementation of GST and analyses their causes. It points to the design flaws which are structural in nature and a bigger problem than the implementation issues.

Chapter 7 presents those aspects of the Indian black economy that are relevant to GST and addresses the question of whether GST would be able to solve this vexed problem. It also analyses the aspects of 'formalization' and 'digitization' which are supposed to help tackle the black economy.

Chapter 8 analyses the impact of GST on various aspects of the economy. What has it meant for the consumers, businesses, markets and their efficiency, states and fiscal federalism, impact of computerization and so on? Importance of federalism for a diverse country like India which is a union of states each with its own unique characteristics is highlighted. It is underlined that most of the Indian states are larger than most of the countries of Europe so that there is a lot of diversity across states and also within states. GST is undermining fiscal federalism and that will have long term consequences. It is also pointed out that computerization is distinct from GST and the benefits of the two should not be mixed up. Computerization could have also been introduced under the earlier system of indirect taxes with benefits similar to the ones claimed for GST.

Chapter 9 looks at the social and political aspects of GST. What impact will the decline of the unorganized sectors of the economy have on employment? What does formalization imply? How increased disparities will make the country more unstable politically and socially. The Chapter also presents the global scenario in which 'marginalization of the marginal' has taken place due to the spread of marketization. It is pointed out that this underlies the implementation of GST in India even though it does not benefit the vast majority of Indians. It is reinforcing the policy of 'trickle-down' which has prevailed in India since independence.

The concluding chapter presents the overall conclusions and a possible alternative to GST which would overcome many of the problems being presently faced by Indian businesses.

CHAPTER 1

WHY TAXES?: UNDERSTANDING THE ROLE OF GOVERNMENT IN AN ECONOMY

GST is an indirect tax that is levied on goods and services. It is supposed to cover the entire chain of supply from raw material to the final stage of sale. By themselves, indirect taxes result in an increase in the prices of the goods and services on which they are imposed. So, why levy such a tax? And, what is the importance of putting a tax on goods and services?

In modern day economies, governments have to perform a variety of tasks which the markets are unable to perform efficiently. As societies have become more complex, the markets have not been able to perform many of the essential tasks and the public sector has been given a larger and larger role in the economy in most countries. A key task in a poor country like India has been promoting development to overcome poverty and deprivation.

For a majority of the poor, the market does not provide a solution in crucial areas like education, health, drinking water, food, sewage and energy. So, the government has to provide these services in addition to what the individual cannot provide like defence, foreign policy, security and functioning of money. All these activities need to be financed and taxes are a source of revenue. So, people pay for the services that the government provides. In effect, services become available collectively rather than each one creating services on their own.

Kinds of Taxes: Direct and Indirect

GST has run into a plethora of problems from day one. But, there were difficulties with the earlier forms of taxes which were replaced by GST and that is why the need was felt for introducing the new tax. So, one could ask, why not do away with indirect taxes altogether. But then resources for running the government would be short. Are there other taxes that could substitute for indirect taxes? To understand whether one should replace one kind of taxes by another or not, it is necessary to understand the nature of the different kinds of taxes.

Broadly speaking there are two kinds of taxes—direct and indirect. Both fall on the income of the citizens but there is a difference as to how they work. As the name suggests, direct taxes fall on the income, the moment an income is earned. That is why they are called direct taxes. The indirect taxes fall on incomes when the goods and services are purchased/used.

Differences between Direct and Indirect Taxes

The implication is that direct taxes cannot be postponed while the indirect taxes can be postponed by not purchasing goods and services. As soon as an income is earned a direct tax becomes due. Due to this difference which at first glance appears to be small or inconsequential, the macroeconomic impact of these two kinds of taxes on the economy is different.[1] So, one is not equivalent to the other. Thus, one cannot replace direct taxes by indirect taxes without some (adverse) macroeconomic consequences.

Why do these differences arise when the tax is paid either way by the citizen? In the case of direct taxes, cost of production is not directly affected. It is paid on the income after costs are subtracted from the revenue earned. To explain better, let us consider this in greater detail. In the process of production, economic entities (individual and firms) earn an income—it can be profit or wage and salary. Out of profit, interest, rent and dividend are paid.

Profits are calculated as revenue minus costs, that is, revenue of the firm from the sales less the cost of production. When a tax

---

[1]   Kalecki (1971)

(corporation tax) is levied on this business income, it does not change the cost of production. It only affects the firm's income in hand (called disposable income). Similarly, when a worker gets a wage or a manager the salary, an income tax on this income does not impact the production cost. The employer does not adjust the wage or salary when the income tax changes (except in rare cases).

An indirect tax like excise duty or sales tax is levied on the value of the good or the service being sold and that raises the price of the good or the service. No wonder each time an excise duty is raised, the price of the good on which it is levied, rises. This leads to inflation and a fall in demand. All else remaining the same, indirect taxes are 'stagflationary', that is output stagnates while prices rise.[2] No wonder, when the government wishes to stimulate the demand for a good, it cuts excise duty or sales tax on that item. During the global financial crisis starting in 2007, the Government of India cut excise duties.

In brief, indirect taxes add to the cost of a good or a service while direct taxes do not do so. Thus the former impacts production while the latter does not do so.

Progressivity and Regressivity of Taxes

There is another very important difference between the two kinds of taxes. It is generally the case that direct taxes are progressive while indirect taxes are regressive.[3] What is meant by progressivity or regressivity?

When the rate of tax rises as the income rises then it is said to be progressive. If it remains unchanged with income it is called proportional and when the rate falls as the income rises then it is called regressive. For example, if one earns Rs 5 lakh and pays a tax rate of 5 per cent while another who earns Rs 50 lakh and pays a tax rate of 30 per cent then this is a case of a progressive tax. If both

---

[2] Kalecki (1971)

[3] Kumar (2013)

paid 5 per cent only then it would be a proportional tax while if the one who earns Rs 50 lakh paid only 3 per cent then it would be a regressive tax.

In India, currently, those earning above Rs 3 lakh fall in the income tax net. If advantage is taken of various concessions and deductions, then one need not pay taxes at even Rs 5 lakh. This is about five times the per capita income of the country. Thus, very few people fall in the income tax net. That is why it is said that the income tax base is narrow in India. This is in contrast with the advanced countries where the income tax starts at a fraction of the per capita income. There almost everyone falls in the income tax net.

There are several other reasons for the income tax base to be narrow in India. Agricultural income does not bear income tax so that a large number of people with such incomes are outside the tax net. But to be fair, very few in agriculture earn incomes which fall in the taxable bracket and there are many difficulties in taxing agricultural incomes. An even more important reason is that there is a large black economy in India[4] so that many who should be in the tax net do not pay an income tax or they pay much less than they should pay. I will explain more on this later in the chapter.

In India, as mentioned above, direct taxes are paid by those who earn relatively high incomes (usually more than 5 times the per capita income) and a vast majority with lesser incomes do not fall in the taxable brackets. Also there is a rising tax rate as the income rises. It increases from 5 per cent at the lowest level to 30 per cent at the highest level. Thus, theoretically direct taxes are progressive in character and can result in a more equitable distribution of after tax income. They can lower the level of inequality in the country. But due to the existence of the black economy, the well-off partly or wholly escape taxation and a progressive tax turns regressive.

To understand this let us think of an example. Someone with Rs 50 lakh of actual income declares only Rs 20 lakh of income. So, she/he generates Rs 30 lakh of black income and on this does not pay any

---

4   Kumar (1999b)

income tax. The top tax the person has to pay is 30 per cent. This is called the marginal rate of tax. But on this declared income the person also takes advantage of various concessions and deductions and pays Rs 1 lakh of tax. So, the average tax rate on the declared income is 5 per cent. But on the actual income the average tax rate comes to 2 per cent.

Consider another person who earns Rs 7 lakh. This person declares the full income and pays 10 per cent marginal tax rate. After various considerations, she/he pays Rs 28,000 of tax and the average tax rate comes to 4 per cent. So, on the declared income, the tax seems to be progressive but if the actual income is considered then the tax becomes regressive. This is the impact of the black income generation. What appears to be progressive on paper becomes regressive in reality.

Indirect taxes fall on everyone's consumption whether rich or poor—everyone has to pay them. It is argued that the rich consume different items than the poor and their items of consumption bear a higher rate of tax. So, it is argued that they end up paying more tax than the poor. In fact, many items of consumption of the poor are not taxed at all. For instance, cereals and vegetables or cheap variety of cloth does not bear any indirect tax. The finer variety of clothing bears a high per cent of tax. The processed foods that the well-off sections consume bear a tax but these items are hardly consumed by the poor. Thus, it would appear that progressivity is built into indirect taxes also. However, this picture is not as clear cut as it appears.

Items that bear no indirect tax also are affected by taxes on other items. For instance, wheat has to be transported so if tax on diesel is increased it raises the freight charges and the price of wheat in the market is also affected. Thus, the point of levy of an indirect tax and where it is felt can be quite different. Basic and intermediate goods and services are used in the production of all goods and services so that if indirect taxes are levied on them they impact the prices of all goods and services whether they themselves bear an indirect tax or not.

It may be argued that this indirect impact on prices of goods used by the poor may be small. But the point is that it is the same for the rich and the poor person so that as a per cent of the income of the rich it is smaller than as a per cent of the income of the poor so that it becomes regressive. For instance, on salt if there is a 10 per cent tax, then on a packet of salt of Rs10, the tax is Rs 1. It is the same for a poor person and for a rich person. But as a fraction of the income of the poor it is much higher than that for the rich person. Further, if the poor person eats 1 kilo of salt in a month, the rich person earning a hundred times more than the poor would not eat 100 kilos of salt. So, the tax on salt would turn out to be regressive.

In brief, when tax as a per cent of the income is taken item by item, indirect taxes turn out to be regressive. The rich consume many more things (like cars, luxury travel, stay in five star hotels and diamond studded pens) than the poor do and on many of them they may pay more tax but the comparison has to be of likes. That is why one needs to take into account items that are commonly consumed by both the rich and the poor and work out the tax paid on this common bundle of goods and services.

Progressivity or regressivity is defined with respect to income and not consumption. This makes a big difference. The rich consume a small part of their income while the poor consume almost their entire income. The richer a person, the smaller is the per cent that is consumed. So, if a rich person consumes 10 per cent of the income and pays 30 per cent indirect tax on it, then he/she is paying 3 per cent of the income as indirect tax. A poor person consumes the entire income and because of exemptions only pays 5 per cent as tax then he/she pays 5 per cent of the income as tax. In other words, the tax becomes regressive. Thus, if the aggregate consumption is taken into account, the indirect taxes remain regressive.

In brief, the direct and indirect taxes differ in two broad ways. The former are progressive (assuming no black incomes generation) while the latter are regressive and stagflationary. It is because of these characteristics that it is preferable to have more of direct than indirect taxes. But, India has had the opposite with more of indirect taxes than the direct taxes. Currently the indirect taxes (all levels of government) are two thirds of the total taxes. Back in 1991, they were 87 per cent of all taxes (See Tables 1.1a and 1.1b and Figure 1.1).

Which Taxes Are Direct or Indirect?

There are a variety of direct taxes in India. They are:

a. Personal Income Tax (PIT)
b. Corporation Tax
c. Wealth Tax
d. Estate Duty
e. Property Tax
f. Gift Tax, etc.

Wealth Tax, Estate duty and Gift Tax are no more applicable or collect negligible amounts. Yet, they are important for overall collection of direct taxes and should not have been eliminated.[5] Other than the property tax which is collected by the local bodies, the other taxes mentioned above are collected by the Central government. A profession tax can be collected by the states but they hardly collect any amount of it. Most of the direct tax collections are from the first two taxes in the list (See Table 1.2a and b and Figure 1.2).

Prior to the introduction of GST, indirect taxes consisted of (See, GoI 2015a):

Indirect Taxes Levied by the Centre

a. Central Excise Duty
b. Duties of Excise (Medicinal and Toilet Preparations)
c. Additional Duties of Excise (Goods of Special Importance)
d. Additional Duties of Excise (Textiles and Textile Products)
e. Customs Duty

---

[5] Kumar (1994)

f. Additional Duties of Customs (commonly known as CVD)
g. Special Additional Duty of Customs (SAD)
h. Service Tax
i. Cesses and surcharges insofar as they relate to supply of goods or services

The relative importance of the different taxes is given in Tables 1.3a and b and Figure 1.3.

Indirect Taxes Levied by the States:

a. State VAT
b. Central Sales Tax
c. Purchase Tax
d. Luxury Tax
e. Entry Tax (All forms)
f. Entertainment Tax (not levied by the local bodies)
g. Taxes on advertisements
h. Taxes on lotteries, betting and gambling
i. State cesses and surcharges insofar as they relate to supply of goods or services

Tables 1.3a and b and Figure 1.3 show that sales tax has been the most important indirect tax.

A cess is calculated as a per cent of the tax on which it is levied. Like, there is the education cess on income tax or the highway cess on petrol and diesel. The money collected from a cess is designated to be spent on the specific task for which it is collected.

Some of the items on which excise duty or sales tax are levied yield negligible amounts of taxes. Such items, only complicate the tax collection and add to the administrative burden. These could be eliminated.

All these indirect taxes, except the customs duty, have been brought under the ambit of GST.

Direct tax collection as a per cent of the GDP is low in India. It is one of the lowest in the world (Table 1.4). Thus, to meet its expenditures without creating a deficit in the budget, the government has been increasing its collections of indirect taxes as shown in Table 1.1. Not only more of indirect taxes had to be collected but many kinds of them had to be created to tax different items and give resources to different tiers of government (Centre, states and local bodies). This made the structure of indirect taxes complex and led to a range of problems for the economy. That is why, it was felt that GST would resolve some of these problems and help generate more revenue.[6]

Why is Customs Duty Treated Differently under GST?

The only indirect tax that has not been integrated into GST is the customs duty. The reason is that customs duty is unlike the other indirect taxes which relate to the internal production structures in an economy. Customs duty provides protection to the internal production from production in other countries (that is, from imports).

Nations try to capture the markets of other nations by selling their products cheap in the latter's markets. For instance, when India exports any item, all the internal taxes that Indian consumers have to bear on such an item, are refunded to the exporters to lower their cost. So, any excise or sales tax paid on any item of internal production is refunded to the manufacturers if they are exporting that item.

Further, a subsidy may be provided to sell at a low price in the foreign markets. This is called dumping. It means that one country is selling a product in another country at a price less than the cost price in the producing country. Recently, the USA accused China of dumping solar panels—Chinese producers were selling them very cheap in the US markets. The US complained in the World Trade

---

[6] GoI (2002) and GoI (2009a)

Organization (WTO). In brief, customs duties are used to protect internal production against foreign competition.

Recently, the US and China have levied customs duties against each other's products starting with US imposing duties against imported steel and aluminum. The Chinese reacted with their own duties against US exports to them. This has been characterized as a trade war. WTO was precisely set up to prevent such damaging trade wars and also to open up markets so as to enable more trade to take place among nations.

A country can also out-compete another and sell cheaply without giving subsidy. This advantage may be due to several factors. A country can produce a certain good cheaper than others for several reasons. It can be any combination of better technology, higher labour productivity, low wages, cheap infrastructure provided by government and so on. All this is considered legitimate under the WTO. In the WTO negotiations, there is a process of bargaining between countries. Each country offers lower tariffs in some commodity in return for lower tariff in other countries for its goods. Thus, globally, customs duties have been reduced and this has been the case in India also.

Developing countries may have had low wages but because of lack of technology, they could not compete with the advanced countries in many of the products and services. This was an important reason for the levy of high customs duties on imports in India. With this protection, the Indian industry diversified considerably in the 1960s but it also led to high costs of production. Thus, a balance needs to be struck—technology needs to be rapidly developed and upgraded and infrastructure created. What are the problems and why this has not happened rapidly enough needs to be understood.[7]

A nation may try to catch up with the advanced technology of others but that may not be easy since technology is forever changing. It is a moving frontier that a less developed nation is trying to catch up with. So, today's advanced technology becomes tomorrow's

---

[7] For a more detailed exposition of this point, see, Kumar (2013)

intermediate technology and day after it becomes a low technology.[8] It requires a huge effort to catch up and great emphasis on R&D. If not, one can advance but remain backward for a long time compared to the advanced nations. That is why customs duties may be required for a long time to protect one's industry. Further, with regard to other under developed nations, there is competition to get markets for similar items. This may require lowering prices.

Be that as it may, fairly high customs duties prevailed in India and they provided protection to Indian production. This changed after the introduction of the New Economic Policies (NEP) in 1991 and further after 1 January 1995 when WTO was created and India became a part of it.

Further, because the Indian production used to bear various indirect taxes, its price tended to be higher than that of the foreign production which bore no indirect taxes since the exporting country refunds any indirect tax levied in that country. To overcome this disadvantage for internal production, a Countervailing Duty (CVD) called Additional Duties of Customs was levied on imports to compensate for the difference in the indirect taxes levied on internal production and the imported goods. Similarly, there were the Special Additional Duty of Customs (SAD). These two components of customs duties which related to internal indirect taxes are now included in GST.

In brief, while customs duties are not included in the GST scheme, the CVD and SAD are a part of the GST since they relate to internal indirect taxes.

Different Ways of Calculating Indirect Taxes

Later in the book I talk about the history of introduction of GST in India. There it is explained why VAT could not be introduced earlier in India because of its complexity. A large part of the Indian production structures consist of small and cottage sectors which

---

[8] Kumar (2013)

cannot handle such a complex tax. Unlike other ways of calculating an indirect tax, VAT is levied on 'Value Addition' (explained below). So, data is required on all input costs and output revenues. The difference between these two gives the value addition on which the tax is levied. What are the other ways of calculating indirect taxes?

There are three ways of calculating an indirect tax, whether it be excise or sales tax:

a. Specific Tax
b. Ad Valorem
c. Value Added Tax (VAT)

Specific Tax

A 'specific tax' is calculated on the basis of the quantity of the good produced. This is simple to calculate. So, a tax on tires will only be on the number of tires produced whether they be tires for cycles or cars or tractors. The value does not matter. So, a specific tax is not 'buoyant' and is highly regressive. Buoyancy is like the extent to which something bobs up in water.

'Buoyancy' of a tax means how much does its collection rise as the value of the production rises. The value of production rises when the price of the product rises. But, in the case of a specific tax, the amount of the tax paid remains the same. So, such a tax is said to lack buoyancy. If the government wishes to collect more tax, each time the price of a good rises, the government has to adjust the tax levied on it. This makes the tax tedious—it has to be adjusted time and again.

Further, the cheaper version of a good bears a higher per cent tax. So, if there is a tax of Rs 20 on tires, then a cycle tire at say Rs 200 bears the same tax as a tractor tire of say Rs 20,000. Consequently, the per cent tax on the cycle tire (10 per cent) is much higher than that on the truck tire (0.1 per cent). In this sense, the tax is regressive.

In the case of a specific tax, black incomes may be generated by showing lower output—misinvoicing of production and sales. When a lower production and sales are shown in the books of accounts, then various taxes are saved on the part of the production/sales not shown. The incomes corresponding to the under invoiced output are the black incomes.

Ad Valorem Tax

In the case of an ad valorem tax, the tax is levied on the value of the good. So, in the above example, a 10 per cent tax on a cycle tire would be Rs 20 while on the tractor tire it would be Rs 2,000. This tax is buoyant since as the price of tires rises, more tax is collected automatically. It is also not regressive in the sense mentioned above.

There is always the possibility that the manufacturer or the dealer or the trader may misinvoice the good to generate black incomes (See Chapter 7). As in the case of the specific tax, the amount of production may be under stated. In addition, the price may be misstated. A tractor tire of Rs 20,000 may be shown as a tire priced at Rs 18,000. Especially when there are multiple tax rates on any good, as used to be the case with textiles, this kind of mispricing becomes even easier and black incomes are easily generated.

In the case of textiles, in 1984, there were 124 different rates of tax depending on various factors, such as whether it was coarse cloth or fine, whether it was hand processed or machine processed, whether it was spun on handloom or power loom or in an integrated factory, etc.[9]

In the case of services, under valuation of the output is even easier compared to the physical production. Most of the black incomes are generated in this sector and not in agriculture or manufacturing.[10] For instance, the worth of the software that is being sold in a CD is hard to judge. One may be sending only junk or showing a low price while charging a high price. Similarly, a lawyer's fee is hard to tell off hand.

At the time of Independence, most indirect taxes were calculated as specific tax. More and more goods were switched to 'ad valorem'

---

[9] NIPFP (1985)
[10] Kumar (1999b)

tax after independence. This gave buoyancy to the indirect taxes since when prices rise, more tax is collected. Also, after independence, the number of goods that bear indirect taxes has increased. It was found that basic goods, like, iron and coal, which are used in production of other goods yield more of taxes with little effort. Thus, the net of indirect taxes was expanded to cover most basic and intermediate goods. This leads to 'cascading effect' of taxes. Cascading is like the waterfall which falls from one rock on to the next.

Cascading Effect

Indirect taxes cascade from one tax to the next. There are two kinds of cascading effects—a tax on tax and a profit on tax.[11] It leads to a higher effective rate compared to the declared rate. How does this happen? A tax on a good used as an input into the next stage of production, raises the cost for the second stage of production. So, the price of second stage good rises. This product also pays an indirect tax. The tax rate is levied on the higher price. Thus, the earlier stage tax is also taxed. This leads to a higher effective tax rate on goods and leads to higher prices. An example would clarify this sequence of increasing taxes.

Consider the chain of iron ore converted to pig iron from which steel is made and which is used to produce utensils. Assume a 10 per cent ad valorem tax at each stage of production (See Table 1.5). This is a very simplified version of indirect taxation with no services used and no sales tax paid.

Let us start with Rs 100 of iron ore. At 10 per cent, it pays a tax of Rs 10.

Assume for simplicity that there is no other input for producing pig iron.

So, for the pig iron producer the cost is Rs 110.

Assume that Rs 110 of iron ore is converted to Rs 150 worth of pig iron.

---

[11]   Kumar (1986) and GoI (1978)

It pays a tax of Rs 15 so that the price becomes Rs 165.

The steel producer buys this pig iron worth Rs 165 to produce steel worth Rs 200.

It pays a tax of Rs 20 on it and sells it to the utensil manufacturer for Rs 220.

The utensil manufacturer buys steel of Rs 220 and converts it to utensils worth Rs 250

It pays a tax of Rs 25 so that the selling price of utensil becomes Rs 275.

Table 1.5 Pricing and Tax at Ad Valorem Rate

Raw material	Raw material cost	Value added	Price of the product	10% tax on the product	Sale price	Tax on tax	Effective tax rate (%)
Iron ore	0	100	100	10	110	0	
Pig iron	110	40	150	15	165	1	
Steel	165	35	200	20	220	2.5	
Utensils	220	30	250	25	275	4.5	
Total		205		70		8	34.15

Note, each time the cost price is higher because of the tax paid at the previous stage. So, the tax at any stage is calculated at that higher price so that the amount of tax to be paid becomes higher and that is the 'tax on tax'. This is shown in the second last column in Table 1.5.

Table 1.5 shows that the Value Added in the production process is Rs 205 but the final product is sold at Rs 275 since the tax at the various stages adds up to Rs 70. The tax on tax component is Rs 8. What it also shows is that the more basic a good, like, iron ore, the more stages of production it enters and it is repeatedly taxed. The intermediate product like steel is also taxed more than once.

In effect, as has happened in India, with more and more of the basic and intermediate goods taxed, the cascading effect has increased. If the tax was only on the final good utensils, then the cascading effect would not be present. Its value would have been Rs 205 and a 10 per cent tax would have meant that it would have paid a tax of Rs 20.5 so that the sale price would be Rs 225.5 and not Rs 275. With the ad valorem tax and cascading effect, the effective tax rate becomes 34.15 per cent while the notional rate was 10 per cent. Thus, if the cascading effect can be removed or if the tax is levied only on final goods, prices would be much less than at present.

As already argued, indirect taxes are regressive and if the effective tax rates are higher, the regressive component increases. Further, even if utensils are considered essential and no tax is levied on them, the earlier stage tax remains. The tax of Rs 25 on the last stage (utensils) would not be collected and the price would be Rs 250 since the tax of Rs 45 would be collected at the earlier stages.

There is another element of cascading effect which may be called 'profit on tax'.[12] In the case of most industries, price is determined as a markup on prime costs.[13] If the prime costs rise because of the taxes on the earlier stage then with a given markup, the price becomes higher and the profit rises. This is the 'profit on tax' cascading effect.

Additionally, as Table 1.5 shows, there is an extra tax due to repeated taxation of the basic goods. Consider, the tax on the entire chain is Rs 70 while it should have been Rs 20.5. There is an extra tax of Rs 49.50. Of this, the tax on tax is Rs 8.

Where does the remaining Rs 41.5 of tax come from? It is from the repeated taxation of the basic and intermediate goods. Rs 100 of iron ore pays the tax four times, pig iron pays the tax thrice, steel pays twice. However, they should have paid the tax only once. Thus, the extra value on which the tax is paid is Rs 300 + Rs 80 + Rs 35 = Rs 415. Ten per cent tax on this is precisely Rs 41.5, the missing tax.

In brief, there are two undesirable effects of the ad valorem tax. They lead to three different kinds of cascading effect which raises the effective tax rate and makes it more regressive. Further, it makes

---

[12] Kumar (1986)
[13] Kalecki (1971)

it easier to generate black incomes through misinvoicing of the production.

Input Credit to Eliminate Cascading Effect

Cascading effect raises the effective rate of tax and also leads to higher levels of inflation. How can this be avoided? An 'Input Tax Credit (ITC)' mechanism helps reduce the cascading effect. This is shown in Table 1.6.

Table 1.6 Pricing and Tax at Ad Valorem Rate with Input Credit

Raw material	Raw material cost	Value added	Price of the product	10% tax on the product	Input credit	Tax to be paid	Sale price
Iron ore	0	100	100	10	0	10	110
Pig iron	110	40	150	15	10	5	155
Steel	155	35	190	19	15	4	194
Utensils	194	30	224	22.4	19	3.4	227.4
Total		205		66.4		22.4	

An input credit means that the tax paid at the earlier stage is deducted from the tax to be paid at the present stage. So, the tax paid on iron ore is subtracted from the tax to be paid on pig iron (Table 1.6). Next, the total tax paid, up to the pig iron stage, is deducted from the tax to be paid on steel. And so on. As can be seen from the Table, the total tax collected comes down and so does the price charged to the consumer.

However, it is possible that the benefit of the input credit may not be passed on in the final price by keeping the price unchanged. The result is a higher profit for the producer. This is not just hypothetical but has happened in the past when excise duty cuts have not been passed on by the manufacturers to the consumers. The manufacturers have at times argued that they have had cost increases because of which they had to keep prices at the earlier levels rather than reducing them. They have also argued that their margins were under pressure earlier and so on. So, the governments have had to be cautious when cutting indirect taxes. This is also a concern with GST being implemented now and that is why an anti-profiteering clause exists in the GST Act. More on this in Chapters 3 and 4.

In the examples given in Tables 1.5 and 1.6, only one indirect tax was considered. But there have been a plethora of indirect taxes as mentioned in an earlier section in this Chapter. Each of the tax was administered by a different agency. Excise duty was collected by the Central Board of Excise and Customs (CBEC) while the sales tax was collected by the sales tax department of the state. So, input credit for payment of excise could be granted by the CBEC but not for the sales tax paid. Similarly, the sales tax department could give the input credit for sales tax paid in the state but not for what was paid in another state or for the excise duty paid. Thus, the cascading effect continued. The scheme of GST by bringing all taxes on one platform is supposed to enable input credit to be given for all the indirect taxes paid.

Value Added Tax (VAT) and Elimination of Cascading Effect

What is a Value Added Tax (VAT)? It is a tax on the value addition by a producer. So, what is the value addition? When a producer sells her product, she gets a price but that is not the value of what she has produced. She had bought raw material and incurred other costs and these need to be subtracted from the price received to figure out what is the value added by the producer. So, addition of value over and above what has been purchased by the producer is her 'value added'. The value of the purchased inputs is the value addition at the earlier stages of production.

VAT removes the cascading effects that are present in the ad valorem taxation and thus lowers the effective rate of indirect taxes. As shown in Table 1.7, this happens since the tax on the earlier stage of production is not taxed. However, as the Table shows, less of indirect tax would be collected and all else remaining the same, the deficit in the budget would increase. Unless of course, the rate of VAT is kept higher than that of the ad valorem tax, as shown in Table 1.8. But then the prices would not decline.

Table 1.7 Pricing and Tax at VAT Rate

Raw material	Raw material cost	Value added	Price of the product	10% VAT	Sale price
Iron ore	0	100	100	10	110
Pig iron	110	40	150	4	154
Steel	154	35	189	3.5	192.5
Utensils	192.5	30	222.5	3	225.5
Total		205		20.5	

Table 1.8 Pricing and Tax at RNR VAT Rate

Raw material	Raw material cost	Value added	Price of the product	Tax to be collected	VAT rate (%)	VAT collected	Sale price
Iron ore	0	100	100	10	10	10	110
Pig iron	110	40	150	15	37.5	15	165
Steel	165	35	200	20	57.14	20.00	220
Utensils	220	30	250	25	83.33	25.00	275
Total		205				70	

It should be kept in mind that VAT is somewhat different from the ad valorem tax with input credit (Chapter 3 discusses the various methods used to calculate VAT). The tax collected under the former is even lower than in the latter case as a comparison of the two Tables 1.7 and 1.6 shows. This is a result of the fact that in the former the input price is reduced while in the latter only the tax paid is reduced at the end but it is calculated on a higher price. This difference leads to lower tax collection under VAT but results in enormous complication in the calculation of VAT.

While the 'ad valorem' tax is calculated on the value of output and an input credit is given for the tax paid at the earlier stages of production to get to VAT, in the case of pure VAT, all the input costs have to be subtracted from all the revenues and on the net the tax is to be levied. Thus, the first method of calculating VAT is much simpler than the second method.

Under pure VAT, the situation is far more complicated than that depicted in Table 1.7. When actual production takes place a lot of inputs are needed in addition to the raw material. To produce pig iron or steel, energy and chemicals are used. There is also transportation, finance, advertising and many overheads. Output is also not simple since there may be by-products like, in the case of thermal power production, there is ash which may be sold for producing bricks or in the case of sugar, molasses are produced which are used to produce alcohol and there is bagasse which is used to produce energy by burning. Thus, the value of all the inputs and outputs have to be taken into account which is not the case in the example given in Table 1.7.

Thus, for a proper implementation of VAT, the entire chain of production and distribution has to be under the tax so that input tax credit can be given for each input. GST attempts to do precisely this. If the entire chain is not there, the cascading effect reappears. Further, if there are different rates of taxes on different commodities, then again the cascading effect may reappear (Annexure 1.1).

If the entire chain of production and distribution has to be under GST, all its stages have to be computerized. Deduction of costs from the revenues has to be almost automatic.

The large and the medium sectors or even the modern small scale sector have this facility but the micro sector consisting of the large number of cottage and home based producers cannot afford this detailed accounting and computerization. The costs increase for all sectors but for the micro and small sectors, disproportionately so. They would have to raise their prices more than others and they would become uncompetitive. This has been the reason that VAT could not be introduced in India earlier (See Chapter 3) even though attempts were made to do so since 1978.

Revenue Neutral Rate (RNR) under VAT

A comparison of the Tables 1.5 and 1.7 shows that if the rate of tax under ad valorem and VAT are kept the same, then as the shift takes place from the former to the latter, there is a drastic fall in the tax collection. In the example presented, it falls from Rs 70 to Rs 20.4. If the government does not wish to lose revenue then it would have to raise the rate of tax under VAT. Table 1.8 shows that if the same amount of tax is to be collected from the various stages of production then the rate of tax has to rise at each of the stages. For the final stage it rises to 83.33 per cent.

This brings in the concept of 'Revenue Neutral Rate' (RNR). It stands for that rate of tax at which the collection of the tax would be the same as in the earlier system of ad valorem tax. The question is whether to go in for overall revenue neutrality or commodity by commodity at each stage of production. In the former case, an overall tax rate would apply to all goods while in the latter case, there would be different tax rates on each of the goods.

I have shown in an earlier article[14] that with RNR rates of taxes, while the cascading effect is removed, the prices do not fall since the same amount of indirect tax is collected, as shown in Table 1.8. The example given in this Table pertains to the case when the same amount of tax is collected at each stage of production of utensils as in the case of ad valorem rates of tax.

If the VAT rates differ across different stages of production and distribution, the situation becomes complex and the cascading effect reappears when VAT is implemented as ad valorem rates with input credit (See Annexure 1.1). It disappears only if there is one tax rate

---

[14] Kumar (1986)

on all goods and services. This is a result of the complex system of production in a modern economy. Some product is usually an input into some other thing. So, transport, finance, trade, energy and so on are not only produced but are used in the entire chain of production.

In the example being considered, if steel is used to produce utensils, it bears a VAT RNR of 57.14 per cent. But for producing lathe machines or for use in cars the RNR may be different since the value addition differs across different uses. So, two complications arise. First, on the same good (steel here) depending on its use, many different RNR would be required. Secondly, if different rates are applied on different goods and services, then the cascading effect reappears since the tax rates differ and do not compensate for each other (See Chapter 4 also).

In an earlier article,[15] it was shown that there is an equivalence between an ad valorem tax regime and a VAT regime. It was shown there that if in the earlier regime of ad valorem tax there was one common rate of tax then on shifting to a VAT regime in which one would like to collect the same amount of tax at each stage of production and distribution as earlier, then there would be different rates of VAT (See Table 1.8). A given fixed ad valorem rate translates into a variable VAT RNR. Similarly, a given fixed VAT RNR will translate into a variable ad valorem rate.

Thus, in implementing VAT as ad valorem tax with input tax credit and many tax rates, too many complications are introduced. So, introduction of VAT regime makes sense only if the government is willing to give up tax revenue to help reduce prices. But under GST the government is not willing to give up revenue and is experimenting with different RNR and multiple rates. So, the issue hinges on how much revenue the government needs?

This brings one to the issue of expenditures of the governments at different tiers of governance—Centre, states and the local bodies—and how to finance them? This is the subject matter of Public Finance which is presented in the next chapter.

---

[15] Kumar (2005b)

CHAPTER 2

GOVERNMENT BUDGET: EXPENDITURES AND REVENUES

Governments have a variety of tasks to perform. As societies have become more complex, the extent, variation and number of tasks they have had to perform has increased substantially. The key task in a poor country like India has been promoting development to overcome deprivation. For a majority of the poor, the market does not provide a solution whether it be in education, health, water, energy, rural development and so on[1]. In fact many of these areas are cases of market failure—that is, markets cannot provide optimal amounts of these items to society.[2] Further, the government has to provide for defence, money, public goods and so on. All these activities require revenue to finance them.

There is a debate on what is the appropriate size of the government and what kinds of activities should it be involved in.[3] Some see not only market failure but also existence of policy failure[4] due to the working of the black economy or due to inefficiencies in the functioning of the public sector. Thus, globally, there has been pressure for a retreat of the government from the markets and this is termed as the Washington Consensus.[5] This was pushed under Thatcherism and Reaganism from the late 1970s. It was pursued via the global financial institutions like the IMF and the World

---

[1]   Kumar (2013)
[2]   Tresch (1981)
[3]   Cullis and Jones (1987)
[4]   Kumar (1999b)
[5]   Williamson (1989)

Bank and later after 1995 it was pushed by the WTO. This has been characterized as marketization.[6]

It has been argued that the government expenditures are often wasteful or unproductive or non-developmental. Government requires an administration just like any corporation does. But its task is far more complex than that of any big corporation. The complexity comes out of the goals that a government has to achieve compared to those that a corporation pursues. For the latter the goal is simple profit maximization and that too most often in the short run.

For the government there is a multiplicity of goals and often they may be contradictory[7]—clearly, short-run profit maximization is not a goal for the public sector. In more marketized economies since the late 1970s there is a confusion about the role of the public sector. Namely, their performance is increasingly judged by how much profit they earn. If they do not earn a profit or earn low profits then there is pressure to privatize such public sector units.

The size of the government is a political decision. How much army to maintain, how much to spend on public education and health, what kind of social security to give and so on are political decisions. Some countries like the Scandinavian countries have high levels of government services while the US has a lower level but higher than in most developing countries. (Table 2.1 presents data on government expenditures/GDP in select countries).

One way to limit the size of the government is to limit its revenues so that any increase in expenditures would lead to an increase in the deficit. Of course, it goes without saying that whatever the government spends should be efficiently done, that is, there should be no wastage. How is this efficiency to be judged remains undefined? How much should a government spend then becomes a political issue. Tables 2.1a and b and Figure 2.1 give

---

[6]   Kumar (1991), Kumar (2000b) and Kumar (2002a)
[7]   Kumar (2013)

the government expenditures in India and its break up since 1990–91.

Current and Capital Account Expenditures and Revenues

Government has to achieve long term objectives which the private sector often does not take up. For instance, in a poor country like India, it must eliminate poverty, provide for high quality education and health to the vast numbers of the poor who cannot afford to go to the market to get them. It must develop the physical infrastructure (power, roads and so on) of the country to promote industry. To achieve all this, it has to incur administrative expenditures but these are often characterized as non-developmental or wasteful.

A more useful separation of expenditures than the developmental and non-developmental is to talk of the capital and current account expenditures. Analytically also this is the correct division to use. Revenues can also be divided between these two categories. Thus, the budget is presented not only as a totality but also as Current Account and Capital Account budgets. The composition of the expenditures since 1990–91 is given in Tables 2.1a and b and Figure 2.1.

Capital account budget reflects the link of what the government is doing this year with the future. Investments, borrowings, buying equipment and the like have a link with the future since they lead to economic flows over time. These are crucial for the growth of the economy. Current account does not have a link with the future periods (years). So, administrative expenditures, subsidies, interest payment from the budget, salaries, grants and tax revenue are over in the current period (year) being considered and do not have a link with the coming years.

In brief, the distinction between the current and capital accounts is how they play out over time. The former has no implication for the future while the latter is linked to economic activity over the coming periods. This is like the distinction between investment and consumption in macroeconomics.[8]

In macroeconomics, investment has a leading role to play since it determines the size of the national income via a multiplier. That is, national income is a multiple of the investment. This is not to say that consumption does not play any role; it determines the value of the multiplier. Thus, both investment and consumption are important but the former is more so.

Similarly, it is not that the current account items in the budget are unimportant but it is the capital account items that are more important from the point of the future growth prospects of the economy. So, how much is the government investing (capital account) in education, health, roads, power and so on is crucial. However, it is not that salaries paid to teachers and doctors in the public sector, police men, army men, railway personnel and post office employees (current account items) are not important. If these salaries are not paid, none of these functions would be performed. The current account expenditures maintain services while the capital account items lead to expansion of these services. So, investment in schools, primary health centres, roads, power plants and so on lead to increased capacity and future expansion.

The broad categories in which the government expenditures may be classified are:

Current Account (See Tables 2.3a and b and Figure 2.2 for Data since 1990–91)

a. Establishment expenditures
b. Expenditures on schemes and projects
c. Interest payments
d. Subsidies
e. Pensions
f. Grants to various entities
g. Other transfers including to foreign governments

---

[8] Bhaduri (1986)

Capital Account (See Tables 2.4a and b and Figure 2.3 for Data since 1990–91)

a. Budgetary support to projects and schemes
b. Loans to various bodies and foreign governments
c. Internal and Extra Budgetary Support (IEBR)

The broad categories into which the revenue may be classified are:

Current Account

a. Tax Revenue
b. Interest Receipts
c. Dividend and Profits of PSUs
d. External Grants
e. Other Non-tax Revenue

Capital Account

a. Recoveries of loans and advances
b. Disinvestment receipts
c. Market loans
d. Short term borrowings
e. External assistance
f. Securities issued against Small Savings
g. Provident Fund receipts

Data on some of these broad categories are given in Tables 2.5a and b and Figure 2.4.

Government's Finances

The main focus here is on collection of taxes under GST, an indirect tax. As mentioned above, a tax is a current account item. It is what the government gets without any future obligation. However, the government can also raise finance by borrowing but that has the obligation of future interest payments, so it is a capital account item. Thus, broadly speaking, government can raise resources for its expenditures both on capital and current account.

The sources of revenue of the government may be categorized as tax, non-tax, grants and borrowing. As mentioned earlier (Chapter 1), taxes are paid by the citizens out of their incomes.

The government also gets a return on past investments, say in the public sector. Further, it collects fees or charges for the services it renders to the citizens. These are called the non-tax resources.

Borrowings are from those who are willing to lend to the government. Only those who save can lend. These are the businesses and well-off members of society. Borrowing can also be from the Central Bank (RBI) which prints notes to lend to the government. This kind of borrowing was ended in the late 1990s. The RBI can buy government debt and finance it indirectly.

Borrowings are not government's own resources so not only does it have to return the money over time but also pay a return (interest) on them. So, it must try to earn a return on the money it borrows to meet its future obligations. If it does not earn enough return to pay back the borrower then it gets into trouble since it would have to use the tax and non-tax resources to pay the interest and return the loan taken. If this continues for a while it puts the finances of the government into a debt trap—namely, the borrowing and the interest to be paid on the debt keep on increasing as a share of revenue from year to year. This squeezes the funds available for development and other essential tasks of the government. This is similar to a bonded labourer who borrows to consume and is unable to repay the lender so that the debt keeps increasing.

Tax and non-tax sources and grants the government may get are its own resources and do not have any future obligations. These can be used to finance administration and other current requirements of the government which do not earn a return, like, paying salaries, subsidies and defence. If there is a surplus from these funds, it is a happy situation since they may be ploughed into development and government investments to build a variety of infrastructure required by the economy and also by the poor in the country. On such investment even if the return is low it does not matter. If the government borrows to invest, it must earn enough to pay back the interest, which can be quite high. Thus, many development projects with low return get ruled out. Some of these may be very useful because of the wider social implications they have (externalities).

Deficit in the Budget

The gap between the government's expenditures and its *own* revenues is the deficit in the budget. Borrowings are not considered as the own revenue. The budget deficit plays an important role in the economy since it boosts demand.[9] When government raises tax revenue, it reduces the purchasing power of those it taxes and that reduces their demand in the economy. When it spends in the economy it raises demand. Thus, the difference between the two, the deficit in the budget, gives the extra demand that the government creates in the economy.

If the economy is running well and capacity of industry is fully utilized then this may lead to inflation. However, if the economy has slack, that is, capacity is underutilized, then this can help give a boost to demand and to improved capacity utilization and faster economic growth. This was seen globally in the period after 2007 during the global financial crisis. Almost all the economies in the world ran a deficit in the budget and that boosted demand so that the world economy did not go into a depression. In the Indian economy also the deficit went up from 3 per cent to 12 per cent of GDP.

There are different kinds of deficits and not one. For some data on the deficits in the budget since 1990–91, see Table 2.6 and Figure 2.4. Each plays a different role in the economy. Borrowing from the Central Bank (RBI) is the budget deficit. It is the difference between the expenditures and revenue, including borrowing from the market. Next, there is the revenue deficit which is the excess of

---

[9] Keynes (1936) and Kalecki (1971)

expenditures on current account and the current account revenues. So, it is the deficit in the current account part of the budget. Third, there is the fiscal deficit which is the budget deficit plus the borrowing from the market. Fourth, there is the fiscal deficit less the interest payment by the government and it is called the primary deficit. Interest payment is the transfer from the government to the lenders who had leant to the government. So, it is like borrowing from one hand and returning with the other hand. Finally, there is the modified primary deficit which is the primary deficit less the other transfers from the government to the profit earners in society.[10] It has been shown that it is this last one that boosts demand in the economy and not the fiscal deficit.

In the literature, the focus has largely been on the fiscal deficit. The IMF and the credit rating agencies monitor this parameter of the budget to assess the health of the government finances. Under the Fiscal Responsibility and Budget Management (FRBM) Act, the goal is to keep the fiscal deficit below 3 per cent of GDP. This is an arbitrary figure. What is important is that the interest obligations should not exceed the return that the government gets on its investments which are used to make the interest payments.

The argument for keeping the fiscal deficit low is that it reflects the borrowing of the government and if there is excess of it then it prevents the private sector from borrowing. This is called crowding out. It is supposed to lower private investment in the economy. However, equally there is the argument that public investment crowds in private investment by generating demand in the economy. Clearly, which situation will prevail depends on whether demand in the economy is adequate or inadequate. So, there can be no general rule that fiscal deficit be kept low.

The crucial deficit is the revenue deficit. It implies that borrowings are used for the current account expenditures on which there is no return. So, repayment of borrowing becomes difficult and they start to rise faster than repayments. The FRBM Act argues

---

[10] Kumar (1999a)

for a zero revenue deficit and that is fine. Tax revenue are crucial to reduce the revenue deficit to zero. This is where the importance of the indirect taxes comes in. They help reduce the revenue deficit.

Expenditures, revenues and deficits are all interlinked. More importantly, they impact all other aspects of the economy—both macro and micro. Thus, they are crucial to the understanding of not only the economic role of the government but the way a modern day capitalist economy functions[11] and this is discussed in the next section.

Fiscal Policy Regime

As mentioned above, the various expenditures and revenues are interlinked via the deficit to the macroeconomy.[12] The model is based on a modification of the national income identity.[13] Usually, when fiscal policies are studied they are taken in pairs, like, indirect taxes and subsidies or direct taxes and the deficit in the budget. However, as shown in Chapter 1, each of the expenditures and revenue are made up of various components. In the budget, the government makes policy regarding each of the variables and that then determines their impact on the economy.

All these variables[14] together constitute the fiscal policies. All of them together impact the deficit in the budget. In effect, if one takes each of them one by one, keeping the other variables constant, one can figure out their impact on the deficit. In turn, that impacts output and prices in the economy. Further, as mentioned earlier, there are many kinds of direct and indirect taxes and each of them also has a somewhat different impact on the macroeconomy. Policies for each of the separate items when combined together constitute the fiscal policy regime.

---

[11] Kumar (1988)
[12] See Kumar (1988)
[13] Kalecki (1971)
[14] Listed earlier in Chapter 1

It is argued that the fiscal policy regime as a whole impacts the macroeconomy. As each variable in the fiscal policy regime changes, it impacts output and prices via the impact it has on the deficit in the budget. For instance, the ratio of direct to indirect taxes determines the inflationary impact of the budget and its impact on output in the economy. The greater the share of direct taxes the greater the output enhancing role of the budget. This is somewhat counter intuitive since an income tax or a wealth tax is considered to be a disincentive to production.

This result is due to what is called the balanced budget multiplier. It means, if the government increases its expenditures by raising resources so that the budget remains balanced, that is the deficit does not increase, it raises demand in the economy and leads to an expansion of output.[15] It also shows that an increase in the subsidy from the budget while keeping the budget balanced is only a transfer from one to the other and has no impact on the output. But in this case, prices do not fall if indirect taxes are raised to keep the budget balanced. However, prices will fall if the direct taxes are used to raise the resources to keep the budget balanced. Thus, with different combinations of policies, different results follow.

The elements of the fiscal policy regime are the broad categories of revenue and expenditures given in Chapter 1. These can be further categorized as:

a. Establishment expenditures including salaries and pensions
b. Net Interest Payments
c. Subsidies
d. Net transfers including to foreign governments
e. Public investments less disinvestments
f. Direct Tax Revenue
g. Indirect Tax Revenue
h. Dividend and profits of PSUs

---

[15] Kalecki (1971)

i.   Net borrowings and grants
j.   Modified Primary Deficit

In brief, the full impact of the fiscal policies of government can only be understood if the fiscal policy regime is used for analysis. So, a study of GST and its economic impact cannot be in isolation but as a part of the fiscal policy regime.[16]

Black Economy, Taxes and the Budget

All the variables included in the fiscal policy regime (listed in the previous section) are impacted by the black economy. Consequently, the fiscal policy regime is substantially determined by the black economy.

Due to the existence of the black economy, expenditures are higher than necessary since there is leakage of funds. For instance, when the government awards contracts for the construction of a school building, due to leakage of funds, for a given quality of construction, the cost would be higher or for a given allocation, the quality delivered would be lower. This would raise maintenance costs. Another example is of road building, as discussed earlier. In this case, since the quality of construction is sub-standard, when the rains come it would get washed away and become pot holed so that repairs would be required. Thus, rather than building new roads the funds would be exhausted in maintenance. Pot holed roads lead to more consumption of fuel and higher maintenance costs for vehicles which tend to break down more. In the case of the above and other similar examples that can be given, there is a waste of resources. As was said in the budget speech in 2005, 'expenditures do not lead to outcomes'.[17]

Black economy implies that people do not reveal their true incomes and avoid paying taxes. This is true for both the direct and

---

[16]   Kumar (2015)
[17]   Union Budget (2005)

indirect taxes. This reduces the tax base of the economy. It can also mean that direct taxes can become regressive (as argued earlier) since it is those with high incomes who evade more taxes and pay a lower tax rate. Further, since fewer entities pay the taxes, the base of the tax narrows. It results in shortage of funds for essential expenditures.

Thus, the revenue collected is much less than what it could potentially be. With the current estimate of black economy of 62 per cent of GDP,[18] at current rates of taxes (direct and indirect), 40 per cent of this could have been collected as taxes. So, the budget could have had an additional 24 per cent of GDP as taxes while it collects only 16.5 per cent currently. Thus, there would be no shortage of resources for development.[19]

The current fiscal deficit of 5 per cent of GDP (Centre and states) could have become a surplus of 19 per cent of GDP. Thus, borrowing requirements of the government would become zero and the interest payment on borrowings would decline dramatically freeing tax resources for further expenditures on development. Indirect tax collection which is inflationary could be reduced, to lower inflation. This would reduce the need for subsidy to the poor and other subsidies.[20]

In brief, the black economy results in higher expenditures, lower revenues, higher deficits, more of borrowings, higher interest payments, higher level of prices and more subsidies. All this results in lower levels of development.[21]

The impact of the black economy on so many fiscal and macro variables results in policy failure. The state is unable to achieve its goals. It gets discredited and there is demand for the retreat of the government from the economy.

---

[18] Kumar (2016b)
[19] For a more detailed discussion of this point see Kumar, Chattopadhyay and Dharan (2007)
[20] See Kumar (1994) for a scheme along these lines
[21] Kumar (1999a) and Kumar (2005)

So, tackling the black economy is crucial for accelerated development of the Indian economy. Governments in India have tried various ways to tackle the black economy,[22] like, lowering tax rates, reducing controls, acquiring undervalued properties and demonetization. None of them have been able to check the growth of the black economy.

As will be discussed in greater detail in Chapter 7, GST is supposed to help tackle the black economy by preventing double book keeping by businesses. It is also said that due to the massive computerization under GST, the human interface would be reduced and that would also lower the opportunities for corruption. For a variety of reasons these best laid plans can fail and it remains to be seen how much of an impact GST would have on illegality that underlies the black income generation process.

---

[22] Kumar (1999b) and Kumar (2017a)

CHAPTER 3

HISTORICAL EVOLUTION OF GST AND VAT IN INDIA

VAT to GST: The Progression since the 1970s

It is said that GST has been introduced in more than a hundred sixty countries starting with France where it was introduced in 1954.[1] In other words, a lot of experience has accumulated over more than sixty years and that it has been operational in other nations, so, India has little to worry about. However, it is also the case that full GST has been implemented in only a few countries. It is also said that wherever GST has been introduced, prices have risen. In the case of Malaysia, when GST was rolled back after the new government took over in 2017, prices fell.[2] This is expected since GST is an indirect tax and such taxes tend to be inflationary.

GST has three important components, namely, it is levied as Value Added Tax (VAT), it brings goods and services together on the same platform and it is levied on transactions from production to the final sale of any product or service. Of course, it is an indirect tax but it is not levied on the 'act' of production, sale and so on. It is levied on all transactions (called 'supply') from the start to the end. So, the earlier excise duty, sales tax, service tax and so on, which were on the 'act' of, are eliminated (with a few exceptions like petroleum products).

In India, the history of introduction of GST begins with the attempt to introduce VAT for the collection of the indirect taxes

---

[1] GoI (2015b)
[2] *Malay Mail* (2018)

so as to eliminate the cascading effect.[3] However, it is a complex tax so it could not be introduced for a long time. The first proposal for introducing it was made in the Indirect Taxation Enquiry Committee Report 1978.[4] It was to be introduced as Manufacturing VAT (MANVAT) since the Indian production structures are very complicated and it was realized that the small and cottage sectors would find it difficult to implement VAT. The idea was that VAT could be implemented for the manufacturing sector because it could cope with the difficulties. However, even this could not be implemented since there are inter linkages between manufacturers in the large, medium, small and cottage sectors.

Next, this idea was pursued in the Long Term Fiscal Policy (LTFP) Report in 1985.[5] Since the difficulties of implementing full VAT had become clear, a Modified VAT (MODVAT) was proposed. It was to be implemented on certain goods which were produced in the large scale industries with inputs largely from the large and medium scale industries. Since input and output in these sectors are recorded, value added could be calculated. This is not the case for the small and cottage sectors which do not keep detailed accounts and so, they had to be left out.

In 1986, MODVAT was applied to thirty-seven chapters out of a total of ninety-one chapters contained in the Excise Act at that time. It was suggested that the list of industries to which MODVAT would be applicable would be increased over time as these industries matured and began to maintain more detailed accounts. Indeed, the list was expanded over the next decade and more and more industries were brought under MODVAT. Initially, to calculate VAT, only the subtraction of the value of input of raw materials from the value of final goods was permitted. In 1994, the scheme was expanded to include the deduction due to capital goods also.

---

[3] Cascading effect described in Chapter 1
[4] GoI (1978)
[5] GoI (1985)

Services were brought into the indirect tax net in 1994 by imposing a service tax on them. It was argued that just as goods pay an indirect tax, services should also pay these taxes. This became important since the government was in need of more and more resources for development. The services sector had been expanding rapidly since independence and yet it was outside the indirect tax net. By the start of the 1980s this sector had become the largest sector[6] and it was recognized that it could yield a lot of taxes. It was decided to go slowly so initially only a few services were brought under this net but the net was expanded over time. This tax was calculated as VAT. Over time, as more and more services were brought under this tax and due to the rapid expansion of this sector, it became the fastest expanding (most buoyant) indirect tax in the economy (Table 1.3b and Figure 1.3).

MODVAT on goods was also expanding as more and more commodities were brought under its purview. Its name was changed to Central VAT (CENVAT) on 1 April 2000. Full-fledged CENVAT came into operation on 1 July 2001. Further, changes were brought about from 1 March 2002. The Kelkar Committee Report[7] recommended moving towards a comprehensive VAT on goods and services.[8] Thus, it became necessary to bring goods and services on the same platform, so that credit for inputs could be given across goods and services and not just separately for goods and separately for services. To implement this scheme, on 10 September 2004, new rules of CENVAT credit were introduced. Simultaneously, new rules for credit on service tax were also introduced. All these changes were a precursor to introducing GST.

Why was CENVAT called that, and not VAT? That was done to distinguish it from sales tax to be levied by the states as VAT, to overcome the cascading effect of sales tax. So, the name CENVAT distinguished it from the name VAT to be used by the states.

---

[6]   Kumar (2013)

[7]   GoI (2002)

[8]   This was first suggested in (GoI, 1978)

VAT was introduced in the states largely from 1 April 2005. Some states delayed their entry into VAT fearing a loss of revenue and a loss of autonomy. There was to be a single rate of VAT as far as possible which reduced the autonomy of the states. Since independence, the states under the sales tax regime were free to levy this tax on goods and services at the rate they thought suited their requirement. They were also free to not impose taxes on certain items. They could also use it as a concession to attract business to their state (backward area concessions).

This made the sales tax regime in India complex. People could buy from those states which offered a lower sales tax rate. For instance, the sales tax rate was lower in the states of UP and Haryana compared to Delhi so many Delhi residents bought their cars in the two neighbouring states and paid a lower sales tax. This led to a loss of revenue for Delhi. While a car is a big ticket item and one could gain considerably even if the tax saving was 2 per cent, but for day to day consumption items it did not pay to go to the neighbouring state to buy one's necessities.

Across the various indirect taxes—sales tax, services tax and excise duty—input credit was not available so the cascading effect continued. It is to eliminate this that GST was proposed. In the budget for 2006–07, Finance Minister P. Chidambaram, proposed that GST be implemented in the nation from 1 April 2010. It was recognized that a Constitution amendment would be needed to implement GST since the federal structure would be altered by the introduction of GST. The states would get some additional powers and lose some powers.

An important change that was to come with the introduction of GST in the country was that earlier the indirect taxes were imposed on the 'act' of production (excise duty), sales (sales tax), transportation (Octroi) and so on. Now under GST it was going to be on the transactions (supply), that is, on the value in the invoice. So, in lieu of the old taxes a new tax was being introduced.

As already argued, VAT is a complex tax and its method of calculation reflects that. A method of calculation had to be devised for GST which could overcome the practical difficulties.

Methods of Calculation of VAT

Chapter 1 described how VAT is calculated in India. However, theoretically, three methods for calculating VAT are mentioned in the literature:

1. Addition Method
2. Subtraction Method
3. Invoice Method

In all these cases, the tax is levied on value addition at any stage of economic activity. The difference between the methods lies in the way each of them calculate value addition. While conceptually, value addition is simple, calculating it is complex.

In the first method, value addition is calculated as it is often defined in the context of national income, namely, as the sum of factor incomes—profits plus wages and salaries.

In the second method, value addition is taken as the difference between the price at which the item (good or service) is sold and value of inputs that go into it. Here one could either take the value including the tax paid or excluding the tax paid on purchases and sales. So, these two constitute the sub categories of this method—the gross or the net method.

In the third method, value added is not calculated but the tax due on sales (good or service) is subtracted from the tax paid on the purchased inputs. That is, the ad valorem tax on inputs and outputs is calculated and then the difference between the two is taken and that is treated as VAT. It is this method, the simplest of the three and the one most often used, which is used in India. But in this case the cascading effect continues, if the tax rates on inputs and outputs differ.[9]

The first method is rather difficult to implement since one needs to know the profit in advance. This is tricky since profit is earned

---

[9]   See Annexure 1.1

only after sales have occurred. While the manufacturer may print a Maximum Retail Price (MRP) on the package that is sold, the price charged may be less. In fact, the manufacturer selling to the trader would be charging less than the MRP which is what the consumer is supposed to pay. Similarly, what the dealer charges the retailer would also be less than the MRP. So, at each stage of production and sale, calculating in advance, the profit that would be earned proves to be difficult.

Further, profit also includes the factor incomes, rent and interest paid by the business. But to the business it is a cost which she nets out of the profit declared. So, this adds to the confusion.

The second method also requires the knowledge of the price to be charged at each stage and from that the value of the inputs has to be subtracted. Again, as mentioned above, at each stage of production and distribution, the price is not so well defined even though the final retail price may be announced as MSP.

In the third method, there is no guess work involved. The actual invoice at each stage is used. As mentioned in Chapter 1, this is the method used in India to implement VAT and now GST.

Summary of Reports

India's experiment with the introduction of a GST-like tax began in the late 1970s. The Jha Committee Report[10] was the first one and was highly influential since ideas from it are also reflected in later Reports. One of the important suggestions in this Report was the proposal to introduce MANVAT. Long Term Fiscal Policy Report[11] suggested MODVAT—which was introduced gradually so that more and more commodities came under its purview. The seeds of a GST-like tax were present in the L.K. Jha Committee Report in the shape of a 'comprehensive VAT'. The Committee anticipated many of the problems that the current GST is grappling with, like,

---

[10]   GoI (1978)
[11]   GoI (1985)

the problems encountered by the small businesses and multiplicity of taxes required in India.

Subsequent reports like the Tax Reform Committee of 1992[12] and the Report of the Task Force on Indirect Taxes[13] also flagged similar issues and pushed for a comprehensive VAT including Services but none of them called it a Goods and Services Tax.

All these Reports expressed anxiety about administration and implementation. They all realized that a 'comprehensive VAT' would be a complex tax, difficult to implement in India. This was also linked to the prevalence of a large black economy and evasion of taxes. None of the Reports properly focused on this problem and how to overcome it—there was only a cursory mention of this problem and faith was expressed in improvement in administration. In later reports a solution was sought in computerization. But the main problem of taxation in India, the black economy, was not dealt with upfront.

Indirect Tax Enquiry Committee Report 1978: Proposal for MANVAT

This Report was prepared by a Committee chaired by L.K. Jha. It analysed the problems arising out of the indirect taxation in India. It pointed to the importance of the indirect taxes since they were 79.3 per cent of total tax revenues in 1976–77 (Table 1.1b). This is large compared to the figure for most developed countries. Within the indirect taxes, it was pointed out that the share of excise duties and sales tax was rising while that of customs duties was falling.

It noted that to begin with most taxes were collected as specific duties but over time that has changed to ad valorem excise duties. It was stated that indirect taxes were made to fulfil various objectives, like, progressivity and protection to small scale businesses. Thus, it pointed to a variety of exemptions and a multiplicity of rates. This

---

[12] GoI (1992)

[13] GoI (2002)

complicates the indirect tax structure which it suggested was not desirable.

Further, it was argued that there was taxation of inputs with undesirable consequences. It was noted that at that time, the tax rate on basic raw materials was higher than on semi-processed and final products. Since there was no credit for tax on inputs, it was argued that it led to higher prices. So, it was suggested that taxation of raw materials should be lowered and that on final products increased. But, in the long run, the Report suggested a generalized system of tax credit and the need to implement VAT. It stated,

> VAT in its comprehensive form is a tax on all goods and services (except exports and Government Services), its special characteristic being that it falls on the value added at each stage—from the stage of manufacture to the retail stage.

The main features of VAT were listed as:

1. It would be a multi-stage tax unlike the then prevailing indirect taxes and it would be collected at all stages of production and distribution of all goods and services.
2. Thus, it would be a comprehensive tax. And,
3. It would remove the repeated taxation of each input entering the production process which occurs under the ad valorem taxes.

Further, it was argued that there was need to encourage the small producers. Since they do not have scale economies and suffer from other difficulties but give a lot of employment, they could be compensated by making them pay lower levels of taxes. So, it was suggested that for turnover up to Rs 2.5 lakh there should be full exemption from tax. For the range Rs 2.5 to Rs 10 lakh, a concessional rate was suggested, say, 3 per cent less than the tax rate levied on the organized sector producers. It was also suggested that in the long term,

> From the economic point of view and for easily achieving a determinate degree of progression, it is best to have a tax system which covers value added at all stages of processing and trade but which, however, does not create problems of cascading and distortions in relative factor prices.

It was argued that VAT was implementable in India because it exists in not only almost the whole of Western Europe but also in some developing countries like Brazil, Argentina and Ivory Coast.

Further, it was suggested that India should go for a comprehensive form of VAT[14] that would replace the existing indirect taxes like excise duty, sales tax and Octroi. This would have the advantage that

a. Businesses would have to deal with only one indirect tax authority.
b. The cascading effect of taxes would be eliminated since each input would be taxed only once.
c. Exports could be made almost completely free from internal indirect taxes.

The Report pointed to a key difficulty in adopting this comprehensive form of tax. Namely, India is not a unitary system of government but a federal system. In such a system, state and local governments have a certain degree of autonomy to take care of their specific requirements. For this, each level of government has some independent powers of taxation. A comprehensive VAT would undermine fiscal autonomy of lower tiers of government.

The administrative challenges posed not only by the comprehensive VAT but even the simpler VAT would be that small businesses do not maintain detailed accounts so would not be able to implement the VAT scheme. Under VAT all inputs and outputs have to be accounted for. Further, the number of tax payers at the

---

[14] What is GST now

lower levels would be very large though the tax paid by them would be very small. So, the administrative costs would be high for little additional revenue. Finally, traders at different levels buy and sell many goods, so that matching the taxes of output and input is a herculean task for them.

Due to these difficulties, the Report felt that not only a comprehensive VAT but even VAT would be difficult to implement in India. Since some of the difficulties are a little less at the manufacturing level, it was proposed that VAT be implemented only on manufacturing, and not at the retail or wholesale level. It was therefore, called MANVAT (Value Added Tax at Manufacturer's stage). This would minimize the administrative problems. The large manufacturers would also not face accounting problems since they already have detailed accounts. It was suggested that for smaller units there may be special schemes which could simplify matters. Also, since MANVAT would be mostly applicable to large and medium units, the number of businesses that would be under the scheme would not be large.

It was suggested that there may be a few rates (four or five) applicable to consumer goods. But it was argued that petroleum products, tobacco, matches, textiles be kept out of this rate structure. It was argued that the excise system then prevalent for these items could continue for them. Why this special treatment? It was argued that these are final products and would have little cascading effect. Finally, it was said that these products were taxed at high rates for economic reasons so that almost half of the excise duty was collected from them (In 1976–77, 46.4 per cent of total excise revenue) and this should continue. It was stated that Brazil also has special provision for some products like petroleum and liquor and Germany also followed this practice.

A few specific proposals regarding MANVAT were:

1. Given the complexities, its implementation be initially restricted to a few (3–4) industries which produce final goods like automobiles and diesel engines.

2. Since the smaller producers would be at a disadvantage, it was suggested that tax credit on a notional basis be allowed to the manufacturers who purchased inputs from them. This would put them on par with the larger tax paying businesses.
3. Since tax evasion could take place, it was suggested that there be physical checking as well.

For the states, it was noted that the most important tax was the sales tax but it posed a variety of problems given that it was very complicated and allowed only limited concessions for inputs like raw material and intermediate goods. Thus, there was a cascading effect. The Report also pointed to the various complexities in the sales tax scheme. First, different states having different tax rates for the same commodity. Secondly, there was an Additional Excise Duty collected by the Centre in lieu of sales tax on tobacco, sugar and textiles. Thirdly, there is an important excise duty on liquor collected by the states and this is an important source of revenue for them. Fourthly, there is also sales tax on motor spirit and is another important source of tax. Finally, there is also a duty on electricity which did not yield much revenue.

For the local bodies, Octroi was an important indirect tax but it was at varying rates all across the country. The Committee disapproved of the Octroi and suggested its abolition on the grounds that it impeded the movement of goods and also there was a lot of irregularity associated with this tax. To compensate for the abolition of this tax, it suggested that the states should levy an additional tax along with sales tax and pass it on to the local bodies.

The Committee did not quite favour a tax on services since it would be difficult to implement. It also suggested the abolition of the tax on electricity since it did not yield much revenue. The most important thing about this Report is that it was comprehensive and flagged almost all the important issues that the later Committees also addressed. The major lacunae was that while it recognized the difficulties in implementing VAT it was not bold enough to say that it should not be implemented in India till the economy becomes more mature.

Long Term Fiscal Policy Report: Proposal for MODVAT

Government of India set up a committee in 1985 to give a long-term basis to fiscal policies. It was felt that this would stabilize the nation's macroeconomic policies. It was also hoped that focus on the long term would help identify the reforms of taxes so as to accelerate development. It submitted the Long Term Fiscal Policy Report in 1985.[15]

However, in an economy that is buffeted by various shocks like drought and calamities and which was increasingly opening up to the external sector, the hope that there would be greater stability in fiscal policies was belied. 1987 saw one of the most severe droughts in India and that was quickly followed by the oil shock of 1989 and the economy was completely derailed.

The launch of New Economic Policies (NEP) in 1991 completely changed the basis of policy.[16] This required a different structure of taxation in tune with the market forces. So, another Committee[17] was set up to propose tax reforms to bring them in line with the greater opening up of the economy. Given the instability of the Indian economy and the short time span before the next Committee came, not much could be done about the suggestions in the Long Term Fiscal Policy (LTFP) Report. However, one important suggestion in LTFP Report was that VAT be launched and this was initiated in 1986.

Given the complexities of India's production structures, MANVAT could not be launched so an alternative was suggested, a Modified VAT (MODVAT). Some of the main recommendations of the Report in this regard were:

---

[15] GoI (1985)

[16] Kumar (2013)

[17] GoI (1992)

1. Production is impacted adversely by the taxation of inputs. To counter this effect, the producers need to be given a set-off equal to the amount of indirect tax that was paid on the inputs. For instance, excise and countervailing duty (on imports) on inputs are paid and this needs to be subtracted (set-off) from the duty that the producer has to pay. This set-off is referred to as the 'input credit'.
2. It was suggested that the input credit should be as extensive as administratively feasible.
3. The set-off be expanded as far as possible to all excisable products with a few notable exceptions like petroleum, textiles and tobacco, which are mostly final products.
4. MODVAT may be extended to more goods in a phased manner.
5. It should be broadly revenue neutral.
6. If there is loss of revenue then the tax rate on final products could be increased.
7. To mitigate the difficulties of the poor, there should be lower rates of tax on goods consumed by them.
8. Recognizing the difficulties that the small scale businesses would face, it was suggested that there be rationalization of excise concessions.

As pointed out earlier in Chapter 1, a switch from ad valorem to a VAT leads to a loss of revenue for the government unless the VAT rates are revised upwards. This concern has been repeatedly expressed by the states. However, the counter argument has been that since more and more items are brought into the VAT net, the base of the tax expands and that could lead to greater collection of the tax. Research shows that buoyancy fell chapter by chapter as MODVAT was extended to more and more commodities.[18] So, the fear of the states was not unfounded. It was the introduction of the service tax in the 1990s and the high collection from customs duties in the late 1980s that saved the day for the government.

---

[18] Singh (2006)

Tax Reform Committee Report 1992

The focus of this Report[19] was on the new requirements for greater opening up of the economy which was initiated in 1991 under the NEP. The state was to retreat and the markets were to be the new driving force in the economy.[20] So, the issue became how to encourage the market functioning in the economy. As a result, the focus was largely on reduction in both direct taxes (to encourage profits) and customs duties (to allow more inflow of imports). Internal indirect taxes were less important and taxes levied by the Centre were given greater importance.

The result was that MODVAT was discussed but not in much depth. The Committee suggested how to expand the base of this tax, simplify it and increase tax collection via this tax. Simplification was to be achieved via reducing the exemptions granted. Steps were suggested to shift to a comprehensive VAT but this was not discussed in detail. It proposed that the rates of tax could be 10, 15 and 20 per cent. In addition to this basic tax it argued that non-essential consumption could bear taxes at 30, 40 or 50 per cent. Cigarettes could be an exception and be taxed at a rate higher than 50 per cent.

The Committee was in favour of the exemptions for the small scale sector. However, it noted that a large number of registrations have taken place under the excise scheme but not only the tax payment by this sector is low, critically, the department does not have the machinery to monitor these large number of registered units. Further, it opined that there is misuse of the exemption for the small scale sector. Considering all this, the Committee suggested a Simplified Assessment Procedure (SAP) for units with a turnover of less than Rs 25 lakh and a tax rate of 2 per cent for them.

It also suggested a shift from specific to ad valorem rates of tax. It noted that there was a shift from ad valorem to specific rates over the 1980s with the tax collected from specific duties increasing

---

[19] GoI (1992)

[20] Kumar (1991)

from 46 per cent of the total in 1980–81 to 70 per cent in 1991–92. It suggested a reversal of this trend. This shift was also necessitated by the need to move towards VAT. In the context of ad valorem taxes it referred to the problem of valuation and black income generation but also stated that there is 'no fool proof method' available which overcomes these problems.

In the context of VAT it suggested that assessment should be on the basis of the invoice raised by the seller. Further, it suggested that excise should not be levied on the basis of goods leaving the production unit (as prevalent then) but on the basis of returns filed at regular intervals. This was a measure of simplification and reduction of paperwork.

A tax on services at the rate of 10 per cent was suggested to broaden the base of indirect tax. It was stated that this should be levied by the Centre and to begin with only a few services should be taxed. The services chosen for taxation should not enter the production process in a general way, that is, they should be almost like final ones. The logic of the argument was that inflationary pressures that would be generated by another indirect tax should be minimized.

Report of the Task Force on Indirect Taxes 2002

This Report[21] came almost a decade after the Chelliah Committee Report. MODVAT had been converted to CENVAT and states were being prepared to move towards VAT. Service tax had been introduced and its coverage widened considerably. Since indirect taxes are stagflationary, this impact was being felt in the economy. The Empowered Committee of State Finance Ministers was already in place to move towards VAT, so the Committee benefitted from their deliberations.

The recommendations made by the Task Force were to 'combine together to simplify and rationalize the tax system, effectively reduce

---

[21] GoI (2002)

transaction costs, encourage voluntary compliance and, in short, bring our indirect tax system and administration at par, if not better, than the best international practices'.

The Task Force looked at the international practice on VAT rates. It concluded that there is no reason to go in for a single Central VAT (CENVAT) rate. There could be a three-tier duty structure and a surcharge on tobacco and petroleum products. It was also recommended that the exemption for small scale units should be lowered to Rs 50 lakh. Actually in principle, the Committee was not in favour of any exemption to small units for a variety of reasons.

Regarding VAT, the Report acknowledged it to be a major reform and wanted its speedy implementation in the states. It also suggested that all the local taxes be discontinued. But it did not say how the local bodies would earn revenue and what would be the consequence of their greater dependence on the transfer of resources from the states. This erosion of the autonomy of the local bodies was ignored. It suggested the setting up of a VAT Council to sort out the problems that may result from the implementation of this tax.

It made recommendations for service tax so that it could be smoothly integrated into the more comprehensive VAT that the Task Force wanted India to move towards. It suggested integration of the goods and services input credit schemes and enhancement of service tax rates to bring them on par with the CENVAT rates. It also suggested speedy automation of the administration since without that, integration of various indirect taxes into a more comprehensive VAT (or GST) was not feasible.

First Discussion Paper on GST, 2009

'An announcement was made by the then Union finance minister, Mr P. Chidambaram, in the Central Budget (2007–08) to the effect that GST would be introduced with effect from 1 April 2010 and that the Empowered Committee of State Finance Ministers, on his request, would work with the Central Government to prepare a road map for introduction of GST in India.'[22]

A working committee of officials was set up which prepared its draft after several rounds of consultations across the board. This resulted in a detailed proposal which was presented as the 'First Discussion Paper'[23] for wider public consultation.

The Report noted the problem of cascading effect of indirect taxes and saw VAT as a means of overcoming this problem. It noted the difficulty posed by the substitution of sales tax by VAT in the states and how steps were taken in this direction from 1995 when Mr Manmohan Singh was the finance minister and then in 1999 when Mr Yashwant Sinha was the finance minister. It was noted that there was a 'rate war' among the states and that this was not desirable. The need for harmonization of the sales tax rates was the first step suggested for the implementation of one tax rate under VAT.

A Standing Committee of State Finance Ministers was set up to look into the implementation of these steps. Later this Committee was converted into an Empowered Committee of State Finance Ministers. This Committee met regularly and its decisions were taken by consensus. The result was the substantial implementation of harmonization of rates within about a year and a half. Subsequently, the states started implementing VAT beginning 1 April 2005. It was noted that 'The rate of growth of tax revenue has nearly doubled from the average annual rate of growth in the pre-VAT five year period after the introduction of VAT'.

This provided the confidence to move towards a GST. It was felt that this would help bring various state and Centre level indirect taxes onto one platform and allow the input credit to be given across various taxes. CENVAT did not include other indirect taxes so they could not be brought in the VAT net. It was felt that GST would lead to a widening of the tax base via a) inclusion of more layers of

[22] GoI (2009a)
[23] GoI (2009a)

production and trade and b) better compliance. The result it was felt would be increased collection of revenue. A similar argument was made for the state level indirect taxes.

It was argued that under GST, there 'would be a continuous chain of set-off from the original producer's point and service provider's point up to the retailer's level'. The problem was that the states would also have to charge tax on services but they did not have this power. Thus, the need for a constitutional amendment was highlighted. It was felt that all the trouble would be worth it since GST would be a positive sum game. It was seen to benefit the government via higher tax collection, the businesses via simplification and lower tax rates and the consumers via lower prices. This refrain has continued since then. It is only in 2015, when I pointed out[24] a contradiction in this argument, that an alternative argument became a part of the discourse. This contradiction in the macroeconomics of GST is discussed later in Chapter 4.

The Committee proposed a dual GST, that is, the Centre and the states having a GST with their own defined functions and responsibilities. It suggested a harmonious rate structure and a collectively agreed Constitutional amendment.

Salient features of the proposed model were to be:

1. Dual GST model to be implemented through multiple statutes (one for CGST and SGST statute for every state).
2. Since the Central GST and state GST are to be treated separately, taxes paid against the Central GST to be allowed to be taken as input tax credit (ITC) for the Central GST only and it could not be utilized for the payment of state GST. The same principle was to be applicable for the state GST.
3. A taxpayer or exporter would have to maintain separate details in books of account for utilization or refund of credit.
4. Cross utilization of ITC between the Central GST and the state GST would not be allowed except in the case of inter-state supply

---

[24] Kumar (2015)

of goods and services under the IGST model (which is explained later).

5. The administration of the Central GST to be with the Centre and the state GST to be with the states. This would imply that 'the Centre and the states would have concurrent jurisdiction for the entire value chain and for all taxpayers on the basis of thresholds for goods and services prescribed for the states and the Centre'.

6. A threshold was suggested below which GST would not be applicable. Another range of turnover was suggested for the Composition/Compounding Scheme for the small businesses.

7. It was proposed that alcohol and petroleum products be kept out of GST but tobacco products should come under GST.

8. For inter-state transactions of Goods and Service, a tax called IGST was proposed. This was to be collected by the Centre and distributed to the importing state. The IGST rate to be the sum of the CGST and SGST rates.

The Report also worked out and presented various other details regarding the implementation of the scheme. Further, it had an Annexure on the frequently asked questions on GST to explain the scheme to businesses and the public.

International Experience

It is said that now GST is applicable in more than 160 countries in the world[25] and India is one of the last countries to implement this tax. Table 3.1 gives a list of some of the major countries implementing VAT/GST and the year in which they introduced it. Table 3.2 gives the continent-wise implementation of VAT/GST and which countries do not implement VAT/GST. USA is a notable exception.

However, it is also the case, as mentioned earlier, that most countries do not have the full GST. What do they have? A variant of VAT. As has been discussed earlier in the Chapter, in the various

---

[25] GoI (2009a)

Reports on indirect taxes in India, the term used was 'comprehensive VAT' or just VAT.

As mentioned earlier, a full GST ought to have all indirect taxes under it and calculated as VAT. If services are not included or various exceptions are made then it cannot be referred to as full GST. In this sense, India also has a variant of GST since many important items are outside its net (See Chapter 6). Also, the small and micro sector in India is very large and not only has it been kept outside the GST net, input credit is not available to it, so for this reason also, the Indian GST is only partial.

Globally, there has been a concern about the progressivity of VAT and its impact on inflation. To reduce its regressivity, the tax rate on essentials, consumed by the poor, has either been kept low or zero. Further, public goods are kept out of the purview of the tax so as to not impose a burden on the poor. For instance, education and health are usually kept out of its ambit.

Experience of a Few Countries:

1. France was the first country to implement GST in 1954. It has had 4 rates of 2.1 per cent, 5.5 per cent, 10 per cent and 20 per cent. The basic rate is 20 per cent which is applicable on most items. This system is now applicable all across Europe.

2. United Kingdom has had VAT since 2011. It has a single rate of 20 per cent. This is the same basic rate as in Europe of which it is still a part.

3. Ukraine has two VAT slabs—20 per cent for most goods and services and 7 per cent for medicines.

4. New Zealand introduced GST in 1986 with a rate of 10 per cent which was enhanced to 12.5 per cent in 1989 and to 15 per cent in 2010. In 1986, the tax was a part of economic reforms and replaced the then existing sales tax. The increase in the rate in 2010 was to compensate for the cut in direct taxes. GST covers all goods and services with a few exceptions like rental income on residential property and financial services.

5. Australia initiated VAT in 2000 with a rate of 10 per cent. It replaced sales tax and several other state taxes like banking tax and stamp duty.

6. Vietnam has three rates of 0 per cent, 5 per cent and 10 per cent for most goods and services, unless stated otherwise.

7. Singapore implemented GST in 1994 with a rate of 3 per cent which was raised to 7 per cent in 2007. There was an increase in the rate of inflation when GST was introduced.

8. Malaysia introduced GST in 2015 with a rate of 6 per cent. Earlier, the tax rate on sales and services ranged from 5 per cent to 15 per cent. There was a lot of criticism of this tax since it was anticipated that it would lead to an adverse impact on the poor and that delayed its introduction. It did lead to an increase in the rate of inflation. Anticipating problems, many essential goods like agricultural products were zero rated (tax rate of zero). Many services and especially those provided by the government and those linked to exports were also zero rated. Education, health and child care were placed in the exempt category so as to protect the interest of the poor.

   Mr Mahatir, the new PM elected in 2018, immediately dismantled GST on assuming power.

9. Canada initiated GST in 1991 amidst a lot of controversy. It has a rate of 5 per cent on all goods and services. In some provinces of Canada, a Harmonized Sales Tax of 15 per cent is also charged. An input tax credit system and zero rating for exported goods are provided for. For equity, low income people can get a rebate on GST when they pay their income tax.

In brief, different countries follow different models of VAT/GST. These differences reflect the diversity of the situations prevailing in the different countries. This has important lessons for India—the country need not have gone in for GST unless it was clear that the vast majority of the people will benefit from it. As discussed in the next chapter, that is not the case.

CHAPTER 4

GST: THE LARGER ISSUES

Benefits of GST: Six Important Elements

Prior to implementation of GST in 2017, as pointed out in Annexure 1.1, there were many indirect taxes, which are now absorbed in GST. So, in the pre GST regime, separate forms had to be filled up for various taxes and filed to different agencies. This multiplicity led to complications and increased costs for businesses. Under GST, it was said that there would be only one tax to deal with so there would be less paper work. This would lead to 'Ease of doing business' and, therefore, to increased efficiency.

Earlier while each tax was calculated as VAT, the input credit was not available across different taxes. For instance, a manufacturer producing an item was liable to pay an excise duty on it. She could deduct the excise duty paid on the inputs but she could not deduct the sales tax that may have been paid on the inputs by the supplier. So, there was a cascading effect of a tax on tax. Under GST, the advantage is that a set-off is available for any tax paid on any of the inputs.

For entry into a state or a city, there was an entry tax and/ or Octroi. Thus, goods transported across states and cities had to pay tax at each of the state and city border that was crossed. It was said that not only was there corruption at each of the check points but also long line of trucks. Thus, movement of goods slowed down and a lot of fuel was wasted due to idling trucks. With GST, it was said, there would be an e-way bill that each truck would carry and it would be tracked by computers thereby obviating the need for checking at each border, again resulting in efficiencies for businesses.

As pointed out in Chapter 3, earlier, each state had its own sales tax so that for the same good there were different rates of taxes in different states. People could then buy the good in the neighbouring state where the tax was less. With a common tax in each of the states it was said that things would get simplified, there would be 'one nation one tax'. It would be like one market and that would unify the country, resulting in greater efficiency for businesses.

It was also argued that since all the stages of production and distribution would be included in GST, tax collection would rise both for the Centre and the states. This would reduce the resource shortage for essentials like education and transportation, thereby benefitting the common citizen. Further, since more tax would be collected, the tax rates on existing items could be reduced, thereby lowering the prices of goods and services.

Another argument was that because GST would be based on invoices drawn up during transactions between businesses, under and over invoicing would be eliminated. Revenue of the seller would be the cost to the buyer. Earlier the seller would under invoice the revenue while the buyer would over invoice the purchases to show lower incomes and pay less tax.[1] Under GST because the two invoices would be automatically matched, this kind of under and over invoicing would no more be possible. Consequently, not only more tax would be collected but the black economy would come under check. Further, as tax collection rises, indirect tax rates could be reduced thereby lowering prices.

The main advantages of GST have been listed as:

a. Bringing together of seventeen indirect taxes on one platform (See Annexure 1.1).
b. Indirect taxes to be calculated as VAT to eliminate the 'cascading effect' and thereby lower the tax burden on goods and services.
c. Due to matching of invoices, the black economy would be curtailed.

---

[1] See Chapter 7

d. There would be economies of scale. Supply chains would be simplified and warehouses relocated resulting in efficiency for large scale suppliers.

e. Transportation would be easier because of elimination of tolls and introduction of the e-way bills. Movements of all goods would be tracked automatically.

Theoretically, the above elements refer to two important considerations. First, all indirect taxes would be on one platform from the earlier separate ones so that there would be less paper work and fewer complications. The other is that all indirect taxes are to be calculated as Value Added Tax (VAT) with input credit available from one indirect tax to the other. Thus, the cascading effect of one tax on to the other is eliminated.

If all the above listed advantages were to materialize, GST would be a win-win for every section of society and hence would be highly desirable. While 'ease of doing business' would be of help to businesses, the consumers would benefit from lower prices. No wonder it has been billed as the biggest tax reform in India and a game changer.

With massive improvements in efficiency of businesses, it was argued that there would be higher production, lower prices, more tax collection and better revenues for the Centre and the states.[2] These are all macroeconomic variables. How taxes impact each of them needs to be discussed in the framework of fiscal policy regime, as argued in Chapter 2. If not, the results remain partial, contradictory and often misleading. This is taken up for analysis below.

Missing Macroeconomic Elements

It is argued earlier in Chapter 2, all the fiscal policy variables work together via the national income identity. They together constitute

---

[2] GoI (2009a)

the fiscal policy regime. It is characterized by the amount of indirect and direct taxes, subsidies, investments, interest payments and so on. These in turn depend on the size of the black economy and its impact on each of these variables. For instance, if indirect tax collections rise and nothing else changes, there would be an increase in prices.[3] Further, since the fiscal deficit is kept unchanged, there is no decline in the output. This is a consequence of demand shifting from those who pay the extra tax to increased spending by the government. In brief, prices rise but output stays the same and that is referred to as stagflation. In other words, indirect taxes are stagflationary.

In contrast, the proponents of GST claim the opposite when they say that GST would lead to higher collection of indirect taxes and lead to lower prices and result in higher level of output. Theoretically, this is contradictory. The result claimed by the proponents is because of their partial and disjointed analysis.

The proponent's take each of these three elements independently—namely, tax collection, prices and output. They believe that since all the goods and services will be under the tax net, more taxes would be collected. Independently, they believe that since input credit would be available, prices would fall. Finally, due to higher efficiency, output would rise. The correct understanding emerges when all three variables are analysed using the fiscal policy regime so that the inter connections between the variables can be taken into account, as presented below.

Impact of GST on Prices

In modern day economies, most products can be stored unlike in primitive economies where most things were perishable. For the latter kind of goods, the producers had to sell sooner than later before it got spoiled. Hence demand mattered a lot. If it was inadequate, the producer would cut the price in order to get more people to buy the good. So, demand and supply were crucial in determining the price.

---

[3]   Kalecki (1971). Also see Chapter 2

When goods are not perishable, as has been the case for some time, most of the goods can be stored and sold later. Even agricultural produce and fish can be stored in cold storage and sold later. Then immediate sale is less important.

Another factor is that most products are sold quite some time after they are produced since there is a long chain of transportation, storage and so on from production to sales. The producer has to print the price on the packaging well before the product is produced. In India a Maximum Sale Price (MSP) is printed on the package. How does the producer determine this price? The producer does not know the demand when the product would be sold. So, the printed price is largely independent of the demand conditions and is based on the costs incurred in production.

Prices are now mostly determined by what is called 'mark up on prime costs'.[4] What are these prime costs? Producers have a good idea about some costs but not all of them (like, overhead costs). There is always uncertainty about being able to sell what is produced since demand may decrease. In that case the producers may have to incur more costs on advertising and sales and also holding inventory; these are all overheads. The producers have a good idea in advance only about wages and raw material costs. These are referred to as the 'prime costs'. The producers put a multiple on these costs to cover the overhead costs and generate a profit for themselves. That is why prices are fixed mostly by a 'markup' on prime costs.

What happens when the product reaches the market and demand conditions change? Say, demand falls. Then, inventory rises and that signals to the producer that now they need to produce less. So, change in demand conditions leads to change in stocks and not prices. It is due to this pricing mechanism that all across the world, prices of goods that can be stocked rise usually when the prime costs go up. For instance, when global commodity prices rise or wages increase, prices go up.

---

[4] Kalecki (1971)

Indirect taxes are also like prime costs. They are levied on the businesses and in turn they pass them on to the consumer. So, when indirect taxes rise, prices rise. This is often seen in the post-budget scenario. For instance, when the government raises excise duty on toothpaste or cars, the price of these goods is raised by the companies and the retailers. Before GST was implemented, the government had increased the service tax from 12 per cent to 15 per cent and this increase was passed on to the consumers. Recall, how the insurance agent and the telephone companies passed on the increase to the consumers.

It is important to note that there is an asymmetry. When the tax is reduced it does not always result in a fall in the price since the businesses tend to absorb the benefit as higher profit. In these cases, usually they claim that costs had gone up earlier and they were holding back the price increase. That has also been the government's worry. With the implementation of GST, any benefit in terms of lower tax rate may be absorbed by businesses as extra profit. So, in the design of GST an 'anti-profiteering' clause was incorporated. How this would be enforced and how profiteering would be determined remain tricky issues. Producers may show increased costs to claim higher prices and thereby claim that the profits have not actually increased.

In effect, if more indirect taxes are collected than earlier, prices would go up since prime cost would rise. However, it may be argued that GST would be applicable to the entire chain of production and distribution—from the raw material stage to the final sale. Thus, more tax would be collected and that is why the tax rate on many items that earlier bore a higher tax rate could be lowered. If that were to happen, would the price of these items not fall?

But, the point is that if some items that were earlier not taxed are now taxed and their prices go up then that would cancel the price fall in certain other items where the tax rate is lowered, assuming that the businesses will pass on the benefit to the consumers. If the total tax collection rises for indirect taxes, the average price would go up even if prices of some items drop. Even in cases where the GST rate is reduced, compared to the earlier tax on that item, the price may not fall because the producers may increase their profit.

For example, tax on services has been increased making all services more expensive. These are often 'productive services' used in production, like, insurance, finance, telecom, transportation and trade. Since these are basic to all production, an increase in their price would raise the prices of all other goods and services even if the tax rate on some of the goods falls.

The argument given here goes against the claim that with GST, indirect tax collection would rise while prices would fall.

RNR and Prices

So, how much tax should be collected under GST? Revenue is crucial for development and especially for a poor nation like India, where a large number of people are below the poverty line (which represents extreme poverty). Those just above the poverty line are also poor and are deprived of the basics of a civilized existence. They all are dependent on government programmes for improving their lot in life. As discussed in Chapter 1, the government, especially the state governments, would like revenue neutrality so that they continue to collect at least as much tax revenue as they were getting under the earlier scheme of indirect taxes. Collecting more would be inflationary as mentioned above so, the goal has to be to collect as much as earlier and not more, if inflation is to be kept under check.

RNR is simple in theory but not in practice (See Chapter 1). As will be discussed in greater detail in Chapter 4, there are many exclusions for achieving various goals. For the sake of protecting the poor the government has left out many essentials from GST. Exports have to be left out so as not to make Indian goods uncompetitive in the international markets. For revenue's sake, some key commodities have been left out. Those who are at the lower rungs of business are also left out of the GST network. So, all this makes GST complex in practice and calculating the RNR has proved to be difficult (and controversial) as will be discussed in Chapter 5.

Be that as it may, what is the implication of leaving out many items in the production and distribution chain? Due to these exclusions, tax collection would be less than it could be and correspondingly the RNR on items that remain in the tax net has to be higher than it could be. The logic is that a given amount of tax has to be collected from fewer number of items in the production and distribution chain so that they have to bear a higher tax rate. The more the items excluded, higher the rate of tax has to be on those items that remain under the GST net. This has other effects as well.

First, many basic commodities and services remain under GST and they have to bear a higher rate because of items being excluded. So, in spite of RNR, inflation would kick up. The reason is that these basics feed into the production of all goods and services, even those that are exempted from the GST net. Hence this factor would cause a general price rise.[5]

Secondly, there is another problem with having one common rate for all goods and services. Usually the basics are taxed at a lower rate than the final goods and services. But one rate on all items would mean that the tax rate on the basics would rise while it would decline for the final ones.[6] Again, this higher rate on the basics would feed into all prices, including those of essentials which are not taxed and the rate of inflation would rise.

Following this logic given by this author, the government went in for five different rates rather than one rate which it was talking of till then. It went in for higher rates of tax on all services and that has spurred inflation since as argued above when productive services are taxed at higher rates, they feed into other prices.

Thirdly, the government was worried about losing revenue and decided to go for a higher RNR. This creates an inflationary situation. Sultan Singh[7] showed in his dissertation that chapter by chapter the rate of increase in tax collection fell as MODVAT was extended to

---

[5]   Kumar (2015)
[6]   Kumar (2015)
[7]   Singh (2006)

more and more commodities. This implied that the likelihood of fall in revenue was great as GST was implemented and keeping this in mind, a higher than required RNR rate was kept.

In conclusion, the government is in a fix. If it collects more revenue than earlier by keeping tax rates higher than justified by revenue neutrality, there would be inflation. If revenue neutral rate becomes the one common rate then too there would be higher level of inflation due to higher tax on basics. If to make the tax progressive and to avoid raising inflation, the essentials are taxed less while the other goods are taxed higher, there would be multiple tax rates and the cascading effect would reappear as argued in Annexure 1.1. Finally, the benefit of input credit or lower tax rates may not be passed on to the consumer by businesses. Hence businesses, by increasing their profits, for items where prices could fall, will ensure that prices do not fall at all.

Impact of GST on Output, Investment and Growth Rate

GST is an indirect tax and it impacts prices as discussed above. It also impacts the government's budgetary position via the revenue it yields. Both these, impact prices and government revenue and through them the level of output in the economy.

If GST leads to an increase in prices, then consumer's demand in the economy would tend to decline. That leads to lower levels of output. However, the government gets more revenue and if it spends that then the demand from the government increases. If the government spends all the additional revenue it gets then the deficit remains unchanged and demand in the economy remains unchanged. The lower real expenditure by the consumers is exactly compensated by the increase in expenditure by the government. So, there is no decline in overall demand and the level of production in the economy would remain unchanged.

However, if the government uses the extra money it gets to lower the deficit by spending less than the extra amount it collects, then demand would be short and production would tend to decline. If it spends more than it collects then the deficit rises and the demand also increases so that the production would tend to rise.

But the deficit could be increased without increasing the tax collection via GST. So, the case of an increase in the deficit can be considered independent of the GST, hence this is not the important case here. The important one is, if increased collection under GST is used to keep the deficit unchanged or to lower it. In the former case the output would not rise but in the latter case it will fall. So, the rate of growth of the economy will either stagnate or fall.

There are two other possibilities. First, if GST leads to a change in the distribution in the economy between the businessmen and the rest. Another case is if GST has a differential impact on different parts of the economy with one part benefitting and the other losing out.

Consider the first possibility. If GST results in an increase in profits because businesses do not pass on the benefit of the input credit to the consumer, then, the purchasing power of the consumers is impacted adversely. This does not change the revenue collection from GST.

The businessmen, being richer than the average citizen, spend only a small fraction of the extra profits they get so that their consumption rises slowly with incomes. The workers and the salaried consume most of their incomes so when they lose incomes due to an increase in GST, they will reduce their consumption by much more than the increase in consumption by businessmen. So, even if the government keeps the deficit unchanged by spending all the extra revenue it gets, it does not compensate for the decline of demand from the consumers. In this case, the businessmen are left with a surplus which they have not spent and that is why demand declines. Unless they increase their investment (which is another form of expenditure) enough to compensate for the fall in demand, output will decline.

However, it is well known that investment does not rise immediately.[8] Investment is a complicated decision and it is very

---

[8]   Kalecki (1971)

uncertain so businesses take a while to decide to increase their investment. They have to be sure that the additional demand is durable and not just a temporary blip and that profits will sustain. Thus, businesses take time to decide on additional investment. After that only they place orders for extra plant and equipment. Most machines are not available off the shelf. So, it takes a while to fulfil orders and for new equipment to be added to the existing capital stock. By definition, it is only when capital stock rises that investment rises.

Take for example the bullet train project being implemented in India. It was conceived in 2014 but its execution is starting in 2018 and it will be delivered not before 2022—eight years later. A nuclear power plant may take a decade or more. One can add a lathe or a milling machine or a welding robot in an assembly line but that may also take months to deliver and install. Thus capital stock begins to rise much after a decision to invest is taken so that investment does not rise immediately after extra profits are earned.

Therefore, in the case under consideration, GST leading to an increase in profits, investment does not rise immediately so that the demand tends to fall and the rate of growth of the economy falls.

It is also claimed that GST would lead to 'ease of doing business' and that would result in an increase in profits and a more conducive environment for investment. If paperwork decreases and harassment of businesses dealing with multiple agencies declines, it would certainly improve business environment. But, investment would only rise with a time lag and not immediately so that the rate of growth would not go up in the short term. Anyhow, as discussed in Chapter 6, in the short run, after GST was introduced, businesses are struggling to cope with its complexity so that 'ease of doing business' has not been evident.

Would the rate of growth rise in the longer term? This would depend on multiple factors. The most important being 'demand'. It is here that the argument given above comes into play—when profits rise demand does not automatically rise. Not in the short run but what about the long term? So, are there other factors that could come into play due to implementation of GST that could constrain or boost demand?

The structure of the Indian economy is highly differentiated. It consists of a very large unorganized sector which works at low wages and low levels of profits. It produces 45 per cent of the output[9] while employing 93 per cent of the workforce.[10] It largely consists of the small and the tiny units. These have been hurt by the complexity of GST and the loss in demand. Why would this happen given the government's claim that this sector has been either completely left out of the ambit of GST or it is only marginally taxed under Composition Scheme.[11]

Unorganized Sector and GST

The large unorganized sector in India which works at the small and micro scale hardly keeps detailed accounts.[12] So, it is unable to calculate what is the value added in its production and therefore, unable to calculate how much VAT it is required to pay. This was the difficulty due to which implementation of VAT could not be undertaken earlier and alternatives like MANVAT and MODVAT were considered (See Chapter 3). The idea, suggested since 1978, that the entire production and distribution chain be brought under a comprehensive VAT from the beginning to the end could not be taken up. Even now this difficulty persists and is hard to overcome.

The proponents of GST deny this argument by pointing to the fact that any unit with a turnover of less than Rs 20 lakh does not need to register or pay GST. Further, those units with a turnover of between Rs 20 lakh and Rs 1.5 crore are under a special scheme called 'Composition Scheme'. They do not have to do detailed accounting and only need to pay a flat tax. But, both these categories,

---

[9]   This point is discussed in detail in Kumar (2017d)
[10] GoI (2018a)
[11] Described in the next section and in Chapter 6
[12] Kumar (2017d). Also see Banerjee and Prasad (2017)

face severe limitations. They cannot make inter-state sales or get input credit or provide input credit to those who buy from them. In effect they are at a disadvantage compared to the organized sector units that are registered and that can provide input credit to those who purchase from them and also take advantage of input credit on their purchases.

Thus, if the small businesses join the GST scheme, their accounting costs rise but if they are outside GST they cannot provide input credit so that those purchasing from them will have to face higher costs unless they drop prices. Either way they lose out.

These units do not get any input credit on their purchases so that their costs rise compared to those who are in the GST net. The consequence is that neither they can give input credit nor can they get input credit and they become less competitive compared to the others. Buyers would then prefer to buy more from the organized sector than the unorganized sector. This would boost the rate of growth of the organized sector at the expense of the unorganized sector.

Since the organised sector is far more mechanized and automated than the unorganized sector, overall employment generation would weaken as production from the latter is substituted by the production from the former. The wages in the organized sectors are much higher than the wages in the unorganized sector but the total wage payment to labour is less. This would impact demand in the economy and lead to lower level of capacity utilization and less of investment (technically it is said that the accelerator stops acting).

GST, Black Economy and Output

Another argument is that GST is transactions based. So that invoices by buyers and sellers can be matched. Thus, under and over invoicing of bills is not feasible. Since this has been the biggest source of black income generation,[13] if it is checked, the size of the black economy would decline. If this were to happen, two things would follow.

---

[13] Kumar (2006a) and Chapter 7

First, inefficiency in the economy due to the existence of the black economy would decline and the rate of growth of the economy would go up. Secondly, what was formerly undeclared output would now be declared so that the rate of growth of the white economy would go up. Since the white economy rate of growth is the official rate of growth, the economy's rate of growth would go up with the implementation of GST.

So, the question is whether GST would help check the growth of the black economy in India and bring down its size which would then boost the growth rate of the economy?

It has been noticed that a large number of establishments are operating without issuing bills even after the introduction of GST. This was true earlier as well. Those who do not issue bills for sales and purchases can be entirely outside the GST net—as it was before. This suggests that there is a complete chain of production and distribution which works entirely in cash outside the system established now under the GST. Such a chain can take advantage of the exemptions for the small-scale sector which does not have to register under the GST network or of the Composition Scheme where a small amount of tax has to be paid.[14]

Further, essential items like electricity and petroleum goods are outside the GST net. Also, many essential items have zero tax on them, so their production and distribution can easily be kept out of the GST net. Thus, the GST chain gets broken at various points and that enables the unscrupulous elements to escape the GST net. In effect, the black economy may be impacted to some extent but is likely to remain substantially unaffected by the introduction of GST.

There are other ways of evading the taxes by misclassifying the goods even if one is registered under GST network.[15] For instance, classifying perfectly fine goods as seconds or scrap has been used by industry in the past and can continue to be used now also.

---

[14] See Chapter 7 also
[15] Kumar (2015)

Doctors may see fifty patients in a day but declare that they have seen only thirty patients. There are as many ways of generating black incomes as the number of businesses (more about this in Chapter 7).

In brief, if the black economy is hardly dented then its adverse impact on the economy will continue. Namely, inefficiencies will continue and non-disclosure of the full output will persist. The actual economy is made up of the black and the white parts. So the total economy's rate of growth is the sum of the white and the black parts. If some of the formerly black (undeclared) output is declared due to reduced misinvoicing, the white (declared) economy's rate of growth will go up without the overall (black plus white) rate of growth going up. It remains to be seen if this small effect on growth rate would be able to counter the decline in the overall growth rate, as discussed in previous sections, due to the adverse impact on the unorganized sector and the more skewed distribution of income in general.

Change from Source to Destination Tax

There are many other major issues that are being raised by GST. One of the most important one is that of federalism which is discussed in detail later in Chapter 8. GST is likely to have a differential impact on the producing and the consuming states and that is taken up in a limited way here since it leads to greater inequality among states and to a shift in distribution.

The way GST is designed, if the production and distribution chain stretches across various states, taxes are passed from the exporting state to the importing state at each stage of production and distribution. So, the tax is finally paid at the last stage by the consumer in the last state where the final sale takes place and that state collects the entire tax paid. Thus, it is said that GST is a 'destination' based tax.

States where the intermediate stages of production and distribution occurred will not get the tax that they got until now under the excise, sales and service tax. India consists of developed states (like Tamil Nadu and Maharashtra) that produce not only in absolute terms but also proportionately much more of the goods and services than the lesser developed states (like Bihar and Assam). The former are called the producing states and the latter the consuming states. The producing states export a larger proportion of their production than the consuming states. So, a larger proportion of the GST would leak out from the former to the latter.

That is why the producing states have been concerned that they will lose taxes to the consuming states. This was the reason for the opposition to the implementation of GST from the former. The Centre assured compensation for any loss to bring these states on board. How this scheme works out in the long run remains to be seen.

However, it is likely that the producing states will gain since they are host to most large scale production which is likely to be the real beneficiary of GST. So, while they may lose in terms of indirect tax collections they would gain with the collection of more of the direct taxes and also due to the generation of more employment. The less developed states have a proportionately higher share of the unorganized sector in their economy and so they will suffer due to a decline in the unorganized sector of the economy.

Thus, GST is likely to lead to greater regional imbalances. This adverse shift in distribution of income regionally will also slow down the rate of growth of the economy in the long term.

Problems with Macroeconomic Data

It may be asked where is the data to show a rise in prices or a fall in the rate of growth or a decline in the unorganized sector demand? This is exactly the same problem that was faced when demonetization was carried out. Official data did not show a sharp decline in the unorganized sector's output so that the rate of growth of the economy did not show a fall. The impact on the prices was also not visible in the inflation data.

I have earlier discussed[16] this issue and pointed out that when there is a shock to the economy then the earlier method of calculating the rate of growth[17] does not apply. This point also applies to GST which administered a shock to the economy and it also impacted the unorganized sectors severely just as demonetization did. During demonetization and immediately after that, the private surveys showed the sharp decline in businesses and especially in the unorganized sectors.[18] This was supported by the data on employment under MGNREGS because large numbers of workers from urban areas went back to the villages and sought work there. It was further supported by the decline in the credit off-take from the banks which reached a historic low.

In India, inflation is measured either using the Wholesale Price Index (WPI) or the Consumer Price Index (CPI). In WPI, services are not represented at all so the rise in prices of services is not captured and this under represents inflation.[19] Since the tax on services has been going up for the last many years, their prices have risen but this is not captured in WPI. In CPI also the representation of services is much less than in the GDP[20] so that this also under represents inflation in the economy.

In brief, official data does not capture either the real rate of growth of the economy after a shock like GST or demonetization, or the true rate of inflation. One has to depend on theoretical arguments or other supporting data as is being done here to explain the impact of GST on output, inflation and investment.

---

16 Kumar (2017d)
17 Kumar (2017b)
18 Kumar (2017d)
19 Kumar (2006b)
20 Kumar (2017d)

CHAPTER 5

GST DESIGN: NUTS AND BOLTS

As has been repeatedly emphasized in the earlier chapters, GST is a very complex tax. It appears to be very simple but when one looks at the details, the complexity becomes apparent. This chapter presents some of the important aspects of GST which will bring out the complexities. If a chartered accountant or a tax lawyer were to write this book she would do it very differently. These experts would go into all the detailed rulings and legal complexities that have been appearing in the press in the last more than a year. They would not look at the structural aspects which lead to the complexity since they as practitioners have to deal with the rules and the changes in them as a practical matter for their clients. This chapter does not deal with the details but presents the structural complexities of GST and the various structural changes that have had to be carried out since the launch of GST.

The structural complexity is a result of the very idea of what is Value Added. No doubt, there is a structural simplification when many taxes are merged into one[1] but other forms of complexity have appeared. In the pre-GST regime, separate forms had to be filled up for each of the taxes and filed to different agencies. This led to practical difficulties and additional costs for businesses. Now there is only one tax to deal with and less paper work to do. But in practice, as will become clear through this chapter, under GST, there is more of accounting work and filing of returns due to structural factors. Hence there is a different kind of complexity.

---

[1] See Annexure 1.1

Report of Task Force on GST of Thirteenth Finance Commission

As pointed out in Annexure 5.1, several dates were fixed for the roll out of GST but its implementation had to be postponed repeatedly due to political differences among parties and criticisms from various quarters. There was also lack of consensus between the Centre and the states on many items. To sort these out two important initiatives were the Task Force of the Thirteenth Finance Commission[2] and the setting up of the Committee[3] to decide the rate structure of GST.

As a part of the Thirteenth Finance Commission, a Task Force was set up to comment and help design the Goods and Services Tax. It is a standard procedure of any Finance Commission that it assesses the revenue that can be collected by the Central and the state governments. Since at that time GST was to be introduced from April 2010, it was necessary for the Finance Commission to study the implications of introduction of GST on the revenues of the different levels of government in the country.

The Task Force Report was submitted on 15 December 2009. It made 'recommendations on various issues relating to the design and implementation of the Goods and Services Tax (GST)'. After studying the paper prepared by the Empowered Committee, it found that

> The contours outlined in this paper do not adequately advance the cause of indirect tax reforms due to a number of infirmities. This initiative seems to be an amalgam of compromises and continued fear of possible revenue losses and adverse impact on the low income groups. Clearly, there are a number of important unresolved issues relating to the design of the GST . . .

---

[2] GoI (2009a)
[3] GoI (2009b)

The authors of the Report hoped that their effort would assist the Union and the state governments reach a consensus that would help bring a 'world class GST regime in India'.

The Report identified the then prevailing indirect tax system in India as 'distortionary and has cascading effects. This leads to mis-allocation of resources, lower productivity and economic growth, and inhibits voluntary compliance.' The Task Force set its task as removal of these infirmities via the proposed GST model. It suggested that, 'A VAT type model will ensure that the different stages of production and distribution are a mere tax pass-through, and the tax is essentially levied only on final consumption within the taxing jurisdiction.'

The Report suggested a dual levy imposed both by the Centre and the states over the same base. It argued that both 'raw materials and capital goods should be treated as inputs for availing Input Tax Credit'.

It wanted GST to be a consumption-type VAT since that reflected the ability of the consumer to pay taxes. Further, it argued that investment would not be discouraged since savings are not taxed under GST. It argued that exports would become more competitive since they would be left out. They were to be zero rated, that is, bear a zero tax rate. However, it suggested that imports would bear GST.

As discussed in Chapter 3, theoretically there are three different methods for calculating VAT. The Report was in favour of the credit method of computation of VAT since it is simple and also more transparent. It also suggested that the tax base should be comprehensive and include all goods and services up to the final stage of consumption. Further, it did not want any distinction to be made between goods and services so as to avoid disputes about classification.

It suggested that all indirect taxes be brought under the GST, including the local body taxes, like Octroi and entry tax. While suggesting that the tax be comprehensive it recommended certain exemptions to essential services and goods. It also wanted a differential treatment of the sin goods. Recognizing the difficulties that would be faced by small businesses, it suggested exemptions to small dealers and manufacturers with a turnover of up to Rs 10 lakh. It recommended that 'the existing exemption up to Rs 1.5 crores of turnover for small-scale industries should not be continued under the GST framework'. Those with a turnover of between Rs 10 and Rs 40 lakh were to be placed in a separate category with a compounded levy of 1 per cent. It recommended that exemptions for units in SEZs be eliminated.

The Report recognized the difficulties in giving credit for inter-state transactions in goods and services. It suggested that this could be accomplished via a bank system where the GST deposited by a dealer in the exporting state gets credited to the state which is importing the good or the service. In this way the GST would be transferred to the importing state and would be finally collected in the state where the final consumption takes place.

The Report pointed to the difficulties in fixing the jurisdiction for administering the tax between the states and the Centre. At the Centre the Central Board of Excise and Customs looked after the indirect taxes while the states had the sales tax department. So, it was suggested that the jurisdiction may be divided between the two (using turnover, etc., as a criteria) so that the taxpayer may have to deal with only one of them.

For ease of functioning under GST, it was suggested that all persons with annual aggregate turnover of more than Rs 10 lakh be required to register and they be allotted a twelve-digit number, an identification number. It was suggested that the first ten places could be the PAN and the last two be the state code. For all others, there should be provision for voluntary registration. For reporting the transactions and payment of the tax a form called GST-1 was suggested. Finally, it was suggested that the basis of administration of GST should not be physical control but audited accounts.

It was argued that the move to GST was not to collect more tax but the same amount of tax as in the earlier system. So, one should move to a Revenue Neutral Rate (RNR). The Report calculated the RNR for Fiscal year 2007–08. It stated that there are five different methods to calculate RNR but it preferred the consumption method.

The average of the five methods gave a rate of 11 per cent for the combined RNR for the Centre and the states. It was further argued that this did not take into account the improved compliance and the increased growth of GDP so that at this rate of tax there would be a revenue gain. The implication was that the RNR could be even lower. Finally, it was in favour of a single tax rate since that is what is practiced internationally. It was recommended that the states ought to transfer some funds to the local bodies.

The Report was clear about the major gains that would accrue due to the implementation of GST:

1. Economic growth would be faster
2. Exports and imports will rise
3. The poor would benefit
4. Prices of agricultural goods would increase
5. Prices of manufactured goods would decline
6. Consequently, terms of trade would move in favour of agriculture
7. There would be better tax compliance
8. Direct tax revenue collection will also increase since GDP will increase, and finally,
9. Balance of power will shift in favour of states after the implementation of GST

To make policies and monitor the GST it was suggested that a council of finance ministers be created. Finally, due to lack of adequate preparedness to launch GST at that time, it was recommended that its implementation be postponed by six months from 1 April 2010 to 1 October 2010. Of course, even that turned out to be too optimistic.

It needs to be said that the Report started by spelling out the need for an ideal GST which could be a model for the international community but it also suggested various deviations from the ideal. This was also the case with the earlier Reports which were criticized by this Report. After criticizing the earlier reports it suggested more or less what they had said. This was due to the complexity of the

Indian situation, administrative convenience, exemptions and the need to treat dissimilar types of businesses differently. All this pointed to the unsuitability of GST for India but as was the case with the earlier Reports, this Report also did not go so far as to say so.

Report on the Revenue Neutral Rate and Structure of Rates for GST

A Committee under the chairpersonship of Dr A. Subramanian, Chief Economic Advisor, submitted its report on 4 December 2015.[4] It was set up ahead of the possible implementation of the Goods and Services Tax (GST).

The government appointed the Committee to recommend possible tax rates, consistent with the then level of revenue collection of Centre and states. Also, it was to develop a dynamic model to assess the impact of the following parameters on the tax rates viz., expected levels of growth of economy, different levels of compliance and broadening of tax base under GST.

The Report opened by stating that VAT or its variants are applicable in 160 countries in the world but most of them face problems. It argued that 'The Indian GST is expected to represent a leap forward in creating a much cleaner dual VAT which would minimize the disadvantages' experienced by other nations.

It listed the same advantages of GST as the earlier Reports and stated the same disadvantages of the then prevailing complex indirect tax system. It importantly added that the tax system then prevailing fragments the nation along the state borders while GST would unite the nation. This was the basis for the slogan 'one India' which constitutes the political import of GST.

The principal task of the Committee was to come up with the RNR and structure of taxes to be levied on broad range of goods and services. So, the Committee decided to first calculate the overall one tax rate for RNR and then the rate structure for specific groups

---

[4]   GoI (2015b)

of goods and services. Given the complexity of the economy and the data bases, it argued that 'Coming up with an RNR is as much soft judgement as hard science'. The reason was simply because data were not available in the form needed to calculate RNR. Many assumptions had to be made. It chose the year 2013–14 for carrying out the calculations.

It pointed to three approaches to calculate RNR. Each required its own assumptions about the data hence gave different results. The approaches are:

1. Macro Approach which gave a RNR of between 9.1 to 11.1 per cent.
2. Indirect Tax Turnover Approach which gave a RNR of 17.69 per cent.
3. Direct Tax Turnover (DTT) Approach which gave a RNR of 11.98 per cent.

The Committee evaluated these approaches and made adjustments to them and recommended '. . . a range for the RNR of 15–15.5 per cent, with a strong preference for the lower end of that range'.

This rate had to be split into a structure of taxes for broad range of goods and services. The Committee recommended very few exemptions from GST. It suggested a three tax rate structure with a standard rate, a lower rate and a higher rate (also called demerit rate) for a few items. The rates proposed were 12 per cent for the lower rate, 17 per cent for the standard rate and 40 per cent for the high rate. The Report compared these rates with international rates to justify them.

The Committee though against exemptions accepted some of them since they were characterized as 'merit goods'. Here too it made a distinction between what the rich and the poor consume. If the bulk of the consumption of some item was by the poor then it could be exempted or kept at the lower rate. Regarding the threshold for taxation, so as to minimize the burden on small businesses, it suggested that a turnover of Rs 25 lakh or even Rs 40 lakh maybe considered.

The Report had sympathy with the idea of some degree of autonomy of the states to raise revenue. It felt keeping petroleum, alcohol, electricity and real estate out of the GST would provide the states some flexibility. Petroleum and alcohol were found to constitute 29 per cent of the total revenue of states.[5] Under GST they would constitute 41.8 per cent of their revenue.

There was a proposal of a band of 2 per cent above the standard rate to give the states some flexibility. But that would again lead to each state having a different GST rate and that would not be good for the GST structure. So, the Committee was not in favour of this proposal and felt that autonomy was already built into the structure by keeping petroleum and alcohol out of the GST.

The Committee justified its proposals for GST rates on the grounds that their impact on inflation would be minimal.

Regarding the issue of compensation for the states in case they lost revenue, the Committee felt that this would be tricky since some assumption would have to be made about the expected growth of revenue under the existing scheme. As such, there could be no certainty about it. If the compensation turns out to be too liberal then the Centre would face a budgetary problem. If it is a bare minimum, the states may not agree to it.

The Committee stated that a shift to GST would mean 'a shift in revenues from producing states to consuming states, from manufacturing to services, and within manufacturing from intermediate and capital goods toward final goods'. This distributional shift is unavoidable because it is in the structure of the GST. This would impact the revenues of the states with some gaining and some losing but these were hard to calculate.

The Committee anticipated various uncertainties and difficulties in the implementation of GST and suggested that sooner or later these would need a review. But it prescribed that this should not be done in the short term. At least one to two years should be allowed to lapse before a review is done. It was also suggested that alcohol,

---

[5]   Table 5.1 gives data on the revenue from these exempt items for 2016–17

petroleum, real estate and electricity should also be brought in the GST net at some point. It was in favour of taxing education and health rather than exempting them. Finally, it suggested that the tax rates and exemptions should not be a part of the Constitutional amendment Bill since that would be difficult to change later.

Operationalizing GST

As discussed in Chapter 1, taxation is a part of the constitutional arrangement of India (or of any country). As a union of states, there are specific powers of the Centre and of the states. So, sales tax was to be collected by the states but the excise duty and customs duty were to be collected by the Centre. Under GST, all this was going to change. Sales tax and excise duty are eliminated. Tax on the 'act of production and sale' is replaced by the tax on the 'supply of goods and services'. There is one common tax rate on a good or a service which means that different states cannot decide to have a different rate of tax which they may think best suits their requirements.

The only major indirect tax kept out of the ambit of GST is the customs duty. The reason, as explained in Chapter 1, is it plays a different role than the other indirect taxes. It protects domestic production and this continues to be necessary for a variety of reasons.[6]

An important aspect of GST is that each person supplying and receiving goods and services for business has to register on the GST portal. The person applying with the relevant papers is allotted a unique GST Identification Number (GSTIN). This is similar to the recommendation by the Report of the Thirteenth Finance Commission,[7] presented in an earlier section. It consists of fifteen places with the first being the state code, the next ten the PAN, the thirteenth place is assigned by the website on the basis of the specificity of the state, the fourteenth place is Z and the last place is

---

[6]   Kumar (2013)

[7]   GoI (2009a)

a check code which can be a digit or an alphabet. This GSTIN is to be used for all transactions by the registered person. Thus, all the transactions by a person can be tracked by the authorities.

GST Council

GST has meant changes in the taxation powers of the Centre and the states. This required an amendment in the Constitution which was approved by Parliament (See Annexure 5.2) and also ratified by the states. The Constitution Amendment Act provided for the setting up of a GST Council which would oversee the functioning of the GST—deciding on the tax rates, procedures and rules to be followed. The Council was to consist of all the finance ministers of the states with the Union finance minister acting as its chairperson. The GSTC was notified with effect from 12 September 2016.

Since different states had different interests and the Centre also had its own interest, it took time to arrive at a consensus on various issues among political parties and the states. Differences arose on the powers of the Council since the states were worried that the Centre would dominate in the Council and their interest would suffer. They did not want a very high rate of tax and proposed a capping of the highest rate. They desired greater autonomy while giving up their taxation powers.

Since the states were worried about losing revenue and in spite of the promise from the Centre that they would get compensation for five years in case of loss of revenue, they wanted some important tax sources with themselves. The largest tax collection came from petroleum products, tobacco related items and alcohol for human consumption. While tobacco related items were included in the GST, the other items have been kept out of the GST structure for the moment. It is specifically mentioned that the Council would decide when the petroleum products would be brought into the GST network. But there is no such mention of alcoholic products.

The states were also worried about being overwhelmed by the Centre so it was decided that the Council would function on the basis of voting by all the members of the Council. The procedure laid down was:

> Every decision of the Goods and Services Tax Council shall be taken at a meeting, by a majority of not less than three-fourths of the weighted votes of the members present and voting, in accordance with the following principles, namely:
>
> a. the vote of the Central Government shall have a weightage of one third of the total votes cast, and
> b. the votes of all the state governments taken together shall have a weightage of two-thirds of the total votes cast, in that meeting.

All the states, big or small, have the same weight in the total votes.

This voting structure was designed so that neither the Centre nor all the states together could take a decision on their own. To achieve the required majority of 75 per cent of the votes, the Centre and a minimum of twenty states would be required. So, in principle, states would continue to have a major say in any policy decision by the Council. However, the bigger states worry that the smaller states may side with the Centre given its clout.

The Council was given a wide mandate so that it could take decisions on all manner of issues that may arise from time to time. For instance, it could set a band of taxes, floor rates of tax and go for a special provision in case of a disaster.

The GST Council has met many times since its inception and especially since the launch of GST on 1 July 2017. A list of its meetings up to March 2018 is given in Annexure 5.3. It has met often and has had to take a large number of decisions and especially after GST was launched since a plethora of problems in the design of GST became evident.[8] Like, the extent of accounting and monthly returns to be filed or the date of launch of the e-way bill or the claiming of

---

8　A list of changes brought about up to 31 May 2018 via Notifications, Circulars and Orders is given in Table 5.2. There were more than 390 changes.

input credit without passing it on in the final price in the case of restaurants.

The problems faced by small businesses were severe so GSTC simplified matters for them, like:

a. The threshold exemption limit for registration was kept at Rs 20 lakh but for special category states it was kept at Rs 10 lakh.

b. For the Composition scheme the threshold limit for businesses was raised from Rs 75 lakh (initially fixed) to Rs 1 crore. It was also decided that this limit shall be raised to Rs 1.5 crore after necessary amendments in the Act. For special category states the threshold exemption limit was kept at Rs 75 lakh.

c. Instead of the requirement of monthly returns, these businesses were allowed to file quarterly returns.

The setting up and the functioning of the Council is presented as a case of cooperative federalism, where the states and the Centre are willing to compromise for the wider good.

GST Network (GSTN)

As repeatedly stressed till now, GST is a complex tax. It requires masses of data and this cannot be handled without computerization. So a GST network has been set up. It is at present a private body but a decision has been taken to make it a 100 per cent publicly owned body[9] since potentially data may be misused. It is important to understand why a computerized system is essential for the success of GST and why, this system, if not properly designed, will lead to the failure of GST.

As already argued earlier, modern day production is very complex with various inputs required to produce an output. A shirt bought in the market may have come from Vietnam, its

---

[9]   FE (2018)

thread may have been made in India, the spinning and weaving machines may have come from China, the colours (dyes) used may have come from Indonesia, the input for the polyester used in the thread may have come from Malaysia, the company which sells the product may be incorporated in Ireland but the management may be based in the USA, the shipping of the product from Vietnam may be by a ship registered in Liberia, the transportation of the product from the port (say Chennai) to Delhi may have been by a trucker based in Mumbai, the finance for the export by the Vietnamese company may have been provided by a bank in Singapore and finally the retail store may be manned by people recruited from UP. It is possible that the IT infrastructure used to manage the supply chain may have been created and may be maintained by a firm in Poland and the importing company may have raised its finance from a UK bank.

When such a shirt is sold, calculating the value added at each stage and levying the tax at each stage becomes very complex. While the example given above is of a global product, a similar example for an entirely Indian product may be created for the various stages of production and distribution of a product. Starting with buying raw material for producing the thread, spinning it, weaving it, processing it, buying dyes, packaging the product, transporting it, selling it to the shirt maker who then buys the other ingredients like buttons, again packaging it and transporting it, selling to the dealers and retailers and so on. At each stage there is need for buying machinery, getting working capital, IT infrastructure, accounting, advertising, marketing, transportation and storage. Thus, the value added in the entire chain from start to finish is hard to calculate.

At the aggregate level it is simple because the final price of the product paid by the consumer incorporates the total value added at each stage. But if one tries to add the value added at each stage and get to the total value added by summing up then it gets horrendously complex. Computerization helps in keeping track of the various stages and that is where GSTN comes in.

Entire Chain of Production and Distribution to Be under GST

GST attempts to tax each stage of the production and distribution cycle of each of the items of goods and services produced in the economy. That is why GST becomes so complex. As explained in Chapter 6, when there are a variety of exemptions because of the intricate and diverse structures of the economy, the complexity of implementation of GST increases further.

Be that as it may, to calculate the value added at any stage, one has to calculate the value of the output of each item and subtract from it the value of the inputs purchased. The inputs can be other goods or services. They can be raw material or overheads. For an average business, there may be tens of thousands of vouchers to calculate the expenditures. It becomes very difficult to keep track of these manually. So, software is required to automatically keep track of wages paid, cost of transportation, purchase of various inputs and so on. Such a programme can help calculate the value added and also the amount of tax due.

Further, since each of the inputs may have paid a tax it has to be subtracted from the tax that is due on the product made by the company. Each voucher for purchases is supposed to mention the tax paid on the purchased items. This needs to be aggregated and so on. This is difficult to do manually and requires automation via computerization.

When all individual businesses are aggregated to form the economy, then the complexity increases further since the businesses are tied together via sales and purchases and each taking input credit for the tax that has already been paid at the earlier stage. The sale by one business becomes the purchase by another business (B2B). The tax paid by the first has to match the input credit claimed by the purchaser. If a business buys 100 different input items then it would have to chase up 100 other businesses to ensure that it is getting the correct amount of input credit. That needs computerization. If one tries to physically chase up sellers, costs will go up.

GSTN Structure

As argued above, production in a modern society is complex with inputs coming from within the nation and/or from outside. There are global supply chains for any production and especially in the case of Multi-National Companies (MNCs). That is why computerization is essential for implementation of GST. Businesses' accounts have to serve two purposes. One is to prepare their own profit and loss statement and another for the tax they have to pay on their income. The same set of accounts produce both the profit and loss statement and the statement for the tax payment.

The government worries that the businesses resort to double book keeping—one account for the tax authority and another for their actual profit and loss statement. Different sets of accounts are used by the businesses to hide their income and generate black incomes. To prevent this from happening the government wants the same accounts to be presented for both purposes and computerization can help in this. But computerization also adds to the complexity for small businesses. When all the businesses are aggregated, the flow of data becomes massive and requires not only automation but complex programmes. Billions of transactions are required to be processed monthly.[10]

Earlier it was suggested[11] that the job of collecting the tax and tallying the accounts could be done by a bank. However, the Empowered Committee decided in its meeting in July 2010 to set up a sub-committee to go into the question of how to manage the expected massive flow of data. The Committee realized that giving input credit for inter-state sales would be tricky and this had to be figured out. That is when the idea of a GST Network (GSTN) emerged.

GSTN was envisaged as a clearing house. It was suggested that every business would feed its data automatically into the various

---

[10] Srivastava (2017)

[11] GoI (2009b)

forms devised for the appropriate purpose and kept electronically on the GSTN platform. The sales by one business would automatically then reflect as purchases by another business. The tax paid by the first would automatically appear in the account of the other. The tax to be paid at each stage of the transaction would be automatically generated and it would then be paid by each business into the government's accounts. This would, in theory, prevent any fudging of accounts and reduce black income generation.

Under the scheme, each business had to register on the GSTN platform. It would then be allotted a unique number which would be its identification for all its transactions and for the payment of GST. Since SGST accrues to the states, each business is required to register in each of the states it operates in. Further, each business registered under GST is required to file three returns each month by the 10th, 15th and the 20th of the month. The data for sales for the previous month's transactions has to be fed in by the 10th of the next month in the form GSTR-1. By the 15th, the business has to validate that its suppliers had correctly filled in their data for the supplies it had received (GSTR-2). All this has to be finalized in a monthly return by the 20th (GSTR-3).

In effect, each business has to carry on a massive amount of accounting. After the monthly returns, an annual account has to be prepared at the end of the year. So, for each state that a business operates in, there would be thirty-seven returns to fill up or cross check. For thirty-one states and Union Territories, there would be 1147 forms. This does not look like simplification. Even big business has difficulty dealing with so much data processing, even if it is not on paper.

It was expected that there would be a crore of registered businesses on GSTN and billions of transactions each month—a mammoth task. Finally, 1.1 crore businesses have registered even though only about 65 lakh filed return and paid tax as on 1 April 2018.[12]

---

12 See Annexure 5.4 for details of the registrations and returns submitted

With such mass of data being fed into GSTN, glitches were expected. No trial runs were done on a small sample to see how it would all work out. GSTN systems went down many times due to system overload. The overload typically occurred around the time the dates for filing the returns came—the 10th, 15th and the 20th. Even on 30 June 2017, one day before the launch of GST on 1 July, the GSTN site crashed as a large number of businesses tried to register. There are also potential problems which may occur if hacking occurs or malicious attacks take place on the system by those interested in disrupting the systems.

For reasons that are not clear, the GSTN was set up as a Special Purpose Vehicle (SPV) with 51 per cent ownership by private financial institutions. The remaining 49 per cent was to be equally shared between the Centre and the states. There were practical reasons suggested for this structure of GSTN which was to be entirely funded by the Central and state governments. The Empowered Group of Ministers which recommended this also suggested that the strategic control of GSTN should be with the government. The proposal for setting up of GSTN as a private sector company was approved on 12 April 2012 by the Government of India.

The Central government agreed to give a one-time non-recurring grant-in aid of Rs 315 crore to start the GSTN. The pre-operative fund requirement was Rs 550 crore in 2016–17, just before the launch of the GST. This was to come from a commercial loan from a commercial bank. It was to take care of initial requirement of funds including payment to Infosys which was to provide the software and the hardware and provide the services for the functioning of GSTN.

It was decided by the Empowered Committee that the GSTN SPV would be self-financing. It would charge a fee for the services it provides to the users, namely, the tax payers and the tax authorities. However, it was later on decided that the government would bear the entire cost and the tax payer would not have to pay any user charges. The Central and the state governments would share this cost equally. The states would divide their share among themselves in proportion to the number of tax payers in their jurisdiction. It should really have been in proportion to the tax share since a poor state may have many small businesses registered who hardly pay any tax but this will cost the state much more proportionately.

It was also decided that GSTN SPV would be the sole agency responsible for the functioning of GST. Its designated task was to deliver all the indirect tax related services via one portal. This portal was to be the front end of the system. CBEC and the State Tax Departments were to have their own IT systems which would function as the back-end and provide the tax administration functions that they normally perform, like, audit, assessment and registration approval.

GSTN was designated to provide the IT infrastructure needed by the tax payers, like, 'the filing of registration applications, filing of returns, creation of challan for tax payment, settlement of IGST payment, generation of business intelligence and analytics'.[13]

GSTN was designed to provide a common registration to the taxpayers for both Central and state GST. Thus, businesses were required to file their application at only one place and not in each state. The role of GSTN is to check the application for completeness and validate the data in the application like the PAN data.

Regarding the return to be filed by businesses, there would be a common return for CGST, SGST and IGST. The return filed would be automatically checked for the input tax credit (ITC) claimed by any business. This procedure would also facilitate the inter-state transactions under IGST. In the case of inter-state sales, transfers of tax from the exporting to the importing state would then take place automatically, simplifying the work of the businesses and states.

In brief, the GSTN is to play the most crucial role in the smooth governance of GST. Any lacunae in this would doom the GST to failure. At present, a large number of businesses are registered under GST but only about 70 per cent of them are paying tax (Annexure 5.4).

---

[13] GST website at GoI (2018b)

CHAPTER 6

COMPONENTS OF GST

According to the GST website,[1] 'The GST Bill provides for a levy of GST on supply of all goods or services except for Alcohol for human consumption.' It provided for exclusive power to Parliament to levy GST on 'inter-state trade or commerce (including imports) in goods or services' under the Integrated GST. The Central government was to 'have the power to levy excise duty in addition to the GST on tobacco and tobacco products. The tax on supply of five specified petroleum products namely crude, high speed diesel, petrol, ATF and natural gas would be levied from a later date on the recommendation of GST Council'.

After the Constitutional Amendment Act was approved, five laws namely CGST Law, UTGST Law, IGST Law, SGST Law and GST Compensation Law were passed. These provided the basis of the functioning of GST in the country. These laws pertained to the Central GST, Union Territory GST, Integrated GST, state GST and finally to the law for providing compensation to the states in case their revenue falls short.

Dual GST

GST has three aspects and corresponding to each there is a tax. As already discussed, GST has to be a comprehensive indirect tax yielding resources for the Centre, each of the states of the Union of India and the Union Territories. Correspondingly there is a Central component (CGST) and a state component (SGST). That is why the Indian GST is called a Dual GST. So, on any transaction

---

[1] See GoI (2018b) and Annexure 5.2 on the Constitution Amendment Act

anywhere in the country a CGST has to be paid to the Centre. Since that transaction takes place in some state or Union Territory, a SGST has to be paid. As explained in Chapter 1, to eliminate cascading effect, an input credit (ITC) is given for the tax paid in the earlier stages of supply. Under the rules, ITC is given for CGST to be paid by the supplier out of the CGST paid at the earlier stage. Similarly, SGST paid at one stage of supply can be adjusted as ITC at the later stage only against SGST. This simplifies the accounting requirement of GST.

In accounting terms this is simple since the CGST and SGST accounts are separate on the GSTN platform and each can be adjusted separately for the ITC. If the system was a unitary one, as in some countries, where the Centre collects on behalf of itself and the states, the Centre would have to apportion the appropriate amount to each state according to some formula. This could cause some complications and disagreements among states.

Some of the Committees had earlier suggested different rates of tax for CGST and SGST but it was finally decided by the GST Council to keep them equal. The total rate for GST approved by the GST Council was fixed at 0, 5, 12, 18 and 28 per cent. Half was to go to the Centre and the remaining to the states. So, the 12 per cent rate means that 6 per cent each would go to the Centre and the state in which the transaction took place. There would be one common tax in the invoice with the two components mentioned separately. Via the GSTN the respective amounts would automatically be credited to the Centre and the state in which the transaction took place.

For instance, if a retailer in Rajasthan sells paint to a client worth Rs 20,000 then she/he has to charge a tax of 18 per cent, consisting of 9 per cent for the SGST and 9 per cent for CGST. The bill will be for Rs 23,600 and will show Rs 1,800 each under CGST and SGST. These will go to the Centre's account and Rajasthan government's account. This is the final sale so there is no input credit (ITC) on the sale.

Let us extend the above example to understand ITC. The paint was made by a local producer who sold it to the retailer for Rs 18,000.

On this he would have to pay 18 per cent GST with 9 per cent each going to CGST and SGST or Rs 1,620 each. The retailer will pay Rs 21,240. But, she knows that she would get back the tax paid by the producer at the previous stage, Rs 1,620 plus Rs 1,620 = 3,240 as ITC. So, her cost remains Rs 18,000 and the sale price remains Rs 20,000. On this price, GST of 18 per cent has to be paid, that is, Rs 3,600. Out of this, she can subtract Rs 3,240 as ITC and pay only Rs 360 as GST with Rs 180 each going for CGST and SGST. The collection by the Centre and Rajasthan is Rs 1,620 each from the manufacturer and Rs 180 each from the retailer. That is Rs 1,800 each. This is 9 per cent of the final price for both the Centre and the state.

Note, the accounting is reasonably simple since the two components of GST paid are credited separately to the accounts of Centre and Rajasthan state. Input credit (ITC) is given from CGST to CGST and SGST to SGST. This simplifies the accounting process as mentioned earlier.

IGST on Domestic Sale and Input Credit

But what about a transaction that takes place across states—supply by a business in one state to another business located in another state. Say, the paint is made in Madhya Pradesh (MP) but sold in Rajasthan. The SGST accounts of each state are separate so how does one state give the ITC to the other? An arrangement had to be worked out for how the exporting state would collect the tax and how the ITC could be given to the importing state.

To take care of the complications involved in inter-state transactions, a third tax called Integrated GST (IGST) was devised for inter-state supplies. It is collected by the Centre. Out of the amount collected, the Centre keeps its share and passes on the state's share to the importing state (Rajasthan in the example) where the supply is made. Further, the exporting state (MP) is to give to the Centre the entire GST it has collected on that supply which is to be passed on by the Centre to the importing state (Rajasthan). An example may make this clear.

The paint was made by a producer in MP who sold it to the retailer in Rajasthan for Rs 18,000. On this he would have to pay 18 per cent IGST, Rs 3,240 and that would be collected by the Centre. The Centre would keep 9 per cent of it and pass on the remaining half to Rajasthan. The retailer would sell the paint for Rs 20,000 and charge Rs 3,600 as GST with Rs 1,800 each due to the Centre and Rajasthan state. Since the tax on inputs is already paid, ITC would be due. Out of the Rs 3,240 of IGST paid, the Centre's account would be adjusted by Rs 1,800 and the balance Rs 1,440 would be adjusted against the SGST. So, the retailer would only pay Rs 360 as the SGST to Rajasthan. So, both the Centre and Rajasthan state get Rs 1,800 each, 9 per cent each of the final price paid by the consumer.

Add one more layer of complication. The producer in MP bought raw materials to produce the paint and paid GST on them. For that she should get input credit out of the Rs 3,240 GST she paid. Say the inputs cost Rs 10,000 and the tax paid on that was Rs 900 each to CGST and SGST. So, the IGST on sale from MP to Rajasthan would be Rs 3,240 less Rs 1,800. That is Rs 1,440. This would be collected by the Centre. Now when the product is sold in Rajasthan for Rs 20,000, Rs 1,800 each is due as CGST and SGST. The Centre has already got Rs 900 as CGST on this plus now it gets Rs 1,440. So, it gets a total of Rs 2,340 which would be adjusted against the CGST of Rs 1,800 due. The balance of Rs 540 would be adjusted against SGST due to Rajasthan state so the amount to be received by the state becomes Rs 1,260. But Rs 900 SGST is already paid to MP so the amount of SGST to be received by Rajasthan would be Rs 360. So, Rajasthan gets Rs 540 plus Rs 360 which is Rs 900. But that is only 4.5 per cent of the price.

IGST has another rule, that is, the Rs 900 received by the exporting state MP has to be given to the Centre which is then passed on to the importing state Rajasthan. It is because of this transfer that Rajasthan gets Rs 900 plus Rs 900, a total of Rs 1,800. It now becomes 9 per cent of the final price. Note that the producing state MP does not get any GST while the importing state Rajasthan gets the full 9 per cent GST. This is the reason that it is said that GST is a 'destination tax' collected by the consuming state and not the producing state which is the originating state.

The sequence in which ITC is to work is the following:[2]

a. ITC of CGST allowed for payment of CGST & IGST in that order;
b. ITC of SGST allowed for payment of SGST & IGST in that order;
c. ITC of UTGST allowed for payment of UTGST & IGST in that order;
d. ITC of IGST allowed for payment of IGST, CGST & SGST/ UTGST in that order.

IGST on Imports, SEZs and Exports

Imports into India also used to bear various taxes in addition to the customs duty such as the Countervailing Duty (CVD) and Special Additional Duty of Customs (SAD).[3] These are also being replaced now by GST. So, an input credit (ITC) is due on this tax payment also. The question is who gets this tax? The state where the good lands from foreign shores or the state where the good is finally sold? This issue is similar to sale across states. Since GST is a destination tax, the tax collected should accrue to the state where the final sale takes place. IGST can play this role and that is what is in the design of GST.

Imports bear IGST which is collected by the Centre and then passed on to the state where the good is sent from the port. If it is a service that is imported then it either comes directly to the consumer or via an intermediary to the consumer. Again an IGST is to be paid on this.

Exports are also a part of the chain of production and distribution. So, they also bear GST but this is refunded back to the producer. In effect there is zero tax on exports. This is so that

---

[2] GoI (2015a)
[3] See Chapter 1

Indian exports remain competitive in the international markets. The idea of levying a tax and then reimbursing it is that the entire chain comes under the ambit of GST. Refund of the ITC occurs only after the export is carried out. There was a danger that businesses could misclassify their production for export and sell it in the internal market. That is why, only when proof is given of export having been carried out is the tax paid returned. Unfortunately, this has become a complicated process and a large amount of refund of the tax (ITC) remains pending. This has increased the requirement of working capital for the exporters and raised their costs.

India introduced Special Economic Zones (SEZs) in 2005 to boost the country's exports. So, supplies to SEZs are to be treated as exports with a zero rate of tax (zero rated). Tax paid at the earlier stages of production can be claimed as ITC. Supply to SEZs is treated as an inter-state transaction. So, an IGST is due on it which is then refunded back to the supplier. Two other ways of supply to SEZs are on the basis of a Bond or a Letter of Undertaking so that there is no refund involved. In the reverse direction, a supply from an SEZ to the rest of the country (called Domestic Tariff Areas) is treated like a normal supply and a GST has to be paid on the supply.

Compensation to the States for Loss of Revenue

As mentioned earlier, the states were worried that they would lose revenue due to the enactment of GST. It was a new tax, its structure was complex and implementation likely to pose problems. Given the poor governance in the country things could go wrong (as has happened after the introduction of GST) and revenue could fall short. The producing states were especially worried about short fall in revenue because this tax is supposed to be a destination tax. The Centre assured the states that they would not lose revenue and even if it happened, they would be compensated for any loss. This helped bring all the states on board to agree to implement GST. A GST Compensation Law was passed as a package of laws in 2017. This was one of the four laws that were passed by Parliament.

It was decided to levy a cess over the peak rate of 28 per cent on certain specified luxury and demerit goods, like tobacco and tobacco products, pan masala, aerated waters and motor vehicles, to raise resources to compensate states for any revenue loss due to implementation of GST. The cess proposed at 15 per cent was not on the tax, as was the case earlier, but on the value of the supply. Thus, the tax rate became 43 per cent. An additional cess on inter-state transactions to compensate the states for any loss in revenue was proposed in the first discussion paper prepared by the Empowered Committee[4] but it was not implemented since the states did not agree to it.

The GST Council worked out a formula and mechanism for GST Compensation Cess. It was decided that the average increase in indirect taxes before the implementation of GST would be projected to the post-GST five years to calculate what the revenue potentially maybe. If a state's revenue fell short of this projected amount then it would be compensated from this cess which would be collected by the Centre. The compensation was to be restricted to five years only. A 14 per cent rate of growth of revenue was to be assumed for working out the compensation.

Initially, the growth in GST revenue has been slow (See Table 5.1) so the states have had to be compensated. But the government claims that the situation will stabilize over time and more revenue will be generated once the full system is in place. The elements that had to be modified or held in abeyance due to complications were the e-way bill for transportation, reverse charge mechanism (RCM), matching of invoices (GSTR-2) and so on. Only time will tell as the system stabilizes whether there will be a revenue shortfall or not. This has implication for the deficit of the Centre (See more on federalism in Chapter 8).

---

[4] GoI (2009a)

E-way Bill

As a part of the roll out of GST, there is a provision of an e-way bill for transportation of all goods.[5] The transportation could be by any means—road, rail, air or water. The idea is to track the movement of goods from the sender to the receiver of the goods. So, the person transporting the goods (say, a trucker) would carry the e-way bill with him/her while transporting the goods. It is said that this is necessary to prevent the generation of black incomes by misinvoicing goods. Even under the earlier system of VAT, a similar bill was necessary for transporting goods. Only now, it has become a more elaborate, centralized and computerized system.

The e-way bill would have to be generated before the sender dispatches the goods. It has to be done on the electronic portal, www.ewaybillgst.gov.in, managed by the government agency, National Informatic Centre (NIC). The portal is meant exclusively for generating such bills. The bill can be generated by the person sending the consignment or the person receiving it or even by the transporter.

Persons who are already registered under GST have to also register at the e-way portal by providing their GSTIN (the identification number given by the GST portal at the time of registration). They are then provided a username and password for future use for registering their consignments. An unregistered party can also generate an e-way bill by using their PAN and Aadhar numbers. Unregistered transporters also need to register on the portal and they are allotted a 15 digit Unique Transporter ID (TRANSIN). This is similar to the GSTIN.

Every consignment of value more than Rs 50,000 has to compulsorily carry an e-way bill. In some cases, it is required even for transporting goods of value less than Rs 50,000. It is not required for the goods that are exempt. Its roll out has been postponed several

---

[5] GoI (2018c)

times since it adds one more layer of complexity of procedures to GST. The dates for its roll out have had to be shifted from 1 February 2018 to 1 April 2018 to 1 June 2018.

The e-way bill has to carry the details of the supplier, the receiver of the goods, the details of the goods, the transporter's details and the registration number of the vehicle carrying the goods. If a mistake is made then the bill has to be cancelled and regenerated. There is a time limitation for the validity of each bill. Once an e-way bill is generated, the transporter has one day for every 100 km (or a part of it) of distance to be covered. The counting of the day is not twenty-four hours but the end of the next day. The distance to be travelled has to be approximately given for this purpose.

The e-way bill has two parts. Part A and B. The basic information about the goods to be transported has to be entered in Part A and then the details of transportation have to be added to generate the Part B which would complete the e-way bill.

The portal has the capacity to generate 75 lakh e-way bills a day. However, there are complaints that it is often slow to respond or that traders are unable to access the portal speedily due to glitches or lack of proper understanding of the system.

Complications may arise if the consignment is not accepted by the person who is to receive them. Another e-way bill has to be generated for return. There may be delay due to natural calamity, riots, accident, breakdown of vehicle and so on. In such a case, the transporter has to apply for extension within four hours of the end of the deadline.

Rules have been prepared for all kind of situations like oversize consignments, bulk generation of bills for multiple consignments, delivery to army canteens, movement by public transport, movement by rail and goods of value less than Rs 50,000 while the total value of goods being transported is more than Rs 50,000. The above points to the various complications that may arise in transportation of goods and therefore, in the working of the system of e-way bills.

Complex Tax Structure and Exemptions

The discussion in this and the previous Chapter points to how complex GST is. This complexity is further enhanced by the following features:

a. The multiple tax rates finally adopted
b. The exemptions provided for registration under GST
c. The creation of the category of Composition Scheme and
d. The e-way bill required for transportation.

Many of these provisions have had to be tweaked since 1 July 2017 (like the Composition Scheme) or implementation had to be postponed (like e-way bill system) to allow the basic GST structure to stabilize.

As pointed out in the previous Chapter, there was much discussion on what the GST rates ought to be. As one of the government committees pointed out,[6] the determination of RNR is more of an art than a science. Since the data are not available in the form needed, many assumptions were necessary to work out the RNR. Since assumptions could always be challenged, no rate of tax worked out in advance could be completely defended. There would always be some subjective elements which the critics could point to.

The problem basically was that GST was supposed to have one common rate for all goods and services across the nation, not only to eliminate the cascading effect but also for simplification. That is why the slogan was 'one nation one tax'. It was considered to be politically important because it was said that this action of the government was unifying the nation—a bit of a hyperbole—since India after independence has been politically one nation even if it is a federal one—a union of states. Yes, there were check posts at the state borders but it was not that the market was not one. Note, all committees on indirect taxes after talking of one tax rate argued that India with its extreme poverty, could not have one rate of tax for all supplies.

---

[6] GOI (2015b)

Experts and policy makers have been concerned that the consumption of the poor should not get taxed as that would lower their standard of living which is in any case abysmally low. So, as the finance minister once said, 'chappals and cars cannot have the same rate of GST'.[7]

Further, in an article[8] it was shown by this author that if there was one common rate on all goods and services, the basic goods and services would tend to get taxed at higher rates than at present which would be inflationary even with RNR and that would adversely affect the poor. The reason for this result was simply that the rates on essentials have been kept low to help protect the poor but if there is to be one rate then tax on essentials would have to rise. The poor by definition do not consume the inessentials so if their prices decline it would not benefit the poor. Thus, if the poor are to be protected, the rates of GST for the basics and essential items of consumption need to be kept lower than the average.

Further, this author pointed out in 1986 in a paper[9] that the unorganized sector producers cannot cope with the complexity of VAT which is what GST is based on. So, this sector which is dominant in the economy and society would find it difficult to implement GST. That is why the idea came up of exempting them from GST or keeping them under the Composition Scheme.

GST Rate Structure

The GST rate structure has been impacted by several factors which has made GST a complicated tax and led to unanticipated problems. Some of these factors are:

a. Concern for the poor that they should not have to pay more indirect taxes

---

[7] IANS (2017b)

[8] Kumar (2015)

[9] Kumar (1986)

b. Concern for small business that they may not be able to cope with the complexity of GST
c. Concern for revenue that it should not fall short

To take care of these concerns, the government had to work out compromises and that further complicated the structure of GST so that it has become a half-way house—not a full GST.

For reasons of revenue, the GST Bill provides for exclusion of alcohol for human consumption. This is a constitutional provision and if these items are to be brought under GST a Constitutional amendment would be required and that would not be easy. Further, the Central government is allowed to levy excise duty on tobacco and tobacco products in addition to the GST. Finally, GST would not be levied immediately on five specified petroleum products, namely, crude, high speed diesel, petrol, ATF and natural gas. The GST Council would decide on when these products would come under GST. This would not require a Constitutional Amendment as and when the Council wishes to bring these items under the GST. But given revenue considerations this is not going to happen anytime soon.

These exemptions complicate the structure of GST further. Why were these exceptions made? The reason clearly is that these items are the big revenue earners for the Centre and the states.[10] These exceptions indicate a lack of confidence of the government that GST would yield adequate revenue. In case of any short fall they could get more revenue from these big ticket items.

The concern for the small suppliers led to their being exempted from registration under GST. So, suppliers with turnover of up to Rs 20 lakh have been exempted. But they will not be able to get input credit (ITC) and if they sell to any other business they cannot offer ITC. A very big disadvantage indeed. Similarly, those with a turnover between Rs 20 lakh and Rs 1 crore will fall under the Composition Scheme and will neither get ITC nor be able to offer ITC. They

---

[10] See Table 5.1

would also not be able to make inter-state sales. Further, the tax that they should have paid under GST but did not pay since they are exempt will have to be paid by the business purchasing from them. This is the reverse charge mechanism (RCM). Thus, the purchasers' cost would go up.

To take care of the poor, some goods like food items, have been placed under the list of exempt items. In other words they would have a zero rate of tax. Some items consumed by the poor are placed in the 5 per cent tax bracket. Many essential services that were earlier free from service tax are also kept at zero rate, like education and health. GST Network which provides services is also exempted from the GST. The cost of the GST Network is also borne by the government so that the businesses do not face an additional cost which they would pass on to the consumers.

> Thus, the rate structure under GST is: 0 per cent, 5 per cent, 12 per cent, 18 per cent, 28 per cent and 43 per cent.
>
> In addition, the tax rate on precious metals is kept at 3 per cent and tax on unworked diamonds, precious stones, etc., is 0.25 per cent.
>
> Restaurants pay a 5 per cent tax but ITC is not available to them.
>
> Those under the Composition Scheme can neither claim nor provide ITC. They have to pay 1 per cent tax on the *taxable* turnover. Initially the tax was 2 per cent on manufacturers and 1 per cent on traders' total turnover.

The GST rate on goods and services have been fixed close to the rate they were already paying under the old regime. So, if some good was being taxed at the rate of say, 15 per cent then it was moved largely to 18 per cent under GST. Most services were at the rate of 15 per cent and that has increased to 18 per cent. This has proved to be inflationary.

Thus, GST has eight different rates at present and major items are outside its purview. This has complicated the GST structure and created problems in its implementation. For instance, exemptions break the chain of GST and make it incomplete—the idea of having GST from the start of finish is not valid. Further, those items that are exempted (have a zero rate of tax) cannot use input credit and that raises the prices of these items.

Further, as pointed out in Chapter 1, in the case of indirect taxes, the point where the tax is levied and where its impact is felt are different. So, the price of goods that pay no indirect tax also rises when basic and intermediate goods prices rise due to a higher tax on them. Thus, they also bear the burden of tax even though they are not taxed. Take the case of vegetables on which no indirect tax is directly levied. But when the cost of transportation rises due to taxes, then the price of vegetables also rises.

Given the complexity of the Indian economy, it is difficult to classify goods and services as being for the use of the less well-off and for the well-off. So, one can have a cheap hotel room for less than Rs 2,500 per night and a more luxurious room at over Rs 5,000 per night and they face different tax rates. This enables misclassification of the good or service. For example sweets have a GST rate of 5 per cent[11] but sweets as prasad have a zero tax rate.[12] This can lead to misclassification and evasion of the tax.

As mentioned in Chapter 1, RNR can be applied in two different senses. One can go for an overall rate and then place every good or service in different rates as has been done now. In this case, some prices will rise and some may fall. The other alternative is to place each individual item and at each stage of production in such a tax slab that the same amount of revenue is collected at each stage as was collected earlier. In this case all the prices remain as they were earlier but the rate structure may become as complex as it was before GST was launched.

In brief, the basic difficulty in the implementation and design of GST comes from the fact that India is a very complex nation with vast poverty, differentiated population and differentiated

---

[11] FE (2017)

[12] IANS (2017a)

production structures. Add to that the complexity of GST as VAT. All these together make it a very difficult tax to implement in India.

Procedures and Complications

The complexities pointed to above have resulted in very complex procedures. There are a large number of forms that have to be filled up. For those not in the Composition Scheme, a Form GSTR-1 has to be first filled up for each and every transaction carried out by the business in a month by the 10th of the next month. A Form GSTR-2 is generated by the system which has to be verified by the business by the 15th of the month (this has been postponed for now). It tells the business what it has purchased and what input credit is due to it. These two together then result in the form GSTR-3 which has to be submitted by the 20th of the month.

GSTR-3 is the full account of a business and is the basis of the tax due from the business. Those under the Composition Scheme are only required to file the Form GSTR-1. To simplify matters it was decided by the GST Council that for businesses with a turnover of less than Rs 1.5 crore, the form may be filed quarterly to reduce their accounting burden. Since these businesses are neither to get input credit (ITC) nor can they provide input credit to others, the GSTR-2 and the GSTR-3 forms are redundant. So, for them, GSTR-1 is all that is needed to pay the tax.

The GST Council meeting of January 2018 simplified matters for the small traders and manufacturers since they were facing severe problems. They were also allowed to file and pay the tax quarterly instead of monthly.

For the government also managing the complex tax, large number of returns, details of transactions by lakhs of businesses and collection of tax is a daunting task. Its existing staff in excise and sales tax departments had to be retrained to carry out the new tasks. Usually, the excise payments were from larger units while the sales tax payments were by a large number of small units. So, it was decided that this division of labour would be continued. Thus, 90 per cent of businesses having a turnover of below Rs 1.5 crore would be administratively under the state tax department. The rest would be under the Central administration. For businesses which have over Rs 1.5 crore of turnover, 50 per cent each would be under the control of the Central and state administrations.

To force businesses to file returns in time, a late fee was provided for. Filing in time by businesses is crucial because delay would mean that others in the chain would also get delayed. ITC would not be possible in time. Administrative work of the businesses would increase since they would be chasing others to make them file in time so that they could file in time. To begin with, there was much confusion and the systems did not function properly, so the late fee had to be waived. The last date of filing was also repeatedly postponed.

From October 2017, the following late fees are to be paid by registered persons:

a. Rs 20 per day for those whose tax liability for a given month was 'Nil'. Earlier it was Rs 200 per day.
b. Rs 50 per day for those whose liability was not 'Nil'. Earlier it was Rs 200 per day.

To deter late payment an 18 per cent rate of interest is levied on the delayed payments from the date on which the tax was due to the date on which it is paid. Further, to deter businesses from claiming excess ITC, to lower their tax liability, a 24 per cent interest is to be paid on such false invoicing. If the accounts are fudged in other ways to show a lower tax liability, a 24 per cent interest would be payable on the short payment of tax.

For collecting arrears of tax payment by a business, its goods can be detained and sold or its movable and immovable property can be sold to recover the tax due.

Electronic commerce is posing a variety of problems for the collection of tax since the e-commerce companies are arguing that they only provide a platform/ market place but do not by themselves sell and buy. So, they claim that they are not liable to pay a tax. To sort out this confusion, it was decided that the e-commerce companies would collect a tax at source of 2 per cent.

Due to the variety of complexities and the various provisions made in the GST laws, it was anticipated that there would be disputes about interpretation of the law. So, provision was made for appeals. A Revisional Authority could look at the orders passed by the officers dealing with a case. The Central government is required to constitute a Goods and Services Tax Appellate Tribunal which would look at any challenge to the order of the Revisional Authority. The order of this authority could be challenged in the High Court and after that in the Supreme Court.

Finally, there is a provision of audit of registered businesses so that compliance with provisions in the GST Law could be verified. This is crucial given the propensity of businesses to hide income from tax authorities.

Given the complexity of the GST provisions, a part of the taxes collected by the Centre are to be passed on to the states and the states collect some taxes that are to handed over to the Centre. Hence there is need for a periodic settlement of accounts between the Centre and the states. This has to be done on the basis of information filed by the tax payers.

To ease the pain of the businesses and especially the small businesses who can barely cope with the complexity of accounting and the computerization required, 'GSTN has selected 73 IT, ITeS and financial technology companies and 1 Commissioner of Commercial Taxes (CCT, Karnataka), to be called GST Suvidha Providers (GSPs). GSPs would develop applications to be used by taxpayers for interacting with the GSTN.'[13] The GSPs could also help businesses cope with the accounting and filing.

The role of Central Board of Excise and Customs (CBEC) has changed under the GST regime. So, it is now called Central Board of Indirect Taxes and Customs (CBIC). Its task now is to administer

---

[13] GST website at GoI (2018b)

CGST and IGST Law. But since Central excise duty continues on petroleum products and also on tobacco products (in addition to GST), it would continue to administer this also. Since customs duty is not a part of GST these continue to remain under the purview of CBEC. For GST, CBIC has had to carry out a massive IT project called 'SAKSHAM'.

Difficulties and Rapid Changes in the Laws/Rules

As mentioned earlier, the inherent complexity of GST (due to it being VAT) in India is enhanced by several factors. In addition to the points mentioned there, one may add,

a. Taxation of all transactions involved in production and distribution of goods and services
b. Exemptions of certain goods from GST
c. Provision of the reverse charge mechanism (RCM)[14] for Composition Scheme, and
d. Complexity in the functioning of GST Network

That the GST administration was floundering can be gauged from the various changes that it has had to make in quick succession. On 22 June 2017, the first notification was issued for GST. It notified certain sections of the CGST Law. After that a flood of notifications were issued and they are listed on the GST website. The number of notifications and orders runs into hundreds in the first year of operation of GST (Table 5.2). By 1 April 2018 it is reported officially[15] that

---

[14] Reverse Charge (RCM) is the GST that should have been paid by those under the Composition Scheme but since they are exempt from it, it has to be paid by those who purchase from them. So, it is called a reverse charge.

[15] GoI (2018b)

. . . 95 notifications under CGST Act have been issued notifying sections, notifying rules, amendment to rules and for waiver of penalty, etc.

Thirteen, eighteen and one notifications have also been issued under IGST Act, UTGST Act and GST (Compensation to States) Act respectively. Further 57, 61, 57 and 8 rate related notifications each have been issued under the CGST Act, IGST Act, UTGST Act and GST (Compensation to States) Act respectively. Similar notifications have been issued by all the states under the respective SGST Act.

Apart from the notifications, 41 circulars and 13 orders have also been issued by CBEC on various subjects like, proper officers, ease of exports, and extension of last dates for filling up various forms, etc. . . . The reverse charge mechanism under sub-section (4) of section 9 of the CGST Act, 2017 and under sub-section (4) of section 5 of the IGST Act, 2017 has been suspended till 30.06.2018.

For tracking supplies, e-way bill was considered to be crucial but its implementation was found to be rather difficult and its initiation was postponed. It has been introduced in a phased manner starting from 1 April 2018. For intra-state supplies its launch was to be decided by each state so as to complete the process by 1 June 2018. It has been said that once the e-way bill scheme is implemented then the generation of black incomes will be further curtailed and revenue collection will improve.

A large number of people and businesses have had to suffer due to lack of clarity on their day-to-day matters. For instance, there was complete lack of clarity on the issue of whether GST is payable by Cooperative Housing Societies? Earlier they were exempt up to a certain amount on the concept of 'mutuality'. Further, the question was, should GST be paid by every member of the society if its billing exceeds Rs 20 lakh or only those members are liable to pay GST whose bill exceeded Rs 5,000? It took months of seeking clarifications from various authorities before the matter was sorted out in the January meeting of the GST Council. In the meanwhile, members of the Cooperative Societies continued to pay tax which was not refunded later on.

Queries like the following are coming daily:

a. Will a service tax have to be paid by a private ambulance service provider on service provided to government?

b. Will the sale of a 'going concern' come under GST?

c. What happens if there is a cancellation of a GST Registration Certificate?

d. Are damages paid on cancellation of a contract subject to GST?

e. Would a caterer providing food to an establishment's canteen be treated as an outdoor caterer or as one running a restaurant?

f. How is the interest on the outstanding balance of a credit card to be treated?

g. There are questions about GST on education sector. Are only public sector education institutions exempt from GST?

h. A person in one city paid freight to a transporter in another city. How is this to be treated?

i. Is a person providing PG service liable to GST even though she is renting for residential purpose?

j. A coaching institute registered in one state provides service to students in another state. How is this to be treated under GST?

Effectively, there are many ambiguities due to the complex nature of the tax and the diversity of the economy. These create difficulties in implementation of GST. Will these be transitional or will new problems keep cropping up? Already some cases have gone to the courts due to differences in interpretations.

Conclusion

This Chapter presents the procedures under GST as it has been implemented and depicts its complexity. For instance, it presents the complex rate structure, its rationale, how the ITC, Reverse Charge Mechanism and e-way bill are designed and how they will operate, how audit will be done, how states will be compensated in case of shortfall in revenue, fines to be imposed for delayed payment, process of appeal against orders of the authorities and so on. This complexity caused problems which then led to rapid changes in GST and much confusion. The problems being encountered are not just implementation problems but structural problems.

The earlier Committees that had gone into the issue of reform of the indirect taxes in India since the 1970s had recognized the difficulties of implementing the same in India given the complex structures of production and distribution. From the large scale to the cottage, the economic structures are complex and not conducive to the introduction of VAT all through the economy from production to the final sale to the consumer. Yet, India has opted for GST which is even more complex compared to the earlier VAT for each separate tax.

The Chapter while presenting the procedures to be followed under GST, is not written the way a Chartered Accountant or a Tax Lawyer would write it. They would focus on the myriad of details about each of the components of GST. They are the practitioners who have to advise businesses about what they need to do. Such details are not relevant to the lay public or even an economist specializing in Public Finance. For the average person it is enough to understand the logic of the major components of GST to judge whether it is good or bad for the country; this is what this Chapter focused on. However, the practitioners would also find the logic presented here useful to better understand the procedures that they need to follow.

The Chapter highlights the link between the vast diversity of the Indian economy and the complications in the design of GST. Indian economy is unique among the major economies of the world with its diverse production structures and the vast poverty that exists. Hence the argument that GST exists in 160 countries cannot be the argument for introducing it in India.

The Chapter shows that the desire to collect tax at each and every stage of production and distribution is at the root of the problem for

GST. Further, it points out that the desire to fulfil multiple objectives has led to the multiple rates which has added to the complexity of GST in India. It also points out that the calculation of RNR is based on various assumptions that can be contested. If that is the case then the rate structure can also be contested.

The various exemptions provided under GST not only add to the complexity but they also break the chain of taxation from the beginning to the end that was supposed to be an integral part of the GST. So, many of the gains that were expected to accrue from GST are unlikely to be realized. The question then again arises why go for GST? The design of a simpler indirect tax which will avoid all the difficulties being faced at present will be discussed in the concluding chapter.

CHAPTER 7

GST, BLACK INCOME GENERATION AND DIGITIZATION

I have pointed out in a couple of books[1] that black economy is a reality of Indian society that cannot be ignored since it is so large. It impacts every aspect of the citizen's life. Its impact is political, social and economic. It sets back development of the country and aggravates poverty and inequality. It undermines policies of the government and leads to policy failure which delegitimizes government intervention in the economy. Policy failure leads to lower level of development and as shown in an article[2] in 2005, the economy has been losing 5 per cent rate of growth on an average since the mid-1970s. The society is poorer and less civilized than it could have been. The most recent exposition of the macroeconomic analysis of the black economy is in a book[3] on the subject.

Policy failure has led to the demand for the retreat of the state and dependence on the markets. It is also clear that markets cannot cater to the needs of the poor since not only can they not afford to pay the market price but there is market failure in modern day economies.[4] So, it is the poor who suffer the most due to the existence of a substantial black economy. Hence, there is an urgent need to tackle this menace which like termites hollows the nation.

Various governments have taken steps to tackle the black economy in the last seventy years. Many committees and

---

[1] Kumar (1999b) and Kumar (2017a)

[2] Kumar (2005c)

[3] Chattopadhyay (2018)

[4] Kumar (1995)

commissions have been set up to study the problem[5] and they have made thousands of suggestions and hundreds have been implemented. In 2016, demonetization was announced with a big bang. It caused untold misery to the poor who never generated any black incomes while those generating black incomes and had black wealth went scot free; the problem did not get resolved.[6] The reason is that the underlying cause of the black economy's existence is not technical or economic but political[7] and that remains unresolved.

Proponents of GST have been arguing that it would help tackle the black economy since all inputs and outputs in the entire chain of production and distribution would be computerized. As argued in Chapter 6, this is not entirely true for the Indian GST since it has various exemptions and certain key commodities are kept out of its purview. Further, small and cottage sectors are largely outside its scope. More importantly, Indian businesses are adept at keeping two sets of accounts and they can continue to do so.

Finally, it is believed that digitization would help tackle the black economy. It is argued that the informal sector would get formalized and come under the tax net. This is an incorrect understanding of the nature of the black economy in India. Most of the unorganized sector earns incomes way below the taxable limit. To understand this it is important to know that in India, taxation begins at a multiple of the per capita incomes and income inequality is high. Hence, a vast majority of the people earn incomes way below the taxable limit and do not fall in the tax net.[8] An overwhelming majority of those below the taxable limit belong to the low paid unorganized and informal sector. Thus, whether these people declare their incomes or not, they remain outside the tax net. Further, they are not the cause of black income generation and even if these people get formalized, this process will not impact the black economy.

---

5   Kumar (2017a)
6   Kumar (2017d)
7   Kumar (1985a)
8   Kumar (1999b)

To understand whether GST will be able to help tackle the black economy or not, it is important to familiarize oneself with some key aspects of the black economy.

Key Features of Black Economy—Misperceptions

Not only is the perception that black incomes are generated in the informal sector incorrect, there are other misperceptions about the black economy.[9] For instance, demonetization was premised on the notion that 'black means cash'. This led to the unfortunate conclusion that if cash is squeezed out of the system, then the black economy would disappear at one stroke. The confusion was also about black money and black income. The former is a tiny part of the black wealth that is accumulated over the years while the latter is what is earned every year. Out of the incomes earned, a part is invested which adds up every year and becomes a person's wealth. So, it is shown in a recent book[10] that black cash is a tiny part of the black wealth and it does not impact the generation of black incomes. Thus, demonetization did not manage to curb the black economy.

It has been argued that use of technology can help curtail black economy. It is felt that the human element is incorrigible so it needs to be eliminated from business transactions if the black economy is to be eradicated. The underlying assumption is that the human element can be eliminated in the running of society. This is a flawed notion since it is human beings who operate technology even if the number of human beings running systems can be reduced. As long as human intervention is needed, illegality can persist. Humans can use technology to indulge in illegality which may be of a different kind than that which prevailed earlier. The form of illegality only changes with the use of technology.

The need is to transform the human element itself but that is a difficult political and social task so policy makers think of simpler

---

9   Kumar (2017a)
10 Kumar (2017d)

and more seductive policies which are economic and technological. The easy way out for them is to think of replacing humans with computers and technology since they cannot be corrupted. Or alternatively, police people and if they do something wrong punish them. Often punishment does not reform the person and only makes them hardened and repeat offenders.[11]

The task of society has to be to make itself better by reforming the human element. Replacing humans with technology without reforming them does not create a better society while that should be the goal of reformers and policy makers. It is now well known that with growing computerization, there is more of hacking, phishing, cybercrime, fraud and so on. New forms of crime are fast growing. Has crime decreased in the advanced countries with growing computerization? With easier access to social media there is more of loneliness[12] and multi-tasking which is resulting in more of psychological problems and often leads to crime.

The idea that more laws are needed to check the growth of black economy is also flawed. As explained in a book on the Indian economy by this author[13] there can be no perfect law since human ingenuity can find a way of circumventing any law. It is argued that a law is a law in letter and spirit and if the latter is not willing, ways of flouting the law can be discovered. This is what seems to have happened in India as more and more laws have been brought on the statute books, newer ways of flouting them have also been found. The Income Tax Act of 1960 was a simple document but with time it was found that businesses discovered loopholes or created them and laws were framed to rectify the flaws. Slowly, the Income Tax Act became more and more complex. But that enabled the tax evaders to evade taxes more easily.[14]

Thus, use of more technology and putting more laws on statute books is like chasing a receding target. The harder one tries the

---

[11] GoI (2016b)
[12] Pawlowski (2018)
[13] Kumar (2013)
[14] Kumar (1994)

worse it becomes. It is reminiscent of *Alice in Wonderland*, where the harder Alice runs the more she remains in the same place. As discussed in a recent book,[15] the crux of the problem is to address the alienation of the individuals from society by making them believe that there can be social justice. Neither more laws nor more technology can achieve this. Technology cannot run society by itself and may in fact create more alienation.

The same book discusses the many other misunderstandings about the black economy, like, that all the black money is held abroad and that it can be easily tracked and brought back. This was a promise at the time of the 2014 national elections. However, only 10 per cent of the black incomes generated annually are taken abroad. So, most of the black money is in India. Further, through round tripping a large part of the money taken abroad is brought back. In effect, what is held abroad is nowhere close to what was stated at the time of the 2014 elections. Similarly, it is a mistake to believe that black money is generated in real estate. The white paper on black money[16] by the Government of India stated that it is the biggest generator of black incomes. However, this author showed[17] in 1999 that black money is circulated via real estate but not generated there.

In technical jargon the capital gain in a real estate transaction is a 'transfer income' but not a 'factor income'. The former only transfers savings from one hand to the other without any production taking place. So, in a real estate transaction, no construction is involved but only the transfer of a property or land from one individual to another in exchange of money (another asset). Similarly, bribes are a transfer income from the bribe giver to the bribe taker. The bribe taker is already being paid for the work she/he is required to do. She may exploit her position to extract a bribe but that is not remuneration for the work she is supposed to be doing. Bribery is a

---

[15] Kumar (2017a)

[16] GoI (2012)

[17] Kumar (1999b)

function of lack of accountability. If there was accountability in the system, bribes would become the exception.

Another common fallacy is that black is generated in the public sector. From this it follows that if the state retreats and the markets take over, black income generation would end. Alternatively, it is felt that government intervention in the markets leads to black income generation; so the solution is that markets be allowed to function. A book[18] by a professor of the London School of Economics showed that black incomes are a joint product of the public and private sectors.

Take for instance the case of rapid privatization of health and education. As the private sector has penetrated deeper in these two 'noble' professions, malpractices have increased with leaps and bounds. It all started with capitation fees and went on to fake degrees, manipulation of marks, leakage of question papers, monopolistic pricing, recommending of medical tests that were not needed, stealing of organs, malpractices of various kinds—the list is endless.

Not only the private sector but also the public sector has followed suit. The commitment that existed in these sectors in the past has given way to creation of private interests in both public and private sectors. Most public sector teachers and doctors flout rules just as much as in the private sector where the profit motive drives them to it. Of course, the set of rules flouted by the former is different from those flouted by the latter. The problem is that commitment to one's profession cannot be bought with money and it weakens as more and more examples from the private sector emerge. The dividing line between ethical and unethical behaviour is thin and as alienation increases very few can resist the temptation to cross over.

The problem once again is how to reform the human element by ending alienation and getting commitment to the profession. Privatization, more laws and rules and their enforcement alone would not work. In fact, in India, the enforcers themselves have got corrupted on a large scale thereby weakening enforcement. Corruption has been unearthed in the Medical Council of India

---

[18]   Cowell (1990)

(MCI), University Grants Commission (UGC), accreditation councils, school boards and so on.[19] Corruption in the regulatory agencies has surfaced often enough and this is the tip of the iceberg.

Mechanism of Generation of Black Incomes by Businesses

To understand whether GST would indeed be able to tackle the generation of black incomes and rid the country of this scourge, it is necessary to understand how black incomes are generated. As argued recently in a book[20] there are as many ways of generating black incomes as the number of professions and businesses. Depending on the specificity of the business, methods have been devised to generate black incomes. Clever lawyers and chartered accountants spend much time in devising ways of lowering tax liability and they advise their clients accordingly.

Most of the ways of generating black incomes in legal activities fall into the category of under and over invoicing of purchase and sales.[21] Of course, the entire income earned in an illegal activity is black by definition. So, to eliminate black income generation one has to curb the illegal activities and curtail black income generation in legal activities. For the latter, under and over invoicing of costs and revenues by businesses needs to be tackled. These are not impacted by the various one-shot measures, like, demonetization or Income Declaration Scheme (IDS) that have been resorted to by the governments from time to time. The issue is whether GST would be able to tackle such manipulation.

Under-invoicing of Revenues

Businesses work to earn a profit. For that they have to produce some good or a service which can be sold to earn a profit. Production

---

[19]   See for instance, PTI (2010), Mukul (2009) and Kasturi (2008)

[20]   Kumar (2017a)

[21]   Kumar (1999b) and (2006a)

is an activity which requires inputs like hiring workers, buildings, buying raw material and so on. So, businesses incur costs to produce anything. When the product is sold, revenue is earned. Unfortunately, people often mistake revenue for income. In common parlance we call the money we pay the shopkeeper as his/her income. This is erroneous since to earn the revenue, costs are incurred. So, income is the balance left from revenue after deducting costs and that is the profit/income of any business.

To generate black incomes, businesses declare only a part of their profit and hide the rest. The part declared is the white profit or the balance sheet profit (one shown on the balance sheet) and this is also declared to the tax authorities and tax paid on it. The other part is the off-balance sheet profit. It is not declared to the tax authorities and no tax is paid on it. An illegality is committed to generate this profit and it becomes a part of the black incomes generated in the economy. The illegality involved is the manipulation of the business account which is not allowed by law. To successfully do so, other illegalities may also be indulged in.

It is also possible that a business is indulging in a completely illegal activity which is not allowed by law, like, smuggling or sex work. This income is entirely illegal and no part of it can be declared to the tax authorities. Hence in a legal activity a part of the income may be black while in the case of an illegal activity the entire income is black.

So, to generate black incomes in legal activities, business accounts are manipulated. Since income is the net of revenue and costs, both of them can be manipulated to generate black incomes.[22] While the manipulation of revenue is presented in this section, in the next one, the manipulation of costs is discussed.

A sale has two components—how much is sold and at what price. So, one can sell 100 metres of cloth at Rs 50 per metre for a total sale of Rs 5,000. A doctor may see twenty patients a day and charge them Rs 500 each for a daily revenue of Rs 10,000. So, revenue is price multiplied by quantity.

---

[22] Kumar (1999b) and (2006a)

To show lower revenue one can show lower price and/or lower quantity. So, for instance in the above example, one can claim that one sold 90 metres of cloth at Rs 45 per metre for a revenue of Rs 4,050. The under reporting of revenue becomes Rs 950. This is the black income earned via 'under-invoicing'. If the profit margin was 25 per cent on sales, the actual profit would be Rs 1,250 but what is shown is Rs 1,250 less Rs 950 = Rs 300. So, for 10 per cent under invoicing, the black profit would be more than three times the white profit.

In the case of a doctor, she may claim that she has only seen sixteen patients and charged them a consultation of Rs 400 each. The revenue shown becomes Rs 6,400 and under reporting is Rs 3,600 which is the black income earned. If the profit margin of the doctor is 75 per cent, his total income would be Rs 7,500 but the declared income would be Rs 3,900. Thus, an under invoicing by 20 per cent leads to more than half the income being black.

Under-invoicing may be done in many ways. For instance, one may show some goods as scrap and declare a very low price. In continuous process manufacture, one can claim that electricity failed and the chemicals being produced got spoiled and clogged in the lines and it has to be sold as scrap. One can produce tiles and claim that some of them got damaged and have to be sold at a discount of 25 per cent. One can sell a software and show a price which is much less than what is charged. A school charges Rs 1 lakh as admission fee to admit a student but the management takes another Rs 20 lakh as capitation fee. So, there is under invoicing by Rs 20 lakh.

Under-invoicing is also done in the case of exports. If one exports goods worth $100 million one may show it as $90 million and repatriate this amount back to the country and keep the balance $10 million in an account abroad. Such under-invoicing may be done in various ways like showing sales (of $90 million) to a company owned by a relative who then sells (at $100 million) to the actual buyer.

There can also be over-invoicing of imports. If a machine is imported worth $1 million, its price may be declared as $2 million.

So, $2 million is paid to the foreign seller who keeps $1 million and deposits the balance $1 million in some foreign account of the importer. This can also be worked out through some intermediate company owned by a relative.

Thus, businesses under-invoice revenue by showing lower quantity and/or lower price. Further, with the usual profit margins, small amounts of under-invoicing lead to large black incomes.[23] Examples given above show that there are as many ways of under-invoicing of sales as the number of businesses.

Over-invoicing of Costs

Revenue is one aspect of the income of a business but the other aspect is the cost incurred in producing the good or the service. A business can inflate costs to show higher cost and lower income.[24] Costs are of many kind.

One needs raw material, workers, travel, transportation, storage and overheads of various kinds. One may have to pay rent on the building where production takes place and interest on loans taken. There is also depreciation of plant and equipment. Broadly the costs may be categorized as raw materials, wages, overheads, interest, rent and depreciation. Each one of them can be over-invoiced to show lower profits.

So, to produce the textiles one may buy cotton worth Rs 1 lakh but claim that one paid Rs 1.10 lakh for it. So, an extra Rs 0.1 lakh of profit is generated by the owner. Other raw materials like chemicals may also be over invoiced. In road projects, less of gravel and tar may be put but the cost shown maybe for the standard amounts fixed in the contract. Thus, costs are inflated. In a building project, the workers employed may be less skilled than needed and the quality of the building inferior to what is stated in the contract. Here also costs are inflated.

---

[23] Kumar (1999b)

[24] Kumar (1999b) and (2006a)

Overheads are usually overstated like travel expenses, entertainment, advertising and so on. The managers' servants may be shown as company employees, their family's entertainment at a hotel or vacation in a resort may be shown as company expense. Telephone charges and so on may be shown as company expense.

Wages are manipulated in two ways. One by showing higher employment than actual and the other by showing higher wages than what is paid to labour. So, in the case of Satyam, it was reported that there were 12,000 fictitious employees whose wages were being siphoned out by the management. Similar cases have come to light in other places also.[25] In MGNREGS very often employment is shown to be higher than it is. This is known as 'muster roll fudging'.

Wages paid are also often less than what are shown on paper. For instance, contractors at building sites may show in the labour register that they are paying the minimum wage but actually be paying half of that. In a private school, the teacher may have to bring half the salary in cash to give to the management before they receive the salary cheque. In brief, not only the number of employees may be inflated but also the wage paid, entered in the accounts may be much higher than what is actually paid. So, the wage bill shown is much higher than the actual wages paid. It is important to note that this inflation of the wage bill becomes the additional profit of the management or the contractor or the supervisor as the case may be.

Misinvoicing and Black Incomes

Even if 10 per cent of the costs are over-invoiced, the profit rises by a multiple, as in the case of under-invoicing of revenue discussed above. The two kinds of fudging of accounts lead to a large amount of black income generation with small amount of under reporting of output. In other words, black incomes generated by businesses are a multiple of the under-reporting of output.

---

[25] Kumar (2013)

The logic underlying this result is explained in this author's book.[26] The entire cost of production of the undeclared output is loaded on to the declared output so that it becomes costless production (entire revenue becomes the profit) while the latter is shown to have higher cost and lower profits. This is also the reason that managements may prosper while the businesses go sick since a large part of the profit is siphoned out as black income.

One of the consequences of misinvoicing is that black incomes are largely siphoned out via the services sector and not the goods producing sectors—agriculture, manufacturing, mining and so on. Thus, the under estimation of the contribution of the services sector to GDP is the highest and least in the case of agriculture.[27]

Consequently, a) the sectoral composition of the black economy is very different than that of the white economy and b) the income distribution gets even more skewed than if the black incomes were evenly spread across all sectors.

Another interesting aspect of misinvoicing is that black incomes in legal activities are profits and not wages. The logic of this result is that wages are costs so inflation of wages leads to lower tax liability. The result is wages are shown to be higher rather than lower and that raises the profits.

The implication of the above formulation of misinvoicing is that the data of the economy is vitiated. Official data does not capture reality—output is shown to be less while inputs are shown to be higher. So, growth of the economy given by the government turns out to be incorrect and employment is stated to be more than actual. It has been shown[28] that all macroeconomic and micro variables of the economy are affected by the black economy so that empirical analysis gets vitiated. Theoretically also it is shown that analysis are vitiated because the black economy is not taken into account.[29]

---

26 Kumar (1999b)

27 See Kumar (1999b) for greater details

28 Kumar (1999b)

29 See Kumar (2005c) and for latest analysis on this see Chattopadhyay (2018)

Black economy becomes the missing variable in policy making and leads to policy failure on a large scale. For instance, data on education may show that all children are in schools because the enrolment has become 100 per cent. But, schools may exist on paper because the funds have been siphoned off or enrolment shown higher to get funds. Further, surveys show that many children are not found in schools and of those tested, 50 per cent children in class five cannot read or write or do mathematics of the second standard.[30] Thus, one would have to question the data on enrolment in schools and worry about the quality of education imparted.

Finally, there is a problem with misinvoicing. A business would want to over invoice cost but under invoice revenue. But this poses a problem, namely, the purchase by a business is cost to it but revenue to the seller. So, the seller would like to show lower revenue while the buyer would like to show higher cost. This is only possible if two sets of accounts are maintained by businesses. One which would be the actual and the other that would be the one presented to the tax officials. Fudging of accounts is known to be quite widespread in India.

Manually it was quite difficult for the tax officials to match the millions (now billions) of invoices of the buyers and sellers. This is where computerization can help. As a first step towards computerization, the government went in for Permanent Account Number (PAN) and TIN (Tax Information Number for businesses). However, in spite of these attempts, businesses managed to fudge accounts and generate black incomes. Under GST now a registration is required and a number GSTIN is allotted to keep track of the transactions of businesses (See Chapter 5). Transporters are required to get a number called TRANSIN.

Black Economy—Definitional Issue

As discussed earlier, transfer incomes are not to be counted in black incomes. Only those incomes associated with production, called factor incomes, are to be taken into account when estimating black

---

[30] GoI (2015c)

incomes. The previous sections show that under and over invoicing generate factor incomes on which taxes are not paid.

Factor incomes are broadly divided into two—profits and wages. All other incomes are a part of these two. So, rent and interest paid by a business are a part of profits. Managerial salaries are wages. In India, given the complexity of production structures, there is also the category of mixed incomes. Many production units are small where the owners are also workers. So, a part of their income can be attributed to profit and the rest to wage.

In the previous section it was shown that black incomes in a legal activity are profits and not wages. In illegal activities, even the wages are black incomes. For instance, the income of a sex worker or a pimp is illegal and is black income. The implication is that black incomes are largely factor income, profits.

Where does the chain of black income generation begin for businesses? It starts with the way accounts are kept. These lead to under invoicing of output. What goes out of the factory or office is under invoiced and less tax is paid. Earlier it was excise duty or service tax that was evaded. When the item was sold, less of sales tax was paid. When the good entered a state and entry tax was to be paid, it was again proportionately less and the same was the case with Octroi (where applicable). Since the profit shown is less, corporation tax liability is reduced and so is the dividend declared so that less of income tax (where applicable) has to be paid.

In a nutshell, evasion of income starts with paying less of indirect taxes and there were several of them. It continued down the chain till the final buyer bought the good or service. Thus, a multiplicity of indirect taxes were evaded—excise, service tax, sales tax, Octroi/ entry tax and so on. It ended up with less payment of direct taxes, corporation and income tax.

The above makes clear that black incomes are factor incomes property incomes and not wages.[31]

---

[31] See Kumar (1999b) for a more detailed exposition and the complete definition

Can GST Curb Black Income Generation?

It has been repeatedly pointed out[32] that dozens of committees and commissions have been set up to study the problem of black income generation since Independence. They have made a large number of suggestions to curb it and hundreds of steps have been taken to check the black economy since 1947. The UPA II which was besieged with the problem of mega scams and growing black economy also took many steps like signing Double Taxation Avoidance Agreements (DTAA), Tax Information Exchange (TIE) Agreements and getting the Lok Pal Bill passed in Parliament.

The NDA government, after coming to power in 2014 started day one by setting up the Supreme Court monitored SIT. It brought in the Foreign Money Bill, Bankruptcy Bill, Income Declaration Scheme (IDS) and so on. However, none of them were able to make a dent on the black economy. So, it promulgated demonetization which also failed to unearth black money.[33] As pointed out, black income generation is a process and there is no one-shot-solution, nor a magic bullet which can take care of the problem.

GST as it is implemented in India promises to curb black income generation. The invoice created by the seller can be matched with the invoice shown by the buyer. So, it would become difficult for the seller to under-invoice and simultaneously for the same transaction for the buyer to over-invoice.[34]

As pointed out in Chapter 5, computerization under GST is linked to the registration in the centralized computer network created for the purpose, called the GST Network (GSTN). In effect, GST is attempting to change the process of black income generation and is not a one-shot solution like demonetization or voluntary declaration scheme.

---

[32] For instance, in Kumar (1999b)

[33] Kumar (2017d)

[34] Kumar (2018b)

Great store is laid by the digitization that would take place due to GST. The government has been arguing since the announcement of demonetization that the economy will be forced to digitize due to both demonetization and GST. It is suggested that this would generate a vast amount of data which would then help unearth black incomes. The government has been claiming that due to demonetization a large number of new income tax payers have had to file their return.[35] The government has also been talking of use of big data analytics to catch hold of the black income generators. The question is, will having more data help curb the black economy?

As has happened in the past, many promising schemes to check black income generation have not had the desired effect. The reason is that one has to identify the correct cause of black income generation and plug it but none of the large number of steps taken in the last seventy years have done so. For instance, laws have been changed, more of technology used and better implementation of laws promised, but, none of them attack the root of the problem.

GST does impact the process used by businesses to generate black incomes but does it tackle the root of the problem? If not, new processes will be developed by the unscrupulous to generate black incomes in different ways.

Circumventing GST

In Chapters 5 and 6, it was argued that GST in India is a half-way house and that is leading to severe problems in implementation. It was also argued that it is highly complex and that helps generate black incomes.[36] In other words, the design of GST in India is flawed. Add to that the fact that a very leaky administration is to implement it. Thus, there are several reasons why black income generation may continue despite GST.

---

[35] Discussed in greater detail in Kumar (2017d)

[36] Kumar (1999b) shows how complexity helps generate black incomes

First, businesses are used to working without invoices or misclassifying the product in the invoice. Secondly, businesses could establish a chain completely outside the GST network with inputs and outputs not declared. For instance, spurious drugs, adulterated food, artificial milk, contaminated water and so on mostly function outside the GST net. Thirdly, it is also possible that a part of the sales are carried on with invoices while the rest may be in cash. There could be fake billing and such cases have already come to light.

Fourthly, in those cases where there are several rates of taxes for the same item, misclassification becomes easier. Fifthly, due to exemptions, misclassification is easier. As argued in Chapter 6, exemptions break the chain of input and output and this can be used to evade the taxes. Sixthly, use can be made of the Composition Scheme which again breaks the chain of input and output. In this case also, for a lower tax rate, one can supply one's good. Seventhly, the e-way bills could also be manipulated to generate black incomes via misinvoicing. There would be need for physical checking of goods transported and this could lead to corruption. There are reports that this may already be taking place.

Exemptions will enable setting up of chain of supply outside the GST net. Thus, the pretext of supplies from small businesses and from those operating under Composition Scheme could be used to operate in cash. A part of the supply can be shown as having been made to these small businesses and then whatever they supply can be carried out in cash up to the final sale. This will be facilitated by customers who are willing to buy without a bill to save on the tax.

Many professionals who have little input like architects, advocates, tutors and doctors, can operate in cash since they have few inputs and, therefore, they would be entitled to little input credit (ITC). They would be willing to forego the little ITC that may be available on the few inputs they use. For example, if for an architect the inputs are 10 per cent of the fee of Rs 100 she charges, then the ITC she would get would be Rs 1.8 (at 18 per cent). If she bills her fee of Rs 100 she would have to charge her client Rs 118. The client is likely to protest or shift to another architect who is willing to receive

Rs 100 in cash. For the cash transaction no tax would be paid and the only loss would be the Rs 1.8 not recovered as ITC. The architect could even charge Rs 102 and not Rs 118 and get the client, and even the ITC of Rs 1.8 would be recovered.

Apart from these specific ways that black incomes can be generated under GST, there are also more broad based arguments for why black income generation will not stop under GST. In the Alternative Budget[37] authored by this writer, it was argued that more complex the laws, the easier is it to generate black incomes. So, it was argued that the tax laws need to be simplified.

The reason is that our law enforcement agencies (like police or ED, Enforcement Directorate) and the regulatory apparatus (like Income Tax Department) are unable to cope with complexity, even if their intention is not suspect. Per thousand of population, the size of the Indian bureaucracy is small compared to that in the advanced nations.[38] Thus, the administration cannot cope with the volume of the work and the complexity it faces, even if the personnel is assumed to be honest. If a large per cent of them are crooked, they would not be interested in implementing the law as it stands. In fact, they would be interested in misinterpreting the law so as to help the law breakers and complexity comes in handy to do so—a good camouflage.

All along in the earlier chapters it has been pointed out that GST is very complex and even experts have been floundering to understand and interpret it. It will enable accountants and lawyers to find loopholes to reinterpret the GST laws in ways that suits businesses.

The entire accounting for GST implementation is computerized. The question is whether this complex system can work smoothly? It can get overloaded and crash as has happened several times since

---

[37] Kumar (1994)
[38] OECD (2015) shows that average employment in Public Sector as a ratio of total employment for OECD countries was 21.28 per cent in 2013. For India it was around 4 per cent.

the inception of GST. The system is supposed to be able to deal with about 90 lakh accounts and 3.5 billion entries a month. Whenever there is a bunching of entries around the 10th of the month and then again the 20th of the month, the volume of electronic traffic increases manifold and the system either crashes or slows down causing difficulties.

Then there is the issue of mal-intent. Computer systems can be hacked[39] as has happened with so many very reliable computer systems all over the world, including some of the most secure systems run by the US government agencies. If there are cyber attacks and the computer system collapses, the entire chain of input credit will be disrupted. Further, not only data can be lost, filing returns would become difficult. Clever people can devise ways of fooling the computer systems by creating bugs and software to circumvent the rules? Like, creating software that only records every alternate sale for official purposes. All this highlights the importance of honesty.

Does the tax department have the experience of handling such a mass of data? The Income Tax Department has been computerizing the filing of returns and their scrutiny for the last many years. However, the data handling requirements of this department are far less than what is required under GST. So, it cannot be a guide to handling GST and how the systems would work. Further, the Income Tax Department is only able to scrutinize about 1 per cent of the total tax returns filed, a little less than half a million out of about 50 million returns.[40]

---

[39] Kumar (2018d) presents a list of cases of recent hacking of data and websites. This is apart from the hacking of the State Department data by Julian Assange and Edward Snowden stole masses of data of the most secretive NSA of USA. Now there are accusations of USA, Russia, China and North Korea hacking into each other's systems. Servers of Mossak Fonseca of Panama got hacked and masses of financial data was stolen in the famous Panama Papers case.

[40] GoI (2016c) gives Income Tax Department data for 2012–13. Also see Kumar (2016a)

Computerization can point to problems in returns filed but the replies given to queries would have to be scrutinized by the staff of which not only is there a shortage but there is also corruption among them. This is what makes the implementation of rules problematic in India.

In brief, the difficulties encountered by GST both because of design problems and implementation issues, are likely to result in the continuation of black income generation, as in many other countries. This would undermine the official claims of better compliance under GST. As argued earlier by this author,[41] black income generation would continue in India because it is a political problem which cannot be sorted out by mere technical or economic steps like implementation of GST or digitization; only its form may change.

Triad as the Cause

If GST is not going to deliver on this score, is there an alternative?

Literature lists many causes of black income generation, like, high tax rates or controls and regulations or low salaries of the bureaucracy or election funding.[42] These arguments have been critiqued many a times.[43] India has drastically lowered tax rates after 1971 and again after 1991. Controls and regulations have also been substantially removed/diluted after 1991. Bureaucratic salaries have gone up substantially. But there is no way of determining what would be an appropriate level of salaries or tax rates. In spite of these large number of steps taken earlier, the black economy has continued to grow in India.

The latest estimate of the black economy in India is for 2012 and it has grown to 62 per cent of GDP.[44] It was estimated to be 4–5 per cent

41   Kumar (1999b) and Kumar (1985a)
42   NIPFP (1985) and GoI (2012)
43   Kumar (1985c) and Kumar (2017a)
44   Kumar (2016b)

of GDP in 1955–56.[45] It needs to be remembered that black economy is measured as a percentage of the officially declared GDP. It implies that these are incomes over and above the official GDP.

The implication is that currently there is illegality in 62 per cent of economic activity and this has grown over time. The question to ask is how can illegality be so large? It means that the rule of law is being increasingly subverted. If illegality is so substantial, it is not ad hoc. It is not that one day the businessmen generate black income and not the next day or one week they do it and not the next. It is done every day of the week in a systematic manner.

It is argued that illegality is 'systemic and systematic';[46] systems are set up to misinvoice in a routine way. Once the systems are in place, illegality is committed 24x7. This is only possible if the instruments of the state are party to the illegality. To carry on the generation of black incomes, the businessmen have to create a nexus with the policy maker, the politician, and the executive, the implementer of policies. In brief, there has to be a triad of the corrupt businessmen, corrupt political class and corrupt executive to sustain illegality in a routine way and generate such a large black economy.[47]

Indian businesses are known to be rather innovative and devise ways of circumventing the laws. Clever lawyers and accountants work for them to find loopholes and suggest ways of lowering the tax liability. They offer interpretations to benefit the businessmen and to argue the case legally if required. That is why, in India, a law on paper differs from the way it works.

In a book on the Indian economy, it is argued,[48] a law is law in letter and spirit. No law can be perfect which can take care of all the eventualities. The world is dynamic and the situations are constantly changing. For instance, e-commerce has disrupted both the normal trade and the tax to be levied on the goods sold via their

---

[45] GoI (1956)

[46] Kumar (2013)

[47] Kumar (1985a)

[48] Kumar (2013)

platform. New provisions are required to tax such transactions and governments all over the world are grappling with this problem.

The clever ones in society can find ways of circumventing any law, if the spirit is not willing. There is need for consensus in society so that laws are voluntarily followed. So, the key issue is how to generate consensus, especially among the ruling elite, on how to govern society. This can only be done via social and political processes and not by some technical steps. Implementation of technical or economic policies is also political and requires consensus building.

Is There a Remedy?

Arguments given above imply that the black economy can only be checked if the triad is dismantled. If not, whatever steps are taken will only lead to a change in the form of the black economy and not its eradication. Unfortunately, the triad in India has strengthened over time, in spite of the many steps taken in the past or the promulgation of new laws.

The triad has not only proved to be durable but has become stronger over time because it serves the interest of each of its components. The businessmen gain control over policies which they can then manipulate in their favour. In the recent big scams like 2G or Coal Allocations, those with the right connections got these natural resources.[49] This is seen repeatedly in the case of land allocation, mines, forest areas, coastal zones and so on.[50] Businessmen get advance information about where the infrastructure is going to be located and they buy the land close to it in advance and make a killing at the expense of the local farmers or tribals. They share the gain with the politicians and the executive.

The triad consists of people from the ruling elite and they gain from its functioning. Naturally then there is little interest in checking its functioning since that would adversely affect their own gains.

---

[49] Kumar (2013) and Thakurta (2009)
[50] Ram (2017)

Those in the opposition also do the same when they get to power. Businessmen keep good relations with all the political parties and fund them—the ruling party more than the Opposition. No wonder, those in power pay lip service to eliminating the black economy but are not really interested in doing so.

The members of the triad subvert the rule of law. It is their lack of accountability that fuels the black economy. So, there is need for accountability for each of the element of the triad.[51] Right to Information is crucial for this but in spite of the RTI Act passed in 2005 and setting up of the Information Commission at the Centre and the states, black economy has continued to grow. The reason lies in the undermining of the Right to Information itself. The powerful (including the political parties) have consistently done everything to not come under its purview. The executive has found new ways of not answering by using the ploy 'information not available' or resorting to other dilatory tactics.

Businesses should be accountable to their shareholders but this is systematically undermined. The board of directors are often the handmaiden of the owners. The independent auditors are also often found to be compromised, like in the case of Satyam or the Nirav Modi and other recent scams that have come to light. Thus, the owners are able to pretty much do as they wish.

In brief, as argued in a recent book,[52] tackling the black economy is a political and societal issue which only movements can address. There is a need to change the consciousness of the public at large so that they demand accountability from their elected representatives. But the public is also compromised. It votes for a person from its own caste, region, community, etc., even if they are corrupt and/or have a criminal background.[53] No wonder the number of legislators with criminal cases against them has grown rapidly as Association for Democratic Reform (ADR) has documented. The public chooses

---

[51] Kumar (1999b) and Desai (2008)

[52] Kumar (2017a)

[53] See Vaishnav (2017) and Kumar (1999b)

one who will do their work, regardless of legality, given that policies fail. There is also a growing belief that one community can only gain at the expense of others. People have come to believe that it is a zero-sum game and not a positive-sum game.

GST does not dismantle the triad and hence cannot tackle the black economy. As argued above, ways to circumvent the GST laws will emerge to enable the black economy to continue, even if its form changes.

Conclusion

It has been argued above that there are many misconceptions about the black economy in the public. That is why there is a lack of proper understanding of this subject. The true cause of the existence of the black economy has not been understood, so in spite of the large number of steps taken to check it in the last seventy years, the black economy has continued to grow.

Black income generation is a process and no one-shot policy (like demonetization) will help check it. The process in place has made the black economy 'systematic and systemic'. It has become so because there is a triad in place consisting of the corrupt businessmen, corrupt politicians and corrupt executive. They belong to the ruling elite and since they gain from the black economy they pay lip service to checking it but have little interest in doing so.

The need is to make the elements of the triad accountable. That in turn requires raising the consciousness of the people at large which could lead to a social and political transformation and which cannot be achieved by technological means or by implementing strictly economic policies. People in administration have to implement policies or technological solutions and as long as they do not undergo a transformation, illegality will continue in different forms.

GST theoretically will help check misinvoicing by businesses but given its complexity, it would be easy to devise new ways of misinvoicing. Great hopes are placed upon the digitization that GST will bring about but this can also be circumvented. As argued, if the spirit is not willing, new ways of subverting any law can be devised and especially if the executive and the political class is as corrupt as it is in India.

In brief, GST does not promise a social and political transformation in the country. Reform of the human element is crucial and for that the growing alienation needs to be tackled. This is difficult but necessary. GST and digitization can actually worsen the situation rather than helping.

CHAPTER 8

CLAIMS ABOUT GST: HOW CORRECT?

Introduction

As indicated in Chapter 6, implementation of GST has been beset with problems. It has hit not only businesses but the common people who have had to bear the brunt through higher inflation and inadequate employment for the young (as argued in Chapter 4). The obvious difficulties were not taken care of. So from day one, changes had to be made in the rules and the GST portal ran into problems which had to be fixed. This is what had happened during demonetization[1] where all manner of quick changes had to be brought about creating further confusion. For instance, it was too ambitious to think that every business would be equipped to file 3 forms every month and one annual return for supply to each state it operates in.

Further, the system of input credit and filing of returns had to be computerized because billions of entries every month had to be coordinated. The GST Network (GSTN) was created for this and businesses were supposed to register on its website. More than a crore of businesses had to be registered. But the website crashed on 30 June because of the rush to register on the site and again on 1 July as the new system started. Businesses have complained of delays in filing their data on GSTN.

Analysts had already warned that this may happen and had asked that the implementation of GST be postponed till the systems are tested. But the government did not agree to this. They wanted the

---

[1]   Kumar (2017d)

new law to be implemented immediately. It was even suggested by some experts that the implementation may be carried out in stages. In a way this has happened because the implementation of many of the critical provisions had to be postponed, for example, e-way bill and reverse charge (RCM).

The officials said that there is no option but to start and learn as one goes along. It was argued that the GST was proposed in 2005 and its implementation should have started much earlier. However, due to lack of political consensus and objections by the states it could not be introduced earlier. So, it was high time that it was initiated since the benefits would be enormous and the country was losing by not implementing it. It was also said that no matter when the scheme is implemented there would be glitches. The moot point is what kind of glitches—basic to the scheme or minor ones.

Clearly, some very basic problems hit the implementation of GST. These features will continue to plague GST even if the temporary glitches disappear over time. This chapter will analyse some of the arguments that have been made in favour of GST.

Weak Claims Made for the Advantages of GST

Some of the claims made regarding GST are given on the GST website.[2]

They are:

1. Decrease in inflation due to
   a. Reduction in cascading of taxes and
   b. Overall reduction in prices

2. Ease of doing business due to
   a. Common National Market and
   b. Benefits to small taxpayers

---

[2] https://www.gst.gov.in/

3. Decrease in 'black' transactions due to
    a. Self-Regulating Tax System
    b. Non-Intrusive Electronic Tax System

4. More informed consumer due to
    a. Simplified Tax Regime
    b. Reduction in Multiplicity of Taxes

5. Poorer states to gain
    a. Consumption Based Tax
    b. Abolition of Central Sales Tax

6. Make in India
    a. Exports to be zero rated and
    b. Protection of domestic industry via IGST

These claims are made in simple terms so that they can be understood even by the lay person. Some of these, like, impact on prices and cascading effect were dealt with in macroeconomic terms in Chapter 4. There the analysis was in aggregative terms. The analysis below is in microeconomic terms, looking at the individuals and firms. The black economy aspects are not discussed here since they have been dealt with in Chapter 7.

Impact on Inflation

It was shown in Annexure 1.1 that the cascading effect does not disappear with the presently structured GST. Further, it was shown that

a. If rates of tax are fixed as RNR, then prices will not fall.
b. If there is one common tax rate for all goods and services then the prices of basic goods and services will go up and they would feed into inflation.
c. If more of GST is collected than was collected earlier from the indirect taxes then the prices will rise.

In addition to the above factors there are other aspects that would cause prices to rise:

a. Complexity and increased accounting work for small businesses
b. Absorption of ITC in prices to raise profits
c. Exclusion of energy (petroleum products and electricity) from GST and ITC not being available for them
d. Items that are exempt from GST would not be able to pass on ITC to subsequent stages of production and distribution and the chain would be broken.
e. Multiplicity of tax rates would mean that cascading effect would continue
f. Fixing tax rates to the higher slab in GST, especially in the case of services
g. Difficulty in governance due to complexity would lead to higher costs

For most firms, the cost of doing business will rise since the accounting work will increase under GST. This would be especially true for the smaller businesses which earlier did not employ accountants or did not computerize their accounts. They will have to pass on the cost increase to the consumers.

The confusion about the input tax credit (ITC) and how it is to be accounted is likely to be used to not lower prices but to raise profit. For this reason, the anti-profiteering clause has been provided under GST. But it is difficult to implement as argued in Chapter 6.

To ensure that businesses pass on the benefit of ITC to the consumer, the government would have to be watchful and use strict measures. This is likely to be resisted by industry since it would give powers to the bureaucracy to check their accounts closely and this could lead to increased corruption.

Under the law, there is provision for a National Anti-Profiteering Authority (NAA) and rules for it have been recommended. It was proposed that such an authority would have a chairman (Secretary level post) and four technical members from the Centre and/

or states. The NAA was constituted on 28 November 2017 with the appointment of the chairperson and the technical members. Further, a Standing Committee on Anti-Profiteering at the Centre and a state level Screening Committee have also been set up. There is provision for a Directorate General of Safeguards in the Central Board of Excise and Customs (CBEC).

The process is quite elaborate. A complainant would have to go from the Screening Committee at the state level to the Standing Committee at the Centre and then the matter would go to the Directorate of Safeguards and finally to the NAA. NAA can order the business to reduce prices, return the excess profit, levy penalty and even order revocation of GST registration.

While the basic items of essential consumption are being exempted (as also in the previous indirect tax regime), if the general price level increases, their prices will also go up. Further, there are two important aspects which will continue to fuel inflation. First, the exclusion of energy—electricity and petroleum products—from GST. This would lead to a cascading effect. Second, the use of several tax rates rather than one tax rate for all goods and services will also result in the continuation of the cascading effect, as explained in Annexure 1.1. So, prices will rise by more than the tax increase.

The items which are outside the purview of GST and those that are exempt from GST will break the chain of ITC. The taxes paid on the inputs to these items cannot be deducted from subsequent stages of production and distribution. Take an example.

To produce wheat, the farmer would use pesticide, diesel for pumping water, transportation to take the produce to the market and so on. On each of them a tax is paid. But since wheat does not pay any GST, no input credit would be available to the farmer. So, his price would be higher than it could be. Imagine that the wheat is sold to the miller to make flour which is then sold to the bread maker. Each of these will have to pay GST but the ITC for the pre-wheat production and distribution stage would not be available to the subsequent stages. Their price would also correspondingly be higher.

As was pointed out in Chapter 6, the GST rates were fixed close to the tax rate that was applicable earlier. However, in most cases the rate was moved to the higher rate under GST. So, if some item had a rate of 15.5 per cent under the old system, the rate was moved to 18 per cent under GST. That was the case with most services and their prices rose.

GST is like a tax from cradle to grave—from raw material to final supply to the consumer. This has made it very complex. As pointed out in Chapter 5, modern day production is highly complex with a supply chain stretching globally and certainly across the states of India. Complexity is the enemy of good governance in the Indian context. If the implementation of GST is fouled up due to the complexity then the impact will be felt on prices.

So, there are many factors that have been impacting prices but then why does the data not show an upsurge in prices? The reason is that the services sector is under-represented in the inflation data.[3] The Wholesale Price Index (WPI) does not have services in it and the Consumer Price Index (CPI) only captures about half the services.[4] Thus, some important items of consumption are not captured in our inflation data. So, if school fees go up, the inflation index will not reflect that. That is why while the public feels that the rate of inflation is high, the official data does not capture that.

Thus, whether the macro- or the microeconomic factors are taken into account, the rate of inflation would rise due to the implementation of GST. But, this is not visible in the data since the services sector is under-represented in the inflation data. However, rate of inflation depends on multiple factors. It could fall due to other factors like a favourable monsoon. The point being made here is that GST will give inflation an upward push even if other factors make it fall. In other words, the rate of inflation could be even lower if GST had not been implemented

---

[3]   Kumar (2006b)

[4]   Kumar (2017d)

Ease of Doing Business

It is certainly true that the number of taxes to be paid and the agencies to be dealt with will be fewer. But will the accounting to be done be any less? Registration in each of the states the firm operates in is required. Thirty-seven forms per state have to be filed. This is to enable SGST to be smoothly paid to each of the states and for accounting for input credit.

More critically, to calculate VAT, every input and output has to be accounted for by each of the firms. Further, if there are common inputs into several items being manufactured or sold by a firm their costs have to be proportionately allocated to each of the items. For instance, if a grocer sells 200 items and transports them from the wholesale markets in one lot then on each item the transport cost has to be proportionately shown. The same goes for say, a hardware store.

As already argued, modern day production is highly complex with many stages involved till the product or the service reaches the final consumer. At each stage full accounting has to be done so that there is a massive increase in the accounting requirements.

While the medium and the large scale sectors were already mostly computerized, it is the small and especially the micro units that face the real problems in accounting and computerizing. Thus, there may be ease of doing businesses for the large and medium scale businesses because they were already largely computerized but it may be the opposite for the small and the micro sectors. Even the large scale producers may have to chase up suppliers to fill up their forms and do so accurately. Any mistake by the latter would create difficulties for the form submitted by the buyer. Imagine a large firm which is involved in hundreds of tasks daily of buying and selling and how much would it have to chase up its suppliers. Thus, overall it remains to be seen how much ease of doing business occur.

As argued in Chapter 6, the claim of creating a common national market is an exaggeration. There was always a common market even if the tax rates differed across borders of the states. Goods moved across borders even if there were entry taxes or Octroi. Checking would still be needed at various places so as to make sure the invoices carried by transporters are correct and not fake. E-way bill system is unlikely to prevent these manipulations from happening.

So, overall there would not be any simplification. It is the small and the micro sectors that will bear the brunt of difficulties and for them 'ease of doing business' is proving to be illusory.

More Informed Consumer?

The GST laws are so dense that most experts are unclear and it is unlikely that the common man, the consumer, will have a better idea. As mentioned in Chapter 1, all indirect taxes are paid by the consumer. Earlier when a consumer bought something she was not aware that at the earlier stages there was excise duty or service tax. If she took the bill it only mentioned the sales tax (VAT). Now, often more than one tax is mentioned—CGST and SGST. On a cinema ticket there was an entertainment tax but now there is CGST and SGST. It does not look simpler.

If prices go up (as discussed above) in spite of the input credit and essential goods being kept out of the GST net, it is not clear to the consumer why this happens. So, one cannot say that the consumer is better informed. In fact she/he is perplexed.

It is true that the total tax liability may be more transparent in the final tax that the customer pays but what good is that if the price rises. She is also confused when she goes to the shop to buy things, whether she should ask for the bill or not. Especially, if the shop keeper offers the product cheaper without the bill or her architect is willing to charge less without the bill.

Would Poorer States Gain?

The poorer states produce less and consume more. So, they ought to gain from GST because it is a final stage tax. That is, the tax accrues to the state where the final sale takes place. The producing states will get proportionately less than the consuming states since they proportionately produce more and consume less.

In absolute terms, the better off a state, the higher its level of consumption. So, in absolute amount, the better off states will collect more of the GST revenue even though in relative terms they may get less. Supposing Bihar produces 100 units and Maharashtra produces 500 units. Assume that consumption in Bihar is 80 units (80 per cent) while it is 320 units (64 per cent) in Maharashtra. So, production is five times more but consumption is four times more in Maharashtra compared to Bihar. It follows, assuming one common tax rate, that the GST collected on consumption would be four times more in Maharashtra than in Bihar. How much advantage would Bihar have because it buys more of the goods from outside? Say, for Bihar, 30 per cent comes from outside while only 20 per cent of what Maharashtra consumes comes from outside. So, Bihar gets the advantage of 24 units while Maharashtra gets an advantage of 64 units. Again in absolute terms Maharashtra would gain much more though in proportionate terms it gains less.

Two factors may be added to this. First, the composition of production and the tax rates on the items of production. Bihar mostly produces basic and essential goods for its population and less of the higher value added products. Since these would be either taxed at 0 per cent or 5 per cent, its tax collection from own production would be little. In the case of Maharashtra, proportionately more production would come from higher value added items paying higher rate of tax. An example would make this clear.

To simplify, assume that neither Bihar nor Maharashtra send their goods outside the state. Further, assume that for Bihar 30 per cent of the output falls in the 0 per cent and an equal amount in the 5 per cent tax rate and the balance in 18 per cent rate. The average tax rate would then be 8.7 per cent. In the case of Maharashtra say 10 per cent is at 0 per cent, 20 per cent at 5 per cent, 40 per cent at 18 per cent and 30 per cent at 28 per cent. Then the average tax rate would be 16.6 per cent. In brief, Bihar on its 100 units of production would collect Rs 8.7 while Maharashtra will collect on its 500 units Rs 83.

Thus, Maharashtra would collect 9.5 times more tax than Bihar even though it produces only five times more output.

Second, the adverse impact of GST would be more in Bihar than in Maharashtra given that the unorganized sector is proportionately more in Bihar. Of Bihar's 100 units of production may be 60 per cent is produced in the unorganized sectors while of the 500 units of production in Maharashtra, only 30 per cent may be produced in the unorganized sectors. Thus, the adverse revenue impact of GST would be on 60 units of production in Bihar but will be on 150 units of production in Maharashtra. If there is a 10 per cent decline in the output of the unorganized sector then Bihar would lose 6 units while Maharashtra would lose 15 units. The loss in absolute terms would be more in Maharashtra but in percentage terms, production would decline by 6 per cent in Bihar and only 3 per cent in Maharashtra. So, the rate of growth would fall far more in Bihar than in Maharashtra.

Regarding the abolition of CST, it is being replaced by IGST. The former accrued to the originating state from where the good is sent to another state, the destination state. IGST accrues to the destination state. Yet, as discussed above, even though GST accrues to the consuming states, they are at a disadvantage. Thus, IGST is needlessly being claimed as a new advantage—to whom?

Make in India

The government has launched a programme titled, 'Make in India' which is supposed to promote indigenous production to boost the economy. One can achieve this goal by offering greater protection to indigenous producers by raising customs duties, as has been done in the Union Budget 2018–19 and creating a conducive environment for indigenous production. GST is supposed to do the latter. The idea also is that if Indian production becomes more competitive then exports would rise and this would boost the economy. China has been a successful exporter and its economy has done well.

Even under the earlier system of indirect taxes, exports were given set-off for the internal taxes paid. However, it was difficult to compensate for the cascading effect of taxes. This is where GST may score because the final tax is clearly reported and cascading effect is reduced. But as already argued, to the extent that energy is left out of GST, ITC would not be available for it and this would create some cascading effect. Similarly, due to some items being exempt from GST, the chain is broken and ITC is again not available so that some cascading effect again occurs. Thus, complete transparency in internal taxes is not available.

On exports, under GST, the exporters have to pay the tax and then claim refund of the same. As the system has evolved, these refunds are not automatic and are greatly delayed. This has increased the working capital requirement of exporters and they have claimed that their cost has risen and so exports are less profitable. The government has also recognized this and has held special camps to clear the dues of exporters. Be that as it may, India's exports have not got the boost that was expected since their growth has been tepid after GST was introduced.

It is also claimed that imports have to pay IGST so there is greater protection to domestic industry. This is incorrect. Protection to domestic production is given by customs duty which has not been touched under GST. IGST on imports is only supposed to provide parity with internal taxes, a role that CVD played earlier. CVD is now replaced by IGST. Thus, there is no additional protection due to switch to IGST.

In brief, most of the claims of the ministry on its website are not valid and at times confusing or incorrect. The only purpose seems to be to convince the public that GST is good. Instead of this kind of weak defence, the government should have gone for a more robust defence of what the real advantages of GST are likely to be.

Analysis of Some Robust Factors Favouring GST

Since the implementation of GST some trends in the economy have become apparent. While one can discount the teething troubles, the long term and structural trends need to be commented on.

These could be listed as:

a. Impact on business climate.
b. Impact on overall output taking the impact on small and
    marginal sectors into account.
c. Impact on efficiency; any reduction in distortion compared to
    the earlier taxes.
d. Impact on federalism and long term health of the economy and
    on disparities.

While the first two are discussed in sub-sections below the other two
are discussed in subsequent sections.

GST, Business Climate and Investment

There are innumerable factors that go into defining the business
climate in a country. GST is one of the many factors. As discussed in
the previous section, prices are likely to rise rather than fall, ease of
doing business is unlikely for the economy as a whole and certainly
not for the unorganized sector which is a very large part of the
economy. If the poorer states stand to lose and the 'Make in India'
programme does not get a boost, the investment climate is unlikely
to improve.

Business climate is reflected in the confidence of businesses to
invest in the economy. If they are confident, they increase investments
but if not, investment slows down. Investment in the economy
has various components like in agriculture, industry, services, in
financial form or in physical form. It can be in the organized or the
unorganized sectors. What is the investment climate for these two
important components of the economy?

It is possible that the organized sector may be doing well and
investing more while the unorganized sector facing a crisis may
be investing less. In such a situation, the official data may show an
increase in investment but would the growth rate of the economy
pick up?

There is likely to be a statistical illusion. Most of the data for the Indian economy is based on the working of the organized sectors of the economy. These sectors are required to report data to the official agencies. The data for the unorganized sectors comes with a delay of a few years. Since this data are not available immediately, how is it to be incorporated in making quarterly or annual estimates? This is where the methodology of estimation is important. In the Indian economy, most of the estimates are based on the data reported by the organized sectors of the economy. Regarding the unorganized sector, it is usually assumed that it is also growing at the same rate.[5] Now, this methodology is alright if there is no shock to the economy but it will fail when there is a shock and the parameters of the economy are impacted.

Investment in the organized sectors of the economy has also been low[6] because of low capacity utilization.[7] The reason for such a linkage is that if demand is low, a producer would produce less than she could produce. If one continues to produce to capacity and it does not sell then one is saddled with inventories and that is an expensive proposition since cost is sunk but no revenue comes from that. Thus, when demand is low, producers cut back production and in that case they reduce their investment. If they were to invest more they would have even higher unutilized capacity and would incur greater losses.

Investment in the organized sectors has also been constrained by the high non-performing assets (NPA) of the banks. It has also plagued many industries. Infrastructure, steel, textiles and so on have incurred losses and, therefore, they have not been able to pay back the loans taken from banks. No doubt, NPAs are a complex issue. Did the bank do due diligence or did they succumb to political pressure to give the loans to favoured businessmen (crony capitalism)? This has been a big factor in India. But incorrect business decisions are

---

5   Kumar (2017b) and GoI (2013)
6   Kumar (2017d)
7   RBI (2017)

also a factor. When an economy is doing well, a businessman may invest believing that it would be profitable but it may turn out to be a wrong judgment. In the case of real estate, a lot of the money is stuck because the funds collected by builders from clients were diverted to other projects. Further, there is much unsold stock of real estate so prices are not likely to go up and investors will not get a return for some time. So, the real estate sector and construction of housing and commercial buildings has been in the slow lane since 2012.

Earlier the banks did not show NPAs in their balance sheet and hoped that they would recover the loan somehow. They in fact threw more good money after the bad and the NPAs increased. The RBI cracked down on the banks in 2015 and forced them to disclose the NPAs.

The high NPAs and criticisms have forced the banks to turn very cautious. The pendulum has swung the other way and industry is finding it hard to get loans. This has led to a lowering of the credit off take from the banks which is one indication of lower level of investment. However, there is another reason for why off take of loans from banks has declined; industry is raising funds abroad and from private players. The net result of all these factors is that the organized sector's rate of investment has been low compared to the peak in 2007, just before the financial crisis hit the world.

The shock of demonetization led to a collapse in the unorganized sectors.[8] Many units in this sector closed down and their workers migrated back to the villages due to lack of work. Such units work on small amounts of capital. The definition of the micro sector is that it has a capital of less than Rs 25 lakh. But in reality for most units it is even less than a lakh and the average employment is 1.7 people. Without work, owners of many of these units run through their capital in next to no time. Their capacity to buy new tools or machines declines. To revive, they need capital which they can only get at high cost from the informal money markets. Thus, it is not easy for them to revive production or increase investment.

---

[8] Discussed in Kumar (2017d)

The important point is that even if investment in the organized sector rises, it does not follow that the same is the case in the unorganized sector. So, one needs to know the net investment taking place in the economy but such data are not available. Theoretically one can say that given the macroeconomic situation, the overall investment in the economy is unlikely to grow.

It turns out that even the large and medium scale producers have found GST to be problematic. Firstly, due to design problems like pricing, implementation of reverse charge (RCM) and input credit (ITC). The rates of tax for different products had not been worked out till the very end so that various businesses did not know how to price their products. After 1 July 2017, a large number of changes were announced leading to additional complications. Secondly, as discussed, the GST itself is very complex. These factors have led to a deterioration of the business climate.

Uncertainty is the biggest dampener of investment. The future is uncertain so one cannot accurately predict the return on investment and if the present also adds to the uncertainty then the business climate becomes adverse and investment is hit. There have been a large number of changes in the rules applicable to GST (Table 5.2) and this has added to the uncertainty.

It is true that the number of agencies that a business has to deal with may be fewer and the paperwork to be done for each may also be less but the requirements of GST are onerous. As described earlier, 'Ease of Doing Business' has been a casualty.

Paper work has been replaced by accounting related problems. It is said that the fees of accountants and tax lawyers have risen dramatically over the last one year. This is not only due to the interpretation they provide but increase in filings and the representation they may have to make before the authorities to get clarifications on various changes in the rules. In effect, cost of doing business has risen in the economy.

As suggested earlier, there may be efficiency gains due to reduced requirements of warehousing and transportation. Warehouses do not have to be located in every state to take advantage of taxes and to avoid Central Sales Tax (which now does not exist). This will lead to scale economies. But the e-way bill will lead to problems and also enhance the level of corruption since physical checking would be required. Some examples of the difficulties faced by businesses are given in Chapter 6 and in forthcoming sections.

In economics, efficiency gain is also understood in another way—as minimization of distortion due to taxes, in the market. This is discussed below. Given extensive taxation at each stage, distortions are likely to increase rather than decrease.

GST and Its Differential Impact

India is a highly differentiated country. Any policy usually impacts the various segments of the economy differently. So, ideally, the government has to devise different policies for each of the segments of the economy. In the case of GST, as discussed in Chapter 6, to take care of the poor and the unorganized sectors of the economy, GST provides for concessions to these sectors. However, as also argued there, there are basic problems with GST design and these cannot be taken care of by providing some relief. Given its complexity, it was pointed that the small and cottage sectors would not be able to cope with its consequences even if they are left out of its ambit.[9]

The smaller units kept out of the ambit of GST fall into two categories. The first covers those with a turnover of less than Rs 20 lakh which do not have to register or pay GST. The other category is the one with a turnover of between Rs 20 lakh and Rs 1.5 crore. The limit to begin with was Rs 75 lakh which was raised to Rs 1 crore and then to Rs 1.5 crore. The latter category is referred to as the 'Composition Scheme'. These units have to register under GST and pay a 1 per cent rate of tax on their turnover (restaurants have to pay 5 per cent). This rate was higher but was brought down after protests from various bodies.

---

[9]   See Kumar (2015) and arguments in Chapter 4

There are several reason for why the small and cottage sectors are suffering in spite of being left out or given concessional rates. First, if policy provides benefit to the large scale sector and does nothing for the small and cottage sectors, the former will out-compete the latter. The existing equilibrium between the two sectors would get disturbed. The idea of 'one nation one tax' would be beneficial for the large scale sector since it operates all over the country. A car company may buy some components in Chennai, steel from West Bengal and sell its product in Assam or Gujarat. So, this company would benefit from the prevalence of common rates all over the country. But that would not impact a small business which produces and sells locally; the supply of raw material and the final sale are all local. Their situation would remain as it was in the pre-GST regime, so no benefit accrues to them.

Second, as mentioned above, large companies would benefit from warehousing consolidation. This does not benefit the small sector which directly supplies from the factory without stocking at different points. Thus, the large scale may become more efficient while the efficiency of the small sector remains unchanged.

Third, GST requires computerization. Most micro units and many small units do not have computerized accounts. In contrast, the large and medium units have computerized systems. So, while the former would have to bear increased costs there would be no difference for the larger units. Thus, the smaller units would become less competitive vis-à-vis the large and medium scale producers.

Fourth, the small units that are not registered under GST will neither get input credit (ITC) nor be able to provide ITC to those who purchase from them. This would have two effects. The first part is considered here and the second one in the next point. The cost of inputs for these small units would rise in comparison to those who are able to avail of ITC. Thus, their price would rise unless they cut their profits. Either way they would suffer. If the price is relatively higher compared to the competitors who are able to avail of ITC, they would lose sales. If they cut profits to lower prices and stay competitive, they will be unable to survive. They already operate on thin margins and live in poverty. This would be aggravated and they would close down.

Fifth, since these units would not be able to offer ITC to those who purchase from them, the cost to the buyer would rise. If the larger units buy from the smaller units and do not get ITC their input costs would rise and they would shift their purchase to the larger units who can provide them ITC. There is an even bigger disadvantage of buying from the smaller units.

Sixth, the bigger unit buying from the smaller unit would have to pay the tax that the smaller unit ought to have paid but was not required to pay. This is called the 'Reverse Charge'. Of course, when the purchasing unit makes its sales, it would be able to get ITC for the reverse charge paid. But that would be later. So, the working capital requirement would increase and costs would rise.

Units under the Composition Scheme suffer from all the above problems that the unregistered units face. In addition, they pay a small tax on which no ITC is available to the purchaser. So, the cost to the latter rises further. Again, there will be reverse charge so that the working capital requirement for the purchaser would rise.

Finally, those registered under the Composition Scheme cannot make inter-state sales. In effect, their market gets limited. This would especially impact those units which operate close to state borders.

It is quite likely that many units that do not have to pay GST would nonetheless register under GST so that they can give ITC. That is the reason, the number of registrations has been high with many units paying no taxes.[10] While a high number of registrations was seen as a success of GST, the finance minister complained that many of those who had registered were not paying any tax.[11]

It was pointed out in an article[12] that if the small and the cottage sectors were to take a hit, employment would be hit, and that would impact demand in the economy and lower the growth of the

---

[10] See Table 5.1 and Annexure 5.1.
[11] IANS (2017c)
[12] Kumar (2015)

economy. The rise in the organized sector's output would be at the expense of the unorganised sectors where output would decline.

Thus, GST is creating two separate circles of growth—one expanding at the expense of the other. This is what happened earlier during demonetization and due to the push for digitization.[13]

Its implication is that the net rate of growth is much less than what the official data suggests since the data for the unorganized sector comes with a delay. Similarly, the investment in the economy is less than what the official figures suggest because it is declining in the unorganized sectors of the economy. All this will lead to growing poverty and rising inequalities (more on this in Chapter 9).

Impact of GST on Efficiency

In economics, the term 'efficiency' is used to denote not only efficiency in production but also in the functioning of the markets. The former connotes production with minimum of resources. The latter refers to the markets achieving the best possible outcome with given resource distribution among the population. So, efficiency is achieved when no one can be made better off without making someone else worse off (called Pareto Optimality)—a rather technical idea based on many assumptions about the market.[14]

Under ideal conditions, the free market, without intervention of the government, would lead the economy to this optimal point. However, the ideal situation hardly ever prevails and the markets fail to achieve the optimum point. In this theory, when the markets cannot achieve the optimum, the government should intervene in the economy to take it there.

The government is supposed to be able to achieve what the market could not achieve. Again this is under ideal conditions and is called the 'First Best'. Here the producers and the consumers face

---

[13] Kumar (2017d)
[14] See Tresch (1981)

the same price for any product or service. They use it to get to the best position they can get to and that gives the optimum for the economy as a whole—referred to as 'efficiency'. When these ideal conditions do not prevail as is normal for any economy, then there are said to be 'distortions' and the economy can only get to what is called the 'Second Best'.

All taxes are distortionary. They do not allow the economic agents to face the same price for maximizing their gain. Thus, an income tax means that the individual gets a lower amount of income after tax than what the employer paid him. So, an employee uses a different price for maximizing her welfare than is used by the employer to maximize his profit. Similarly, a sales tax implies that the price paid by the consumer is not the price received by the shop keeper selling the product. Again the optimization by the consumer and the seller are based on different prices. It is said that a tax drives a wedge between the two prices so that the economy cannot achieve the first best optimum position. There is said to be a 'loss of welfare' for society.

So, in the second best there will always be a loss of welfare of society. What can policy do? It can try to minimize the welfare loss due to distortion. This minimization is referred to as achieving 'efficiency' and is with reference to the markets.

This idea is unfortunately also mixed up with the idea that there would be greater efficiency if there is less of paper work and dealing with multiple agencies. But as already argued there may be less paperwork but more of accounting and difficulties. Be that as it may, less paperwork leading to greater efficiency sounds plausible to the lay person who does not understand what is meant by the market efficiency and minimization of distortion in the market. But what the economists mean by GST being less distortionary is the latter and not the former.

Ideally, policy makers should use non-distorting taxes. Income tax is possibly less distorting than the indirect taxes. So, it should be used in preference to the indirect taxes. Do non-distortionary taxes exist? Theoretically, a 'lump sum' tax is supposed to be one such tax but these are not practical.[15] Thus, with government levying taxes for achieving its aims like good governance, faster development or investment, there will be distortions and loss of welfare.

It has been argued that GST is less distortionary than the earlier system of multiple indirect taxes (excise, sales, service taxes, etc.). One possible argument to support this hypothesis can be that each tax is distortionary so if there is a multiplicity of them then the distortion would be more compared to the situation when there is only one tax, GST.

Another argument can be that VAT is less distortionary than the other forms of tax because it eliminates cascading effect. So, the effective tax rate comes down. However, due to fixing a revenue neutral rate (RNR), the amount of tax collected remains the same so that the effective tax rate remains unchanged for the economy as a whole. Hence the distortionary effect remains unchanged. In a sense, the amount of distortionary effect may be measured by how much the price rises above the cost of production. This remains unchanged with RNR.

It may also be argued that the elimination of cascading effect and having one common tax rate reduce distortionary effects. But given that India does not have a full blown GST since there are multiple tax rates and exemptions and cascading effect is not fully eliminated, distortionary effects persist.

More importantly all stages of production and distribution are sought to be covered under GST, so at each stage of this chain, a distortion is created. Thus, cumulatively, there is far more distortion than was the case with the earlier system of indirect taxation when cross linkages did not exist across taxes.

In brief, even though GST may reduce distortions in the markets in three different ways, it does not seem reasonable to assume that distortions will be less. This is because the entire chain of production and distribution is sought to be covered under GST so taxation increases

---

[15] Tresch (1981)

rather than decreasing. Hence it is only an assumption that there is greater 'efficiency' due to GST.

Is GST a Final Stage Tax Collected by Consuming States Only?

One of the arguments for GST is that it is a final stage tax. Even though it is collected at each stage of production and distribution, it finally accrues to the state where the last stage sale takes place, due to the input tax credit (ITC). How true is that?

GST is supposed to be collected as VAT. If it was pure VAT, it would be collected at each stage of production and distribution by the Centre and the various states (in the chain). The tax collected at the intermediate stage is not passed on to the final stage. It is collected at each stage and only the amount of input credit for the previous stage is subtracted from the next stage. So, the final seller, the retailer only pays the VAT due from her. Of course, the customer pays the entire tax in the chain. But it is not that the entire tax is collected at the final stage from the retailer.

Take an example, if iron ore is produced in Orissa, the state collects the VAT on iron ore. The iron ore is processed in West Bengal to make pig iron so VAT on that is collected there. It may be sent to Jharkhand to produce steel and VAT on that is collected there. In between there is sales and transportation and those taxes are also collected in the different states. In brief, VAT by itself is not a final stage tax. The total tax collected at each stage of collection is reflected in the final price paid by the consumer but it does not mean that it is collected at the end.

The GST introduced in India is an ad valorem tax with input credit (ITC). As mentioned in Chapter 3, the ITC is passed on from the intermediate stages of collection to the final stage of collection of GST. If all the transactions take place in one state it is obvious. But when they take place in different states, then it is not immediately obvious. However, given the scheme of IGST as a part of GST, the exporting state passes on the ITC to the importing state so that the

GST entirely accrues to the state where the final sale occurs. It is collected at different points but the consuming state gets the entire amount.

If the chain of production and distribution is broken, ITC would not be applicable and the tax would not be passed on to the final stage. With exemptions in the chain, the entire tax does not accrue to the consuming state.

Indeed as shown in Chapter 6, the Indian GST has many exemptions so that the entire chain is not covered by GST and it is broken at various places. If a large scale unit supplies to a small scale producer who falls under the Composition Scheme, then the ITC is not available as pointed out above. The chain breaks at that point and the tax does not accrue at the final stage. Further, if the Composition Scheme producer supplies something to those under the GST then also the ITC is not available and the chain starts from that point even when there is a reverse charge.

Similarly, if the chain runs through exempt items, it is broken. The tax paid on the previous stages is not passed on to the final stage. For example, if pesticide is used on crops to produce food, then too the tax on pesticide is not passed on to the final stage since there is no tax on food items. It is said by the government that 50 per cent of the items are exempt because they are essential goods. These items are produced by the use of a large number of intermediates and basic goods. In turn, these essentials are used to produce other goods. For instance, wheat is exempt and is used to produce flour and bread which may be used in restaurants and so on which are not exempt from GST.

In brief, the Indian GST based on ad valorem tax with ITC and IGST would have been a final stage tax but the various exemptions break the chain and prevent that from being the case.

Link of GST with Fiscal Federalism

India is a union of states which present a vast diversity in economic, social and political terms. In fact, there is no other country in the world with the kind of diversity that exists in India.[16] After independence from the British, India came together as a Union. Recognizing the vast diversity, it was decided to give considerable autonomy to the states. It was felt that each state should be allowed to choose its own path of development based on its social conditions and practices. To exercise autonomy, it was decided that the states should have their own tax resources. For instance, issues relating to education and health vary across states, so they need to be tackled differently by each state and they need resources. Hence these were designated largely as state subjects.

However, for reasons of efficiency of collection of taxes, the power to collect some of the major taxes was given to the Centre. So, income tax, corporation tax, customs duty and excise duty were to be collected by the Centre. The only major tax left to the states was sales tax.

A Finance Commission was provided for in the Constitution whose task was to work out the formula for sharing of resources between the Centre and the states. It was mandated that it would give an award every five years as to how the resources would go from the Centre to the states. It was also to decide on the formula for allocation of resources among the states.

So, the Centre was to keep a share of the resources it collected for carrying out the tasks that had to be centrally performed like defence, foreign affairs and currency. Some of the tasks were to be jointly carried out by the Centre and the states, like, education and health. The remaining tasks were to be carried out exclusively by the states. The states were to raise their own resources and these were to be supplemented by statutory transfers to them from the Centre.

Under GST the states have had to give up their power to raise their resources in their own way using indirect taxes. The GST Council is to decide on their behalf. Prior to GST, the states could set their own tax rates based on their specific requirements and also choose the resource base to tax. This power is also now with the GST

---

[16] Kumar (2013)

Council. It was said that there is need to harmonize GST rates so as to avoid competition among states (See Chapter 1). In other words, the autonomy of the states is being truncated and federalism is being undermined.

What is Fiscal Federalism?

Most large nations have different levels of government. In India there is the Centre, the state and the local body. As mentioned above, the constitution provides for overlapping jurisdictions. So, some tasks are performed by all three levels of government. As mentioned earlier, education is one such area in which all three levels of government are involved. The same is true for employment generation.

In some cases, like, supply of water or sanitation, only the local body is involved. The Centre has the exclusive task of providing defence or taking care of foreign policy and so on. The question arises as to what is the most efficient way of providing public services to society? Further, which level of government is most suited to provide which services and how should these be financed? Fiscal federalism deals with these issues.

In a modern day state, citizens are under multiple jurisdictions. In a democracy, theoretically, the citizens collectively decide on the role the government should play. The closer the government is to them the more they are able to influence it and the better the provision of services. That is why, 'decentralized' governance is considered the best. However, not everything can be done at the local level. A university or a large museum or a zoo in every village is not feasible. These have to be provided by the higher tier of government for a group of villages collectively. A city may be able to have these institutions but possibly not every city; only in some large cities.

This explains why federalism also involves market failure in the case of certain services. For instance, every village has a road but if it does not link up with the roads of the neighbouring cities or villages then no one would be able to access the village or get out of it. So, left to themselves villages would go for what is the best orientation of the road for their citizens but that may not be what the surrounding villages may agree to. Similarly for a river flowing by its boundary the best way to prevent floods may be by building dykes but what may suit one village may not suit others. In all these cases the market fails and a higher level authority needs to step in and create a joint facility which is the best for all the villages.

Thus, a state with jurisdiction over the villages and the city may need to coordinate the orientation of a road running across various villages or a dyke on a river. This results in creation of state highways in contrast to local roads in a village or a city. Similarly, coordination across states may be needed to construct national highways created by the Central government.

River water disputes and pollution across state boundaries are cases where the Centre needs to step in to resolve the differences across states. The problem also spills across international borders. Say, in the case of rivers between Nepal and India or Pakistan and India. Now there is the emergence of 'global public goods' which affect all nations, like, climate change, ozone hole, use of CFC, plastic pollution in the oceans, over fishing, extinction of some species and global financial transactions. These issues are crying out for a supranational authority to tackle them. Various international bodies have tried to tackle these problems, like, the UN and G20.

GST Denting Fiscal Federalism

As mentioned in Chapter 4, fiscal autonomy of the states has been dented by GST. It is structured around the idea that there should be one common tax rate across all states—'one nation one tax'. So, under GST, car or wood have the same tax rate in all the states. It is the same in Tamil Nadu as in Jammu and Kashmir or in Gujarat or in Arunachal Pradesh. But Gujarat and Tamil Nadu which have large volume of sales of cars may want to keep the tax on them low but Arunachal Pradesh may want to tax cars at a much higher rate. Similarly, Jammu and Kashmir and Arunachal Pradesh may want to tax wood at a much higher rate than other states since for them it is an important source of revenue.

Most states and some political parties were earlier worried about the implementation of GST especially because they understood that their fiscal powers would get truncated. The BJP, was the biggest objector till it came to power at the Centre in 2014. Mr Modi as the CM of Gujarat was the most vocal opponent. The states were also worried that they would lose revenue under GST which would lead to a worsening of their fiscal situation. The UPA II could not implement GST because of the political opposition.[17]

That a compromise has been worked out to implement GST does not negate the fact that fiscal federalism has been dented. For the states to give up their power to levy tax and fix tax rates, a constitutional amendment was required and this came as the 101st Constitution Amendment. Further, to give voice to the concerns of the states, the GST Council was set up. The finance ministers of Opposition ruled states were appointed as the chair of the Empowered Committee which was set up to work out the design of GST and also bring about a compromise among the states and with the Centre.

Among the states, there are Special Category states. These are mostly the border states which have special problems. That is why they are given special grants and higher devolution from the Centre. Under GST also they have been given special dispensation. Except J&K, exemption from registration for GST in special category states is fixed at Rs 10 lakh while for other states it is Rs 20 lakh. This is a bit strange given that they are usually poorer and have less developed infrastructure, they should have had a higher exemption limit so as to exclude more businesses from the purview of the difficult GST. Also, under GST, since it is a destination based tax, the poorer states with a lower proportion of manufacturing and services, are likely to get a higher share of GST. Thus, a higher level of exemption for businesses would not lead to lower collection of GST for them.

---

[17] See Annexure 5.1

There are other issues involved in GST which impact federalism. One of them is the states' fear of revenue loss for which the Centre has agreed to compensate them. The other was the composition of the GST Council. It has been set such that neither the Centre nor the states can unilaterally take a decision which goes against the interest of the states or the Centre. All these have already been discussed in Chapter 6.

Federalism also involves the third tier of governance in the country—the local bodies. They are the most direct interface of government with the public and according to theory they are most able to take care of the needs of the population. Thus, under theory of decentralization, they must be given greater autonomy by providing them with robust sources of revenue.[18] GST does not provide for their revenue while removing some of the taxes they used for collecting revenue, like Octroi and entry tax. This undermines federalism.

Curtailing federalism will not have any great impact immediately but its repercussions will slowly become evident as it impacts the long term health of society and the economy. It will result in growing regional disparities and rise in income inequalities in the economy. It would also impact the delivery of public services and governance in society (more on this in the next chapter). In this sense, implementing GST is likely to prove to be a short sighted policy and GST as 'One size fits all' is not good for the nation.

Efficiency Due to Computerization of All Transactions

One of the arguments for why GST will be efficient has to do with computerization and the setting up of the GSTN. This is a crucial component of GST since it is so complex that it cannot work without computerization (See Chapter 5). All accounts of all businesses need to be computerized and put on one common platform, the GSTN.

However, computerization could have been introduced in the earlier system of taxes also. This would have allowed the cross

---

[18] Panta (2014)

checking of the invoices of businesses. Under and over invoicing indulged by businesses (See Chapter 7) could have been checked which was not possible in the pre-GST regime where such computerization did not exist. Since that system of taxes was less complicated, a simpler computerized system would have worked.

In the present GST system complexity is not only due to the linking of all stages of production and distribution with billions of invoices being filed every month but due to the multiplicity of rates, classification problems and various exemptions granted.

Apart from the difficulties mentioned above, there is much confusion about various supplies to be taxed. Like, which education services will be taxed and which will not be? Which legal services will fall under the GST net and which will be outside it? What happens if goods are transported via bullock cart? Would an e-way bill have to be generated if transportation is by an auto rickshaw and if so what would be the description of the vehicle? The point is that even computerization would not be able to handle such confusions and difficulties.

In brief, the benefits of GST need to be separated from the benefits of computerization. One needs to compare the efficiency of GST with the earlier simpler system if computerization on the present scale had been introduced. It is possible that the latter may have turned out to be even more efficient.

Conclusion

This chapter evaluates the various claims made in support of GST. Like, it would lower prices, lead to ease of doing business, reduce distortions and increase efficiency. None of these are found to be quite correct. In fact, given the complexity of GST and the attempt to bring every transaction in the economy under its ambit, it is more distortionary and does not promote 'ease of doing business', especially for the unorganized sectors. While the organized sector is floundering this may be temporary but the unorganized sector is unambiguously adversely impacted.

Since business climate is adversely impacted, it has a negative impact on investment in the economy which depresses the rate of growth. It is argued that most of the advantages would accrue to the organized sector which would expand at the expense of the unorganized sector and this would lead to a fall in the growth rate of the economy and to greater inequity.

Poorer states are likely to lose due to GST even though it is supposed to be a destination tax rather than a tax at source. Since they have a larger per cent of the unorganized sector and that is the sector that would be most adversely affected, they would also be negatively impacted. Far more than the gain in GST collections will be lost due to decline in direct tax collections. It is argued that GST would dent fiscal federalism and that will also have a negative impact on the poorer states. The impact on federalism is altering the basic structure of the Indian Constitution which had provided the states greater autonomy. The adverse impact on the local bodies has not been taken into account in official discussions.

Finally, it is pointed out that much of the claimed advantage is due to computerization and not due to GST. An alternative system which would be much simpler can also deliver similar efficiency with computerization and this is discussed in the concluding chapter.

Indian GST is a Half-Way House

To get GST accepted by the states, a compromise was worked out which left out certain items like alcohol and petroleum products from the GST net. These commodities collect a large amount of tax for both the Centre and the states.[19] The states felt that if they lose revenue due to the implementation of GST, they could get more from alcohol and petroleum products. The Centre and the states have been collecting large amount of revenue by raising taxes on petroleum products in the last four years as global prices of crude oil fell.

---

[19] See Table 5.1

The advantage of lower prices was not passed on to the consumers but instead absorbed as excise duties and sales taxes.

These and other exemptions have made GST very complex and a half-way house. These are design problems and not implementation problems. That is why, GST in principle and even more so, as it is implemented, is not suited to India given its complex structure of production and distribution and given the complexity of modern day businesses with a vast network of inter connections. While the earlier many indirect taxes are replaced by one tax, since many more stages are taxed, distortion of the markets is increased and not decreased so that inefficiency is increased rather than decreased. That is why there are more adverse effects than beneficial ones. If cascading effect is not eliminated, market efficiency is not achieved.

All this makes the GST a half-way house. The question is then, why go in for it? Finally, if GST is all about a final stage tax, then why tax all the intermediate stages and complicate the tax? Why not tax only the final stage?

CHAPTER 9

SOCIAL AND POLITICAL
IMPLICATIONS OF GST

GST is supposed to be a tax on the entire chain of production and distribution in the Indian economy with some exemptions. The exemptions are a result of the specificity of the Indian situation—it is a very complex nation with vast disparities, widely varying social structures and use of different levels of technology. GST is a tax and taxes not only have economic consequences but also have crucial social and political implications. They impact prices, production, equity in society, social development, regional development, choice of technology, sectoral development, rural urban divide, infrastructure development and so on.

The social and political importance of taxes becomes apparent when the governments present their budgets. There is a high degree of public interest in knowing how they will be impacted. In the recent decades, the media projects more of the reaction of businessmen and the stock markets than the public because of the market orientation of the economic policies but that does not mean that the common person is less affected. Most of the budgets are also incremental in nature and seldom is there a big shift in policies so that the impact on the public is over time and not felt immediately. But, public memory is short and it forgets what was in the previous budgets so it is often unable to link the deeper impact on their life with budget policies.

GST was in the works for at least twelve years before it was implemented and much debate took place over it during this period.[1]

---

[1] See Annexure 5.1

Yet, it had a huge impact on businesses when it was introduced. The economy experienced a shock which affected every section of society. Post-implementation there was a lot of confusion about the tax and the government had to repeatedly announce changes which led to further confusion (Table 5.1). Many believed that the government had not planned properly for the implementation because it was too busy coping with the shock of demonetization,[2] announced nine months earlier.

The government, economy and society were too busy coping with the shock of demonetization to be able to plan fully for the start of GST on 1 July 2017. The rates had not been decided till almost the last minute. So, pricing was not easy for producers. The rules framed for GST were not thought through so had to be changed many times. The difficulties in procedures had not been anticipated and these also had to be changed later. Two shocks in quick succession is hard for any economy to cope with but India had to go through with it. These have had social and political consequences.

The Political Aspects of Introducing GST in India

There is a deep long term social and political impact of GST on Indian society. It was supposed to unify the nation into one market—it was presented as 'one nation one tax'. It was called a 'Good and Simple Tax'. These were very powerful political slogans which the opposition was not in a position to take on and it agreed to the implementation of GST. Thus, the government could claim unanimity for the implementation of GST. In fact, the GST Council consisting of the representatives of all the states passed all the measures under GST unanimously and this was projected as 'cooperative federalism'. Further, since major political parties ruled in different states, it could also be projected as an indication of political unanimity.

The idea of GST was being pursued since the time of NDA I (and even earlier) and was taken up in the budget of 2005 by the UPA

---

[2]   See Kumar (2017d)

I.[3] So, the Congress party was not in a position to mount a major challenge to GST. In fact, its confusion showed when it claimed that it was the initiator of GST and it tried to claim credit for GST. The Congress party and other opposition parties had not thought through the implications of GST so they could not offer any cogent opposition. The BJP which opposed GST during the UPA rule, changed its position after coming to power as NDA II and pushed the implementation of GST, forgetting its earlier objections. Thus, none of the political parties had thought through the problems that GST would pose and they were in no position to oppose it or offer constructive suggestions for an alternative.

In the first chapter, it was shown that different taxes have different impact on each of the micro and macroeconomic variables. It was argued that indirect taxes are stagflationary while direct taxes are the opposite[4] and hence more desirable. Further, it was mentioned in the previous chapter that indirect taxes are more distortionary than the direct taxes. Thus, it would have been more desirable for the nation to collect more of direct taxes than indirect taxes.

In 2005, the UPA I government had also talked of the need to introduce the direct tax code (DTC) to reform direct taxes. However, little headway has been made in that direction. The emphasis has been on GST and collecting more of indirect taxes—indicating a political bias.

It was also shown that indirect taxes tend to be regressive while the direct taxes can be progressive. Thus going for more collection of indirect taxes increases the regressive component of India's tax system. It also does not put greater pressure to tackle the black economy and collect more of direct taxes. Again this benefits the elite sections of society. They can continue to earn large sums of incomes through the black economy on which they do not have to pay taxes.

---

[3] See Annexure 5.1
[4] Kalecki (1971)

As discussed earlier, the black economy is run by the triad consisting of the ruling elite in the country. This elite does not curb the black income generation process since it derives enormous benefit from it. It only pays lip service to eliminating the black economy. As argued, since the black economy is now 62 per cent of the GDP, if it could be brought into the tax net, the government could have collected at the present rates of taxes, about 40 per cent of it or about 25 per cent of GDP extra.[5] So, instead of collecting about 17 per cent of GDP as taxes as at present, it could have collected about 42 per cent of GDP as taxes. With so much of tax collection, indirect taxes could have been cut back[6] with all the associated positive impact on the economy.

In brief, it is a political choice, whether to curtail the black economy and reduce indirect tax collection or to continue as it is with more indirect taxes and its negative consequences.

The triad running the black economy will only act against the black economy if it is politically forced to do so. The UPA II was forced by movements to go for the Lok Pal Bill pending since the 1960s. The NDA government came to power on the promise of curbing the black economy quickly but it has not been able to deliver on that so far.[7] As argued, mere technical steps like GST will not help unless there are social and political movements which change the consciousness of people.

Various political parties at different times have favoured or opposed GST depending on whether they are in power or in the opposition. Partly, the political parties have favoured GST, because they do not wish to go for the difficult route of tackling the black economy. The ruling dispensation has presented it as the biggest reform since independence and a step to tackle the black economy to get political mileage out of it. But, none of them realized that GST is 'neither good nor simple' and would create huge problems. Even

---

[5] Kumar (2017a)

[6] As suggested in Kumar (1994)

[7] Kumar (2017a)

if 160 countries have implemented it, that cannot be a reason for introducing it in India with its own social and economic specificities.

Why GST?

If GST as an indirect tax is not so desirable and a better alternative is available in the form of direct taxes and if it is as difficult to cope with as depicted in the earlier chapters, then why should the entire political spectrum support it? Why has every state government fallen in line to implement GST even though many of the states were ruled by opposition parties?

One reason why state governments have fallen in line (J&K is the only state which resisted till the last) is that one cannot be an exception if all others accept GST. The state that does not implement GST when every other state implements it would lose out in terms of production and distribution. Businesses in the non-implementing state would neither get input credit on their production nor would they be able to provide input credit on their sales outside the state. So, its products would become more expensive everywhere and its sales would decline.

Current Globalization as Marketization

However, there is a bigger reason for the consensus among the mainstream political parties. The nature of current globalization has altered the basic thinking in society.[8] People are increasingly atomized and that has led to a decline in the concern for collectivity. Individuals have become more self-centred so that the perception has spread that each one is for themselves. The wider and long term perspective of society has given way to a narrower and short term perspective. These tendencies are not new but earlier they were at the margins while now they have become dominant or have become the rule. These ideas are now central to the thinking of large numbers

---

[8]   Kumar (2002a) and Kumar (2000b)

who see nothing wrong in them and do not feel guilty when they act on these ideas.

The nature of the current globalization may be characterized as 'marketization'.[9] It implies the penetration of the market principles into all institutions of society. It is not that markets did not exist earlier—they have existed since there has been exchange of goods— even under barter. Marketization has proceeded apace since the mid-1970s as Reaganism and Thatcherism have taken hold in the world. Williamson called it the 'Washington Consensus'.[10] It implies that all the major institutions of global economic governance (largely located in Washington) have been pursuing this common agenda. These institutions include the IMF, the World Bank, WTO (earlier GATT), ADB and so on.

The World Bank has characterized it as 'market friendly state intervention'—state should intervene to help the market. Where markets did not exist, markets have to be created for 'efficiency'. So, air, water, land, coastal areas and so on should be marketized and privatized. Whatever helps capital to grow is considered desirable. So, tax concessions to the well off, cut in direct taxes and elimination of taxes on wealth are considered desirable.[11] Subsidies to the workers are supposed to distort the markets, so they should be eliminated.

What all this has meant is that capital has been strengthened while labour has been weakened. An important factor aiding this is the mobility of capital. It has become exceedingly agile and trillions of dollars move every day. This is far more than the daily trade or the daily production in the world economy. These are purely financial transactions. Thus, the 'Wall Street has come to dominate over the Main Street'. Policy making has slipped into the hands of financial institutions to the detriment of producers of goods and where a majority of the work force of most nations is employed. This has marginalized the common persons in most countries.

---

[9]   Kumar (2013) discusses this in detail and Kumar (2002b) presents it in brief

[10]   Williamson (1989)

[11]   Kumar (1991)

Global Financial Architecture and Policy Independence

The global financial architecture helps in this rapid movement of capital via tax havens.[12] There is not only a lot of illegal movement of capital but the rich, the powerful and MNCs take advantage of the financial arrangements to legally escape tax in their countries. This is called Base Erosion and Profit Shifting (BEPS). While the legal route is widely used, there is also the illegal part which affects the developing countries the most. The latter is referred to as the flight of capital which ultimately funnels capital to the developed countries. In fact, a large number of the tax havens or the institutions based there belong to the advanced countries. The developing countries have lost more capital than the aid they received from the developed world after the Second World War.

As discussed in the previous chapter, market efficiency refers to the situation in which individuals in society are able to get the best outcome they can, given their resources. If the markets are divided between nations then efficiency has to be achieved in each nation. But it would be even better if all the nations could combine together into one market then the efficiency achieved would be the highest. So, potentially, the global market would lead to ultimate efficiency. Multi-National Companies (MNCs) bring together the various markets through supply chains and sales of their products. These firms today dominate the global markets and are the ones that are most sought after and they get concessions in different nation states and that helps them grow faster. They not only have command over capital they also are able to get favourable policies by making nations compete among themselves to attract them.

Policy has slipped from the hands of national governments to global financial institutions who oversee national policies and characterize them as sound or deficient. Credit rating agencies define what is a sound investment. So, national governments have to keep the global financial institutions and the credit rating agencies happy.

---

[12] Tax Haven Team (2014)

The latter represent the interest of international capital and not that of the people of different nations. So, they adopt the 'one size fits all' policies.

Mobility of capital means it can move from one country to another quickly destabilizing the currency and the markets of countries that do not fall in line. To attract it, the developing world has to offer concessions. If one country offers one concession say, a lower tax rate, then other countries have to follow suit. This is called the 'race to the bottom'.

Even the advanced countries have had to give concessions to capital. Post the collapse of the Soviet bloc, the East European countries needed to attract capital for their development and they cut their tax rates. This triggered a race to the bottom with even the advanced economies like Germany and France having to cut their tax rates. Ireland played this well and in twenty-five years became one of the most prosperous country. It attracted big companies like Apple and Google.

Global Financial Institutions and Their Role

Actually, the change in the form of capitalism from welfare state to a pure capitalist state started with the weakening of the Soviet bloc and the 180 degree change in Chinese policies in the mid-1970s. The Western powers realized that the communist bloc was no more able to present an alternative to the rest of the world. This was visible in the negotiations in GATT and in the stance of the World Bank and the IMF in the 1980s.

In the Uruguay round of negotiations in 1986, the advanced nations pushed for new issues like trade in agriculture, trade in services, TRIPS and TRIMs. This resulted in the creation of WTO in 1995. The developing world which was resisting opening up of their economies was told 'to take it or leave it'. The choice for them was to either be coerced multilaterally under WTO or be coerced bilaterally outside it.[13] The former was preferable so they all joined

---

[13] Kumar (2000a)

WTO. Russia and China also clamoured to join it knowing that as capitalist economies they could not stay outside the global capitalist system and do well.

How does the financial architecture help global capital to get its way? Most economies in the world have had to face some kind of economic crisis since the 1970s. Like the Latin American countries and almost the entire continent of Africa in the early 1980s, the South East Asian economies in 1997, India itself has faced crisis in 1966, 1980 and 1990. Each of the countries facing a crisis goes to the IMF for adjustment to ward off the crisis. The IMF then recommends a package of reform for the country, called the 'conditionalities' of the loan it gives. These are short and medium run policies.

It also requires that the country go to the World Bank for Structural Adjustment Loans (SAL) to set its long term policies right. For these loans the country has to agree to other 'conditionalities' imposed by the World Bank. These are called 'cross-conditionalities'. For instance, to give a SAL for reform of the energy sector in India the cross-conditionality imposed by the World Bank was reform of the RBI and implementation of VAT. Cross-conditionalities need not be in a sector related to the sector for which the loan is sought. So, for the loan for energy sector, India had to agree to change its policies on taxation and finance.

The conditionalities basically push for marketization and aim at limiting the role of the government and promoting the private sector. Under WTO, the main condition has been to open up the economy and allow foreign goods and capital to come into the economy. For instance, one of the conditions has been to give 'national treatment' to foreign capital. This opens the way for MNCs to enter a country. Since they have deep pockets, they are able to dominate the markets and also the Indian companies. So, most Indian private banks, like, ICICI are now foreign owned. Ola is largely foreign owned and so was Flipkart even before its takeover by Walmart. Alibaba, Tencent, Softbank and so on are holders of large part of the equity in Indian firms in the technology sectors.

Foreign capital, to enter a country, requires the opening up of the financial markets, like, the stock markets. This enables portfolio investments (FII) in the stock markets. That then makes the stock markets' health dependent on foreign investments—whether FDI or FII. It also enables foreign capital to control Indian companies. All this makes policymakers sensitive to pressures from foreign capital. Credit rating agencies begin to play a bigger role because they signal to foreign capital where it should go.

Even governments of rich countries mount pressure to open up the economy through their ministers and senior bureaucrats. Like, when Enron was trying to enter India in the early 1990s, the secretaries of various departments in US government came to put pressure on Indian policy makers. Even big wigs like Henry Kissinger came in support. Annual meets like the World Economic Forum (WEF) are also places for lobbying by the powerful global financial interests.

Another way this works is via directly influencing national policy makers. There is a 'revolving door policy'.[14] Policy makers are brought from these global institutions and they push the line of the institutions they come from. Indians are recruited in these global institutions and then sent to India to set the agenda. This process of people coming from the World Bank and IMF has been going on since 1975. Many Indian bureaucrats and academics have aspired to serve in these international agencies to not only earn high salaries and pensions but also to become more influential in policy making.

In the prevailing environment of marketization, what these policy makers with connections to global institutions (like IMF, World Bank and ADB) suggest becomes the acceptable agenda for policy. Often when policy makers are criticized for acting under the influence of foreign institutions, it is argued that the policy suggestions are coming from Indian policy makers themselves. In brief, the global financial interests, in a seemingly natural way, see

---

[14] Bhushan, (2010)

that their interest is taken care of while limiting the role of national policy makers.

The pressure for VAT came from reports written by Indian bureaucrats and academics (Chapters 3 and 5). It is interesting to note that many of the authors had either come from the global institutions or had served there. The generalization to GST was also suggested by Indians. Even though each of the reports saw it as difficult in the Indian context, none of them argued that it be deferred; instead rationalizations were offered for its introduction. None of them argued that there is need to wait to implement GST till the Indian economy matures. None of them suggested a simpler form of GST (as discussed later in the Conclusion).

Principles of Marketization

If the policy makers and bureaucrats were subject to global pressures why did the public not realize what was happening or coming? In 1991, the marketization was presented under the garb of TINA (There Is No Alternative). The collapse of the Soviet Union also made the political parties believe that there was no alternative to capitalism. The public accepted this idea. Thinking in society changed from believing that government is essential in economic affairs to government cannot deliver and that the markets are essential to take care of the social problems. That the black economy led to policy failure and that it was a result of the operation of a triad was not realized by the public (or at least the influential middle class). Consequently, India went for a hundred-and-eighty-degrees shift in the policy paradigm.[15]

The subtle penetration of the market principles in the popular consciousness was important in the change of the mood in the country. Some of the market principles that have become a part of the sub-conscious of the people globally and also in India are a) 'dollar vote', b) 'more is better', c) 'rational individual', d) 'homoeconomicus'

---

[15] Kumar (2013)

and so on. Here only a brief exposition of these principles and their societal impact is presented.[16]

The 'dollar vote' refers to the idea that in the market the number of votes an individual has equals the amount of dollars one has. Those who have more purchasing power in the market are able to influence the market more. It is the anti-thesis of democracy where 'one person has one vote'. A rich person with a million dollars is not equal to the poor person with one dollar in her pocket. He is a million times more influential than the poor person in the market and determines the outcome of the market far more. So, the consumption and production pattern in the economy is determined by the dollar vote. A rich person can buy a luxury car but the poor may not be able to buy food or send her child to the school or get proper medical attention.

The implication is that the marginal in society gets more marginalized. Thus, a US citizen equals thirty Indians. So, the USA with one fourth of the population of India dominates in all institutions of global governance. Similarly, in India, the more prosperous states dominate over the poorer states and within the prosperous states the richer areas dominate over the poorer areas. So, for capital, Maharashtra does not mean Vidarbha where a lot of farmers commit suicides due to distress but the Mumbai–Pune belt or the Mumbai–Vadodara belt. For capital, UP does not mean Kanpur (which has got deindustrialized) or Banda but the area contiguous with Delhi–Ghaziabad and NOIDA. Thus, marginalization follows at the international, national and regional levels. This also reflects in the politics of the country which is dominated by the moneyed. Even the parties ostensibly representing the poor are in the grip of those who control the purse strings.

'More is better' implies that the welfare of the individual improves with more consumption. This is the underlying basis of consumerism—consumption for the sake of consumption. It leads

---

[16] For a more detailed description see Kelly and D'Souza (2010) and Kumar (2013)

to higher levels of pollution and climate change. It also means that sacrifice is no more a virtue. Improving one's welfare is important and not how it is done.

Decline of Collectivity and Rise of Individualism

These ideas are supplemented by the notion that humans are 'rational individuals'. The rationality is that they are working to maximize their gains (welfare). Thus, life is all about profit and loss. Marriage is also an economic institution with little of social, cultural and emotional aspects to it. Everyone is to calculate whether they are gaining or losing. They should stay in the marriage if they are gaining otherwise they should quit. No wonder, divorces are increasing.

This makes people 'homoeconomicus' and individualists. Only economics matter; other aspects of life are not important. If one is only working for one's gains, then how one makes the gains is not important. So, greed has been raised to a new high pedestal. It is not that greed did not exist earlier but it is now welcomed. So, use of illegal means for making gains is not necessarily bad as long as one does not get caught. New means of making illegal gains are being sought. In fact, illegality may maximize the gain of individuals which society with its rules is not allowing.

Society and people matter less and less since individuals increasingly think of themselves as atomized beings working for their personal gain. Collectivity and society matter less. Atomization and working for one's gains leads to the idea that one should not feel guilty about what one is doing. To maximize profit, costs are to be minimized. So, feeling guilty at doing something wrong has to be minimized since that is a cost to the individual. All this makes collective action difficult.

Another important idea is that society is subjective while the market is objective. So, society is in retreat while the markets are advancing and with that the market philosophy is gaining ground in society. Collective action through the state is also to be minimized since that interferes with 'efficiency' of the market.

For the market, there are no 'essential' goods or 'luxury' goods. So, government should not make judgments about taxing the luxury goods more and essentials less. There is also a new international division of labour with polluting goods produced in developing countries and clean technology products in the advanced countries.[17] Most of the pollution-causing recycling work is done in the slums of the cities of the poor countries. Thus, if it damages the health of the poor it is immaterial since this is 'efficiency'. It is a part of the marginalization process.

Because humans are taken to be homoeconomicus, history, politics and sociology do not matter. Man is seen as a part of a big machine—a cog in a wheel. So, unemployment is nothing but the switching off of a machine and employment means switching it on. The social aspects of unemployment do not matter. If the children of the unemployed cannot attend school because their fees cannot be paid, that is immaterial.

Models of economics tend to be divorced from history and politics so that they can be mathematized and that takes them away from the real social dynamics and the uncertainty of the future.[18] They only capture incremental change but not the real social changes which come as shocks (like, in the stock market) or as part of social dynamics.

As economic models become ahistorical they at best represent short term dynamics and this goes in parallel with people becoming short-termists. The result is a narrowing of the perspective of individuals and of society. All solutions are short term. People and rulers are only looking for quick fixes. This author has characterized them as non-solutions[19] since what is thought to be a solution for a given problem results in newer problems. No wonder, society does not have answers to its long term problems like crisis in democracy, climate change, regional conflicts, consumerism, growing illegality,

---

[17] *The Economist* (1992)

[18] Kumar (2013)

[19] See Kumar (2013)

crime and immigration. Looking at these problems in the short run and as individual problems (not collective) only leads to strengthening of authoritarianism and polarization of communities. The real need for change is in collective consciousness via political and social movements but for that there is little patience and it is seen as untenable.

To sum up, national policies are not entirely in the hands of national leadership. Due to a sea change in the consciousness of individuals in society brought about by the marketization process, short termism and individualization have taken root with the result that policies are not necessarily in the long term national interest. Marketization also pushes the marginalization of the marginal so that the interest of the poorer sections are not at the centre of policy making. All this underlies the decision to go for GST even if it is detrimental to India's long term interest and marginalizes the majority. It has been pushed by international capital along with India's big business. It represents the strengthening of capital and weakening of labour in Indian politics. Big is privileged over the small.

Two Circles of Growth

As discussed in Chapters 4 and 8, the unorganized sector will be unambiguously hurt. The organized sector is also finding it difficult to cope with the complexity of GST but could conceivably gain over time. This would widen the gap between these two sectors. Can this be good for the country?

Recognizing the difficulties that GST would pose to the unorganized sectors of the economy, they have been exempted from GST entirely (turnover below Rs 20 lakh) or kept under the Composition Scheme (turnover between Rs 20 lakh and Rs 1.5 crore) with marginal tax. As argued earlier, this apparent favour to the small and cottage sectors is actually the cause of their difficulties in their business transactions. They are in a fix, if they are a part of the GST, they will suffer due to the complexity and the need to computerize and if they are outside it, they suffer in any case—a lose-lose situation.

The large and medium scale sectors will gain due to the scale economies that will be fuelled with regard to inter-state supplies, ease of transportation, warehousing and so on. But they will also gain at the expense of the small and cottage sectors.

The economy is increasingly divided into two disjointed circles of growth—the organized and the unorganized sectors. The former has advantage in terms of technology, capital, marketing, monopolistic and oligopolistic power to set prices and so on. Hence it has been growing at the expense of the unorganized sectors. Recognizing the importance of the unorganized sectors in employment generation and poverty removal, the country has been providing protection to this sector through a variety of means, like, reservation and cheap credit. There has also been the Monopolies and Restrictive Trade Practices Act (MRTP) to prevent the buildup of monopolies in the market. But these have not been able to prevent the rapid advance of the large sector.

With the launch of the New Economic Policies (NEP) in 1991, these concessions to the unorganized sectors were diluted and the growth of the large scale sector accelerated further displacing the small sector. MRTP, FERA, small scale reservation are all gone. This trend of diverging growth is being aggravated by GST.

There are inter linkages between the two sectors but these have been weakening. People from each of the sectors have been buying the product of the other sector thus generating demand for each other. The small has also been providing ancillaries for the large scale sector. But these two components of demand have been weakening over time. For example, the local retail stores are being replaced by organized sector retailers like Big Bazar and by e-commerce. Similarly, local taxi stands and private chauffeurs are being replaced by taxi aggregators, like, Ola and Uber.

The small scale was also being misused by the large scale to take advantage of the tax concessions available to the former. Items were produced by the small scale but labelled and marketed by the large scale. So, textiles were being produced by the power looms for the large scale sector which marketed it under its own brand name. That was also the case with electrical appliances and other items. All this is weakening and GST is going to impact these arrangements adversely.

The opening up of the Indian market and the inflow of Chinese goods on a large scale further damaged the unorganized sector. All kind of Chinese goods earlier manufactured in the small scale sector in India have been flooding the Indian markets. Some examples of these are fans, toys, festival items (Diwali and Holi), lights, torches and so on.

GST and digitization accelerate this ongoing process of marginalization of the unorganized sectors. As pointed out in the previous section, marketization marginalizes the weak in the market—it favours the large over the small businesses. While in economic terms this may seem to be 'efficient' with growth being fuelled by the large scale sector, it leads to growing inequality which has political and social implications.

Since it is the unorganized sector that employs the vast majority of the work force,[20] any setback to this sector leads to growing under employment and crisis in the lives of these people. With the growth of the organized sector, while wage rate may rise, employment available declines since the large and medium sectors are far more automated than the small sectors. Thus, the overall wage received by workers would fall. The purchasing power of those employed in the unorganized sectors and of workers as a whole would decline.

This decline in the fortunes of the majority of workers is reflected in the paradox of increasing stocks of food along with persisting hunger and malnourishment (especially among children and women). The poorer families do not have the purchasing power to buy enough so they go hungry and because they are buying less than they need, food becomes surplus and stocks rise. Usually, as prosperity increases, per capita consumption of food rises but in

---

[20] Rajya Sabha (2014) and GoI (2016a)

India, the opposite has happened since 1991.[21] In China, USA, etc., the per capita income and consumption of food are much higher than in India. It is not that the well-off sections in India are eating any less, so the decline in the overall per capita consumption of food is at the expense of the poor.

The inadequacy of demand for food items leads to low price of agricultural produce and decline in the incomes of the farmers. As argued recently,[22] while the cost of production in agriculture has been rising, prices have fallen at the farm gate so that farmers are complaining that they are suffering a loss. The urban consumer does not benefit from this fall in farm gate prices because of high trade margins.

The rise in under employment and decline in the incomes of farmers has led to protests by big sections of people. Youth is agitating for employment and reservation in jobs. In fact, prosperous communities like Jats, Patels and Marathas are in the forefront of these protests. The situation is desperate for educated youth which is not getting jobs commensurate with their degree and training. For jobs of scavengers, people with MBA degree have been applying. For a few hundred jobs of peons, lakhs of BTech and BCom degree holders applied in 2015.[23]

Farmers have been committing suicide due to indebtedness and also protesting against low prices across the country. They have thrown their produce on the roads or allowed cattle to feed on vegetables rather than harvesting it and bringing it to the market. During demonetization, some farmers even gave away their vegetables free to the consumers.[24]

The unorganized sector works with little capital and once it closes down or suffers a loss, even for a short time, it loses its entire capital and is unable to restart production without capital infusion.

---

[21] Kumar (2004)

[22] Kumar (2017d)

[23] Ali (2015). Also see Singh (2018)

[24] Kumar (2017d)

This is true for agriculture as well as non-agriculture producers. The capital needed by them is often provided not by the formal banking system but by the informal credit markets which charge a high rate of interest. Thus, as production is hit in the unorganized sectors, the cost of reviving it is high and incomes of this sector fall over long periods of time.

Rising Disparities

The gap between the two circles of growth is growing and the inter-linkages between them are weakening. Since the organized sector employs only 7 per cent of the work force and has been shedding jobs due to growing automation, there has been a crisis of employment. Youth is forced to go into the unorganized sector with low wages. The result has been growing disparity and failure of expectations of the youth.

Growing disparity and decline in availability of skilled jobs for youth has social and political implications. Since the poorer states have a larger share of the unorganized sector, over time, they will grow slower than the more prosperous states. As argued in Chapter 8, GST intensifies this trend and that will aggravate the rising inter-state disparities.

The undermining of fiscal federalism which reduces the autonomy of the states to deal with their problems in their own way will also further aggravate disparities. Tensions between the better off states and the poorer states are already rising in the context of the Finance Commission awards and they can only get worse over time as disparities rise. The richer states want to have a higher share of the fiscal pie rather than allow the poorer states to have a larger share of the resources. One of the ideas underlying the Finance Commission transfers has been that the poorer states have to be helped to catch up with the better off states by giving them a larger share of the transfers. Of course, in absolute amount the better off states get more but they want to get even more. They are questioning why they should get a smaller share.

As explained earlier, various states are at vastly different levels of development. Some are industrialized and have a large component of production based on advanced technology. There are others which are more dependent on primary products and small scale production. They may also need to spend more on upgrading their education and health systems. So, their pattern of raising revenue and expenditure requirements are vastly different. That is why they need to follow different paths of development.

For instance, a state in a European country and a state in India at vastly different stages of development will of necessity have different paths of development. One size fits all will not do. That is the reason why the issue of autonomy of Indian states has been crucial and enshrined in the Indian Constitution. This is being undermined by GST. Can this be good for the country?

The famous Kesavananda Bharti judgment in 1973[25] is considered a landmark judgment since it propounded the Basic Structure Doctrine of the Indian Constitution. It was argued that the Parliament cannot undo the basic structure of the constitution. A thirteen judge constitution bench gave this judgment by a narrow majority of seven to six. In the basic structure, federalism is as crucial as secularism, welfare state, rule of law and separation of powers. Does GST fall foul of this judgment, given that federalism has been truncated—even if the states have voluntarily done so?

As argued in the previous chapter, the third tier of government in India is the local bodies. They are crucial for providing some of the basic services needed by the citizens. They need autonomy to pursue their different goals. In Maharashtra, the needs of Mumbai are different from say, Kolhapur. The resource base of Mumbai is vast and private sector initiative much stronger than in Kolhapur. The latter cannot do what the former can accomplish. So, different solutions are required. Policies decided by Maharashtra government may not be able to do justice to either of the two cities.

---

[25] Supreme Court Judgment (1973)

As some of the important sources of revenue of local bodies (like Octroi and entertainment tax) have been absorbed in GST, they needed to be also provided with independent source of revenue. This has not happened. There is no mention of devolution to the local bodies. It is not clear whether the Centre or the states are to pass on a share of the resource.

At times it is argued that local bodies face the problem of elite capture and corruption.[26] But it is not that the higher tiers of government do not face these problems. Strengthening of decentralization through giving autonomy in resource raising and expenditures is an important step in making local bodies accountable. Once this is done the citizens are able to more easily demand accountability from their representatives. This is the best way of strengthening democracy, otherwise it will weaken.

Undermining federalism will not have an impact immediately but its repercussions will slowly become evident as it impacts the long term health of society and the economy. It will result in growing regional disparities and rise in income inequalities. It would also impact the delivery of public services and governance in society.

Political Aspects

GST's political message is based on the idea underlying the slogan 'one nation one tax'. It is as if the nation is being unified finally. It is argued that while politically the nation had become one on 15 August 1947, economically it had not integrated. GST is supposed to create one common market and there would be economic integration. This is an overstatement.

Politically the nation has been one since independence even if there have been separatist movements from time to time in various parts of the country or there have been agitations to create separate states and larger states have been split into smaller ones. It cannot be said that due to these various agitations, the country was not

---

[26] Panta (2015)

one politically. Difficulties do not imply that the country was not integrated politically. Similarly, impediments to movement of goods across the nation at state borders or at points of entry to cities do not imply that India was not one market.

Goods and services were moving across state boundaries and cities all the time. Yes, movement may have slowed down at the borders due to entry tax or Octroi but that did not mean that goods were not going across the nation unhindered. People were buying across states depending on where the tax rate was lower.

Even now, goods move on highways and trucks have to stop at toll plazas to pay a charge. Does traffic not slow down due to the rush at these toll plazas? If electronic tagging can speed it up at the barriers, the same could have been done with entry taxes. If e-way bills have to be checked, will traffic not slow down? Is there an alternative to checking?

Without checking of trucks or other vehicles, misclassification of goods being transported cannot be detected (See Chapter 7) and this is rampant in India. Already there have been reports of corruption in checking of e-way bills and misclassification being caught. Thus, the unification slogan was not only political but a hard-sell.

The basic design flaw in GST and massive problems in implementation have let to discontent in the country and the opposition parties have sensed this and attacked the ruling party and the government repeatedly. One opposition leader has called it 'Gabbar Singh Tax'[27] and not what the PM called it, 'Good and Simple Tax'. However, why has the opposition woken up now when it is too late to remove GST without causing severe disruptions?

The government has argued that all decisions on GST have been taken unanimously in the GST Council. Almost all the main opposition parties are represented in it via their state units which are in power in different states—Congress has been in power in several states, Trinamul Congress in West Bengal, CPM in Kerala, TSR in Telengana, Samajwadi party in UP, JD(U) and RJD in Bihar

---

[27] Langa (2017)

and so on. Why did these parties not raise objections to the various provisions that are proving to be difficult to implement, such as, input credit (ITC), reverse charge mechanism (RCM) and e-way bill?

Thus, the opposition parties cannot escape their complicity in the implementation of a very complicated GST. They did not consider the adverse impact it would have on the unorganized sectors of the economy or the problems that arise due to RCM and ITC. Partly, they did not have an idea of what the fallout of GST would be for the nation as a whole and more specifically for the unorganized sectors.

Marginalization of the Marginal

More importantly, the political unanimity in accepting GST across all parties and across the nation indicates the complete marginalization of the marginal. The difficulties that would befall the marginal sections of society were not even considered and such a policy was rushed through. It only strengthens the hypothesis that the vast majority of Indians are disenfranchised. No matter which party gets to power, the interest of these sections is not taken care of. This has led to growing alienation in society with the attendant problems and GST only adds to this trend.

GST has been projected as formalizing the economy. The informal economy which is often outside the pale of government regulations is seen as undesirable. It is felt that if it gets formalized, it would be good for the economy. Demonetization was also said to lead to greater formalization since those in the informal sectors would get into the formal sectors. Data has been presented based on registrations under Employee Provident Fund Organization (EPFO), showing massive increase in registrations and this is taken as formalization of the workforce.[28] However, this is not new employment but just the unorganized sector employment counted

---

[28] Ghosh and Ghosh (2018)

as organized employment.[29] Independent analysis from CMIE[30] shows that employment generation has hardly increased and most likely decreased.

The argument for formalization is based on a limited view of the problem. If the unorganized sector uses bank accounts more for their transactions or their workers get registered under Employees Provident Fund Organization (EPFO) that does not change the status of these workers as being poor and marginalized.[31]

The argument also has a technocratic bias. It is implicit that technology will solve all social ills because the human element is the problem and it needs to be replaced. As argued in Chapter 7, this view is not correct. The person behind the technology continues to matter. This view only marginalizes the poor and alienates them, thus leading to social and political problems in managing society.

The unorganized sector workers still would not have collective bargaining power to protect their interest. They would still have very low wages. Businesses they work for would still not recognize them since they would remain contract labour employed by the contractors who would keep their status temporary. They would still be the reserve army of labour weakening labour's bargaining power. The issue is not formalization but the well-being and the empowerment of the workers as a whole and more specifically of those in the unorganized sectors.

The meaning of marginalization of the marginal is that they have little say in the country. These sections of the population have little voice in the political process and, therefore, they are not able to influence policies. As argued above, they are also the ones who have little purchasing power in the market and therefore, are not able to affect the outcome of the markets. They are at the receiving end of the processes in the market. It should be clear that one is

[29] Kumar (2018a)

[30] Vyas (2018)

[31] Kumar (2018a)

not referring to individuals but groups of people. Individuals by themselves have little say in either policy or the market, even if they are well-off.

Marginals in India would include a vast majority of farmers, traders, youth, cottage and home based businesses, women, Dalits and tribals. The representatives they choose do not represent their interests but those of the vested interests who give them money to fight elections and who help them climb the ladder of success.[32] That is why even the representatives of the poor support policies that benefit the elite groups at their expense.

Anti-Rural Bias in Policy

The farmers, even the well-off among them, are unable to determine the price of their produce in the market. But businesses are able to set the price they charge in the market. So, what would be the price of a car or a tube of toothpaste is set by businesses. However, the price of wheat or cabbage is not set by the farmers. They have to accept the price prevailing in the market. The government tries to set a price for some agricultural commodities through the procurement price or the Minimum Support Price (MSP) determined by the Commission for Agricultural Costs and Prices (CACP). But often the farmer does not get this price since there is no mechanism to enforce it. Further, even the price set by the CACP is based on many assumptions. One of the key assumptions is that the farmer should be afforded a bare minimum existence by assuming a lower cost of cultivation than the one given by the farmers.

There is also an anti-rural bias in policy. Resources are poured into urban development but not into rural uplift. This has led to a growing divide in the country between rural and urban life. So, rural infrastructure is weak compared to urban infrastructure. This has many deleterious effects. It leads to a growing disparity between rural and urban areas. It results in lower investment in rural areas

---

[32] Kumar (1999b)

and therefore, to lack of jobs there and because of that, to migration to urban areas. Since urban infrastructure is far more expensive than the rural infrastructure, far more resources are needed in the urban areas than in the rural areas. This results in pre-emption of resources by the urban areas and perpetuation of the disparity between rural and urban areas.[33]

Due to inadequate job creation in rural areas, there is massive under employment there and that perpetuates poverty. Workers are stuck in agriculture at very low productivity and therefore at low incomes. Inadequate investment also means poor standards of health and education and inadequate telecommunication, transportation and so on. If power is available in cities for twenty hours a day, in rural areas it is often available for four hours a day. The government instals electricity poles in villages and calls it electrification. Whether electricity reaches homes or not, especially of the poor, is another matter. Drinking water is often polluted or of poor quality resulting in health issues.

Trickle Down Model of Development

This philosophy of development is based on trickle down and top down approach. There is an urban bias in this. Since 70 per cent of the population is rural and the agricultural sector employs 45 per cent of the work force, these people are marginalized in our policies. The rural areas (compared to the urban areas) have fewer bank branches, farmers get proportionately much less loan and so on. Thus, development slows down in rural areas. Not only this, the savings from rural areas are channelled to the urban areas via banking.[34] So, not only is there greater poverty in rural areas, poverty is perpetuated in these areas because of a lack of investment and lack of infrastructure.

---

[33] See Kumar (2013)

[34] The Credit Deposit ratio of banks is much higher for Delhi and Mumbai than for the poorer states which have a much larger rural population.

The poor, the farmers, workers, Dalits and tribals are concentrated in rural areas, which are neglected. They are the marginalized and deprived in society. It is not that urban areas do not have the marginalized but their poverty is different and they benefit from the better urban infrastructure. Above all, the marginals migrate to urban areas for jobs since there are few in rural areas. The urban infrastructure is also differentiated with the better-off sections having a vastly better deal than the poor who are forced to live in slums or slum like conditions. So, the urban poor are also marginalized but less so than the rural poor. In effect, the trickle down approach adopted in India has led to the cornering of resource by the ruling elite at the expense of the marginalized sections, the urban poor and the rural areas.

A bulk of the population is marginalized in the economy and has limited purchasing power, so that in spite of their huge numbers, they constitute a small market. This has the twin effect of creating two circles of growth and persistence of poverty among the vast majority. The small and local businesses producing for the poor also have to produce inferior and cheap goods at low margins so that they also have a poor living standard. This marginalized section of population constitutes one circle of growth with low incomes, poverty and low growth. The other circle is that of the elite of society who corner the resources and have a prosperous life style.

Given the small size of employment in the organized sectors (7 per cent of the work force),[35] those in the unorganized sectors are unable to break out and join the former. Models of development[36] have been based on the idea of modernization and trickle down because of the hegemonization of the discourse. But as argued by this author,[37] these are models of European development in the nineteenth century and do not apply to the post-independence Indian situation. There is little additional employment generation

---

[35] Rajya Sabha (2014) and GoI (2016a)

[36] (Lewis, 1954)

[37] Kumar (2013)

in the modern sectors of the economy, given that they are based on automation. So, this sector cannot absorb labour from the backward sectors. Emphasis on developing the modern sector by concentrating resources there has resulted in the perpetuation of marginalization.

Entrenched Poverty

It is argued that with modernization and trickle down, poverty has reduced. It is claimed that as growth has picked up hundreds of millions have been lifted out of poverty in the last seventy years. Unfortunately, two factors are ignored. First, poverty usually refers to 'extreme' poverty where the basics of life, food, clothing and housing are not available to individuals. Second, poverty changes as society changes. In a society where the social values are set by modernity, can poverty still be defined by the old parameters? Earning a few rupees above the poverty line does not make someone non-poor.

Poverty is defined by the 'social minimum necessary consumption'.[38] In the 1960s when poverty line was defined by the government it was accepted that the state would provide education and health so these need not be included in the poverty line. The poverty line was predominantly defined by access to food. The situation has changed since the state either did not provide the poor with education and health or of a very poor quality so that the poor have increasingly had to go to the market and get it at a high cost. The poor realize that they cannot escape poverty without good quality education for their children. Further, the environmental degradation has hurt the poor the most so that their health costs have risen dramatically.[39] Modern day life has also become dependent on communication and forms of entertainment, requiring expenditures.

In effect, poverty line is a changing line and not a fixed one for all times. It is also the case that people are forced to spend more on

---

[38] Kumar (2013)
[39] Kumar (2002a)

health, so, less is available for the basics of life and poverty persists. One major illness in a family or a single large expenditure on a social function pushes the family below the poverty line as defined by the access to basics. Thus, poverty line changes with social development and is not fixed for all times. If measured in relation to the changing needs of the poor, poverty has not declined.

It is not being argued that there is a conspiracy to marginalize a large section of the population. Marginalization is a result of the policy of modernization. Even if it is recognized by the elite that India has not yet reached the level of the advanced countries, the attempt has been to rapidly catch up with them. Resources are poured into modernizing a small section of the population even if the others are left out of it. Modernization is presented as 'nation building'. Anyone criticizing these policies is then seen as backward or even anti-national. The mainstream opposition parties when they come to power follow the same policies so they also do not oppose these policies.

Modernization is very expensive and it preempts resources, leaving little for the so called backward sectors, like, rural areas. Development of the backward sectors becomes a residual and justified by the trickle down theories. It is argued[40] that urbanization is seen as modernization and since it is far more expensive than rural development, it leaves little resources for the rural areas. The modernizers ask what the alternative is or argue that there is no alternative (TINA). Gandhi[41] suggested an alternative path of development from below but even the national leadership of the Congress party characterized it as backward. So, for the modernizers this is not relevant for the present. There is a hegemonization of the discourse with global forces pushing for it. The Indian elite wishing to join the global elite happily push this agenda.

GST is also seen as modernizing taxation and the economy through formalization. The unanimity among the political parties in

---

[40] Kumar (2013)
[41] Gandhi (1909)

pushing for GST even though it adversely impacts the vast majority of Indians is due to the influence of the idea of modernizing the country. Since it exists in 160 plus countries so India must catch up with the world. But the issue is how in a democracy the interest of the vast majority can be ignored? This is where the interest of the big businesses, including the MNCs, comes in and this is what they want. Political parties are tied to the interest of this section and have concurred in the implementation of GST. The government does not tire of proclaiming abroad that GST is the biggest reform and would lead to ease of doing business. This is the pitch made abroad to attract foreign capital.

In brief, GST is backed by a narrow social and political constituency in India. Its implementation indicates the extent of marginalization of the marginal in India and the weakness of democracy. The implications of growing marginalization in society will be serious since it will lead to rising discontent, alienation of the citizens and further weakening of democracy.

Conclusion

GST as a tax not only has an economic impact but also social and political implications. It is argued that major implications will follow the differentiated impact of GST on the unorganized and organized sectors of the economy. The organized sector will benefit at the expense of the unorganized sector and the well-off states will benefit at the expense of the backward states. This will happen in spite of the tax being a destination tax with the consuming states gaining. The organized sector is also facing problems even if they are transitional. On the whole, it is pointed out that GST is strengthening the process of marginalization in society.

An argument made in favour of GST is that it is formalizing the informal sector of the economy and this would modernize the economy apart from checking the black economy. In Chapter 7, it was argued that this outcome is not assured given the nature of the black economy in India. Further, it is argued here that GST and digitization would only further marginalize the unorganized sector which cannot deal with the complexity of the GST.

The impact will not only be in the short run but more importantly in the long run. The short run impact is both due to faulty implementation of a complex tax and design problems. Some of this may be mitigated as the teething problems are overcome. The long term consequences will be a result of faulty design and the marginalization process set into motion. Two circles of growth which have characterized the Indian economy are strengthened— marginalizing the unorganized sectors of the economy.

Big business has been privileged over the small resulting in increasing inequity, growing marginalization and in the long run to greater alienation. This would strengthen the existing trend of growing alienation in India due to the growing black economy and marketization. All this reduces the capacity of the nation to implement policies and achieve goals. Implementation of a flawed GST in haste implies that society and the interest of the majority of the people matter less and less to the political class. People who get even more disenfranchised this way will have even less stake in the nation. The political unanimity shown by the politicians of all hues indicates a decline of democracy where diverse views are not being taken into account in policy making. It reflects a hegemonization of social and political thinking by the idea of western modernity.

The pressure for the implementation of GST has come from large businesses and international agencies who believe GST is good for them. The large scale businesses see in this the possibility of an expansion of their market share at the expense of the unorganized and small and cottage sectors. This is shortsighted thinking because if employment gets hit, the market size would decline and the growth of the overall economy would fall. This can only lead to greater inequality and more entrenched poverty thereby leading to growing political, social and economic instability.

How could a tax with such adverse consequences be implemented in a democracy? It is argued that this is due to the hegemony of the idea of western modernity among the Indian elite and their acceptance of the top down approach to development since Independence. GST is presented as a scheme of modernization and nation building. The top down and trickle down approach to development has been strengthened by the process of marketization in India since 1991. This has led to a basic change in the thinking of the people and of the political parties. Consumerism and atomization have taken hold of people leading to greater alienation and lack of concern for the collective. Alternatives are neither tried nor accepted on the ground that 'there is no alternative'.

CONCLUSION: DESIGN OF A SIMPLE ALTERNATIVE

GST has been in operation in India since 1 July 2017. It was pitched as heralding a new dawn of freedom for the nation and promised much. In this volume, it has been shown that it has not yet delivered on the promises and is unlikely to do so because of design flaws. GST is a complex tax which is levied at dozens of stages of production and distribution of any good or service; from raw material to the final sale of a good (or a service). In a complex country with its vast diversity of producers (large, medium, small and cottage scale producers) and widely diverse states and regions with their own specificities, a single tax creates problems because it cannot cater to the diversities. Thus, the argument that some form of VAT and GST is now practiced in more than 160 countries is not a valid reason for having it in India. No country is as diverse as India. Further, none of the countries have gone in for as complex a GST as India has. Hence comparisons with other countries are inappropriate. There is a need to focus on what India needs.

Unfulfilled Promises and Claims

It is shown in this volume that to accommodate the vast diversities in the production structures in India and also to take into account the high levels of poverty, GST has been modified and that has turned what could potentially be a simple tax into a very complicated one. It is a half-way house with a faulty design so that businesses face a variety of problems and that has set back the economy. No wonder even the government has had to issue more than three hundred notifications and orders in the first year of operation of GST (Table 5.2). The changes being constantly made added to the confusion all around. Even experts have found it difficult to keep track of the changes and the public and businesses have been left feeling lost. The dependence of businesses on tax lawyers and chartered accountants has gone up substantially and along with that the cost of doing business has increased markedly.

The promised 'ease of doing business' is not yet in evidence. Due to the prevalence of several rates of taxes and exemptions to major inputs like energy, the cascading effect which was sought to be eliminated continues (Annexure 1.1). Prices which were supposed to decline due to the provision of input credit (ITC) have not only not fallen but actually risen since tax on all services have risen from 15 to 18 per cent. This increase is not captured in the official data since services are under-represented in our inflation indices. Further, tax collection has been less than expected and that has been a blessing in disguise since it moderated prices somewhat.

Government was supposed to collect more taxes and use that to provide better public services to the deprived but that has not yet happened. The black economy was supposed to be curtailed with the implementation of GST since it should check under and over invoicing by businesses. If this were to happen, then formerly undeclared output would get declared and the rate of growth of the white economy would rise. Reports indicate that the black income generation is continuing as increasing number of businesses are being caught evading GST. In fact, reports are that a chain of production entirely outside the GST network continues. Worse, businesses are using fictitious bills to claim input credit. In that case, the switch from black to white would be small and its effect on raising the rate of growth would be negligible.

The contradiction between collecting more revenue under GST than earlier and the claim that prices would fall is pointed out in this book. GST is an indirect tax and if it leads to increased collection of revenue, prices would rise, even if input credit (ITC) is provided.

However, the biggest claim was that the rate of growth of the economy would rise. This book points to several reasons why the opposite has happened. First, if prices rise and demand falls, the rate of growth of the economy would fall. Second, the organized sector of the economy would benefit while the unorganized sector would lose out in spite of the exemptions and concessions granted to it. Thus, the former would grow at the expense of the latter but overall the rate of growth would be lower than earlier. The shift from the organized to the unorganized sectors would lead to lower level of employment and rising inequality which would also lower demand in the economy and to a decline in the rate of growth. This decline is not captured in the official data due to methodological reasons.

Marginalizing the Marginal

It has been argued that GST is leading to a growing disconnect and divergence in the two circles of growth in the economy. One of them, the unorganized sectors, employs 93 per cent of the workforce, and as it shrinks, demand in the economy would fall further and that would slow down the economy. If the net rate of growth is calculated —adding the growth of the organized sector to the decline in the unorganized sectors—it would be close to zero.[1] Official data does not show this since it calculates quarterly growth on the basis of the corporate sector data. It does not take into account the decline in the unorganized sector. The data for this sector comes when periodic surveys are conducted once every few years. In the meanwhile, it is assumed to be growing at the same rate as the organized sectors—an erroneous assumption after a shock to the economy as was the case with demonetization and now GST.

Third, since the ease of doing business has not taken place, many of the large and medium scale businesses have suffered. The accounting required for GST is very complex. Even though it is supposed to be computerized, the number of forms to be submitted

---

[1] Kumar (2017b)

and the data requirements are large. The reduction of seventeen taxes to three taxes has not meant less of accounting. It is pointed out in this book that no company paid seventeen taxes.

Broadly, there were three taxes (excise, sales and service taxes) which have been replaced by three taxes (CGST, SGST and IGST). Entertainment tax, purchase tax, luxury tax, tax on lottery, etc., are not paid by every producer. For instance, none of them would be paid by a producer of steel. Also the various cesses could all be clubbed together or even eliminated as is the case under GST. These cesses were not essential to the old taxation system and the tax revenue they generated could be collected in other ways, like, charging a higher tax on specific items.

One indirect tax, the customs duty, has not been brought under GST. A part of it which pertained to the internal taxes like Countervailing Duty (CVD), has been incorporated into GST as IGST but the main duty has been left out. It is explained in the book that customs duty provides protection to indigenous businesses and this role cannot be done away with. So, it is on a different footing than the other indirect taxes. No input tax credit (ITC) is available for customs duty paid. Exports are zero rated to increase their international competitiveness. These steps, linked to external trade, have long term implications for growth, technology development and so on.

Computerization which is supposed to make accounting easier is needed by GST but it is not integral to it. It could have also been introduced in the pre-GST system. So, the efficiency in accounting due to computerization should not be attributed to GST. There is a need to compare like with like. GST cannot work without computerization while the earlier system could but with computerization it would have also become more efficient.

The high volume of accounting and computerization required by GST cannot be handled by the small and cottage sector businesses without a significant increase in their costs and decline in their profits. The large and medium scale businesses were already computerized so they face only small additional costs. Thus, the small and cottage sector businesses lose out to the large and medium scale sector if they come under the ambit of GST. If they stay out of the GST as the rules presently provide for, then they can neither avail of input credit (ITC) nor provide input credit to the buyers. Worse, the registered businesses buying from them have to pay a reverse charge (RCM). Thus, they again get out-competed by the organized sector producers who can avail of ITC to lower costs and provide the buyers the ITC which cheapens their produce further. In brief, it is shown that whether the unorganized sector stays out of GST or gets registered under GST, they lose out.

The idea of 'one nation one tax' was to provide ease of doing business and efficiency. This may be true for the large scale businesses who gain in a variety of ways but not for the small and micro businesses who produce locally and sell locally. This will mean that the competitive edge of large scale businesses will increase compared to that of the small and micro sectors. The former will then grow at the expense of the latter.

The marginalization of the small and micro sector has been accelerating with the rise of e-commerce and spread of organized retail stores in India. Business has been shifting to these modes from the small businesses. It is reported that these organized sector businesses have been growing at about 30 per cent when the economy has been only expanding at about 8 to 9 per cent in nominal terms. Thus, e-commerce and other big stores are eating into the share of the small businesses, especially in urban areas.

The above arguments point to the difficulties faced both by the unorganized and the organized sectors. This has set back the investment climate and the result has been stagnation of private investment. Of course, the rising NPAs of the banks and the infrastructure sector are additional reasons for stagnation of the private investment in the economy. GST has added to the pre-existing factors which were not conducive to the increase in the growth rate of the economy.

A major advantage of GST is that it reduces the cascading effect of taxes and thereby lowers the effective rate of indirect taxes. In the earlier system, with the introduction of VAT for each of the taxes, it was reduced for each of them but now it is removed across the taxes also. In Chapter 1, it was shown that there are three types of cascading effects and not two as believed earlier and the biggest one is the multiple taxation of inputs—basics and intermediates. This feature benefited the states coming later (consuming states) in the chain the most. But since this is now eliminated these states will lose the most amount of revenue. Since it is the poorer states that come later in the chain, they stand to lose most of the revenue from elimination of this form of the cascading effect.

In effect, even though GST is a last point tax and the consuming states which are usually the poorer states are to collect proportionately more of the tax, they are the ones who also lose the most when GST removes the cascading effect.

The poorer states are also the ones that have a higher proportion of the unorganized sectors in their output so a decline in this sector will impact them the most. Thus, even if they gain some due to GST, they will lose more due to a decline in their incomes and employment.

In brief, it has been shown in the book that it is the unorganized sectors and the poorer states that stand to lose the most in spite of the exemptions and other features of GST. As discussed in Chapter 3, GST will shift the distribution of income towards the well-off and away from the poor and this will lead to a slowdown in the economy if investments do not rise sharply. There is no sign of that at present. Increased profits do not lead to an immediate increase in investments so that demand tends to fall short. The differential impact of GST is the design flaw (or the intention) in GST which marginalizes the marginals further, as explained earlier in the book.

'Formalization' Only a Name

The proponents of GST point to its role in promoting greater transparency and digitization in the economy. This is referred to as the 'formalization' of the economy and it is supposed to be beneficial because it would broaden the tax base and check the black economy.

However, a bulk of the black incomes are generated in the formal sectors of the economy and not in the informal sectors where the incomes are mostly way below the taxable limit.[2] The formal sectors are mostly digitized by now and yet they generate a bulk of the black incomes using a myriad number of ways. Hence it is not clear that formalization or digitization of the informal sectors would lead to a check on the black economy. This is not to argue that some informal sector units do not generate black incomes. But, even if they are forced to formalize, they can also generate black incomes just as the formal sector units do presently.

Formalization is equated with modernization of the economy and the tax system. Thus, it is not opposed by either the political system or the media. The argument also has a technocratic bias. The idea is that technology will solve all the problems of society and the human element is corrupted and cannot be relied upon. So, technological solutions are to be preferred. However, it is pointed out that the person behind the technology is no less important and if her consciousness is not transformed then problems will continue. The technological solutions often end up marginalizing the poor and creating greater alienation in society. The Indian elite equate technology with modernization and are pushing for it in its narrow interest but that is shortsighted.

Would digitization make the 'informal', 'formal'? If that means a bank account or even computerization or a provident fund account for workers, then indeed there is formalization. But what does that mean? The wages of workers remain unchanged, their job security is not enhanced so that one can be fired at any time, hours at work remain onerous with the working day stretching beyond eight hours, safety precautions at work remain the same, so many work in dangerous conditions, like, a worker spraying pesticide without masks or a worker in a chemical factory with little protection from fumes. The situation of the unorganized sector workers remains unchanged even if they are enrolled under a provident fund scheme.

---

[2]   Kumar (1999b) and Kumar (2017a)

The lot of the informal sector producers also does not change with formalization or digitization. In the country, 99 per cent of the MSME units are micro units and they employ 97.5 per cent of the workers in this sector.[3] They have an average employment of 1.7 persons. Their lot would not change even if they are called 'formal' because they open a bank account. Their incomes and the employment they provide would remain unchanged. They would still be suppliers to the low-income unorganized sector and produce cheap low-quality products. Thus, with a bank account only their category changes but not much else. Since their incomes are mostly below the taxable limits, this kind of formalization may lead to registration but not to increased tax collection.

Distortions Are Not Reduced

Another important point mentioned in favour of GST is that there would be less of distortions in the economy and that would lead to increased market efficiency. Theory says that each tax levied leads to distortion. In this book it is pointed out that since every stage from raw material to the final product is sought to be taxed under GST, there are many more stages of taxation than earlier. At each stage there is a distortion so that the totality of distortion increases.

The fact that seventeen taxes are replaced by one (three) tax is used to argue that distortions in the market will be less. As argued above, this is an overstatement since hardly any producer paid all the seventeen taxes. Most paid three taxes—excise sales and services—and these are now replaced by three taxes—CGST, SGST and IGST. Thus, at the aggregate level, distortions remain the same. Cesses were not integral and could have been eliminated or absorbed.

GST becomes a last point tax due to the shifting of the taxes from the exporting to the importing states. The purchaser of the final good or service (consumer) is to pay this entire tax. In the earlier system also the final consumer/purchaser paid the entire tax.

---

[3]   GoI (2017a)

So, what is the difference? Earlier the purchaser only saw the VAT (sales tax) on the bill (if she asked for the bill) but not the excise duty and other taxes paid at the earlier stages. So, there is supposed to be greater transparency. How does this help the consumer? It does not lead to lower prices or better service.

Yes, it does mean that the consuming states get to collect the tax and not the producing states (See Chapters 4 and 8). Since the poorer states have less of production than the better-off states, one could argue that GST would lead to greater equity. However, it is pointed out that the poorer states have more of the unorganized sector and if this sector declines, the economic well-being of the poorer states would be adversely impacted. The little bit of extra GST received by these states would not compensate them for the loss of employment and production they would suffer due to GST. In effect, in spite of the favourable structure of GST for poorer states, the gap between them and the better off states would only rise, increasing inequality in society.

Not a Simple Tax

Apart from bringing all indirect taxes on one platform, the other theoretical aspect of GST is that it is to be calculated as VAT. It is pointed out in the book that there are three ways of calculating VAT and the one chosen in India (and most parts of the world) is based on ad valorem with ITC. If proper VAT had been used, GST would have been collected at each stage of production and distribution by the state where the tax on that stage is levied. It would not have been passed on to the importing state where the final sale takes place. It is because the tax is calculated as ad valorem with ITC that it passes on to the state where the final sale occurs.

The method chosen leads to several problems. First, with different rates of tax on inputs and outputs, cascading effect does not get eliminated even if it is reduced.[4] Second, input tax credit

---

[4]   (See Annexure 1.1)

(ITC) poses serious challenges, especially for the micro and small businesses. Third, with exemptions, the chain of ITC is broken and cascading effect continues. Fourth, the small businesses that neither get ITC nor can they pass on ITC to their buyers are at a disadvantage compared to the large businesses. This leads to shrinkage of their market. These are design flaws in GST which are another cause of growing disparities and rising under employment in society.

Government had great difficulty in fixing the GST rates. What should the Revenue Neutral Rate (RNR) of tax be? Different committees appointed to suggest what it should be came up with different rate structures. One of the committees admitted that fixing the rate is not an exact science, implying that ambiguity would remain. There are two possibilities, should the same amount of tax be collected from each item as was the case in the pre-GST regime or should the same amount as earlier be collected in the aggregate from all goods and services? In the former case there would be many tax rates and that would lead to complications, like, increased misclassification and continuation of cascading effect. If the government were to exercise the second option and decide on one common rate for all goods and services then the basics and essentials would get taxed higher than earlier and that would make the situation inflationary in spite of RNR.[5] Thus, neither of the two options was promising.

The government decided to chart a middle path. Go for overall revenue neutrality with a few rates and exemptions for essentials. But this led to the argument that the idea of 'one nation one tax' was undermined. While that is not true since the same rate for an item prevails all over the country, having multiple rates creates other problems as discussed above—reappearance of cascading effect, possibility of misclassification, black income generation and so on.

Further, if the essentials and some other items are kept at zero rate of tax or the low 5 per cent rate of tax then the remaining items have to be kept at higher rates of tax like 28 per cent for some goods

---

[5]   Kumar (2015)

and 18 per cent for services. This led to price increase for many items and a rise in the rate of inflation. The GST Council was overwhelmed by representations to reduce the 28 per cent rate of tax. It obliged by lowering the rates for many items.

Another option was to fix a rate lower than RNR so that prices did not rise. But then revenue would fall short and the fiscal deficit of the Centre and the states would rise. Since the states were guaranteed a 14 per cent increase in revenue (for five years) their revenue shortfall would also have to be made up by the Centre. Hence the entire burden of revenue shortage would have to be borne by the Centre. But the Centre is constrained to lower the fiscal deficit under FRBM, so it has to prevent a rise in the deficit and that is only possible if expenditures are cut. Usually these cuts fall on essential social sectors, like, education and health and that impacts the poor adversely. Thus, giving up RNR is a tough option for the government.

Design Flaws

Granting exemptions to essentials and to small producers meant that the complete chain of production and distribution was not under GST. This undermines one of the basic ideas of GST—to have the entire chain of production and distribution under it and make it a last point tax. The break in the chain of input credit that takes place also enables black incomes to be generated. Data suggests that while a large number of businesses have registered under GST, only about 60 per cent are paying any tax (Table 5.1). In fact, the ministry has been arguing from the beginning that only 5 per cent of the units pay 95 per cent of the tax. Thus, registering more businesses only increases administrative costs without commensurate increase in revenue. Is it then worth it to have the entire chain of production and distribution under the GST net?

Chapter 7 on black economy shows that there are as many ways of generating black incomes as the number of businesses and a large number of these methods continue to be used post-GST.

Professionals who use few inputs may not care about ITC and continue to operate in cash as before. Misclassification of goods and services is likely to continue. It was also argued that complexity is used to generate black incomes so that GST lends itself to such income generation.

Key difficulties faced by businesses were RCM, availing of ITC and detailed accounting. Businesses have to chase up their suppliers to ensure that they file their data and also do it correctly. Seeing these difficulties, the government suspended RCM and GSTR 2. However, these are crucial for the design of GST which seeks to cover the entire chain of production and distribution. This is the dilemma faced by the government, if it continues with these features, businesses will have a difficult time and if it drops them then the design of GST would not work. This is another basic design flaw of GST.

Federalism is an important aspect of the Indian Constitution. Because the states are very diverse in terms of their need and their resource base, the Constitution makers granted them considerable autonomy. This is being dented under GST with the same rate of tax prevailing in all the states. Further, the third tier of governance, the local bodies are not taken care in the GST structure and have no independent tax base to meet their needs. Local bodies are crucial for providing services to the citizens since they are closest to them. That is why decentralization is considered very important in a federal structure in a vast country like India. So, GST dents federalism and decentralization which will have long term repercussions.

Policy Makers' Lack of Clarity

The previous sections point to the complexity of GST and that coupled with the complexity of the country created difficulties for the policy makers. There was lack of clarity about what is to be done and that led to design flaws. The compromises made to accommodate diversity ended up creating further complexity. Many critical issues regarding basic design of GST remain unclear and unresolved. So, some of the critical elements like e-way bill, input credit (ITC), reverse charge mechanism (RCM) have had to be postponed and some of them may not get implemented ultimately even though they are considered essential to GST. Are these transient difficulties?

Introduction of the e-way bill was also a method to check the black economy and also automate movements of goods and speed up their delivery. The entry barriers at the state borders would get eliminated. However, policy makers did not think through that checking of goods would remain necessary to check misclassification of goods which is quite widespread in India. Further, trucks do stop at toll plazas. Some other mechanism would have to be thought through.

GST was introduced with little time to discuss the difficulties and sort them out. Due to preoccupation with the impact of demonetization in November 2016, policy makers had little time to focus on GST. So, the real problems with introduction of GST in India remained unaddressed. Namely, what may be good for the large scale and organized sector may not be good for the rest. The small and tiny units producing and selling locally would lose from a unified market which will benefit the large-scale producers.

GST is backed by large businesses even though they too face initial problems. The analysis till recently was mostly based on what the large scale wanted. But a macro analysis needs to take into account the small and cottage sectors also. The differential impact of GST matters little in the advanced countries with their homogeneous economic structures. Their situation is not comparable with that of India. So, it makes little sense to say that because France introduced VAT in 1954, India should also go for it.

The contradictions in the argument put out by the government in favour of GST especially at the macro level suggest that the policy makers did not think through their argument but were intent on pushing for GST. They were perhaps confused. A simple macroeconomic analysis would have shown that either way the government's argument was contradictory, as explained earlier in the book. It was based on a partial analysis with each component analysed separately and not as a whole. The amount of tax collection, its impact on prices and their joint impact on growth and investment were all analysed separately.

The confusion in the thinking of the policy makers and their desire to push through GST anyhow will have political and social consequences over time. These have not been taken into account. Protests by traders and farmers, the dominant sections of the unorganized sectors, have persisted. Other long term issues will manifest themselves over time, even if in the short run all may go smoothly. When they do show up, they will be attributed to other unknown causes at that time.

Proposal for Reform of GST: An Alternative

Since GST has not delivered on the promises made and will lead to complications over time, it is time to think of an alternative. The hurry to implement it was so great that even a trial period was not considered. The ruling elite which formulates policy, and in this all political parties are complicit, did not consider the deleterious impact GST would have on the unorganized sectors.

Can GST be reversed and can one go back to the earlier system of indirect tax? Clearly, the previous system was also not satisfactory since indirect taxes are stagflationary and there was a multiplicity of these taxes. It is better to collect more of direct taxes.[6] India pays very little of those in spite of the high level of disparity. The well-off sections can indeed pay a much larger per cent of GDP as direct taxes if the black economy could be checked.[7] So, the first part of the alternative is to collect a lot more from the direct taxes by checking the black economy.

The second part of the alternative would be that even if more cannot be collected from direct taxes, can something be done to reform GST to make it better than it is? Indeed it can be reformed to improve matters all around.

---

[6]   Kumar (1994)
[7]   Kumar, et.al. (2007)

The hint of possible reform lies in the idea that GST is a destination tax, paid by the final consumer and also collected by the state where the final consumption takes place. Since the complexity of GST arises due to the various intermediate stages of transactions, sales, production, transportation, accounting and so on, why not simplify the tax by eliminating the intermediate stages of tax? These stages are anyway only passing on the tax to the final stage.

So, GST should be levied only on the final consumption leaving out the intermediate stages of production and distribution. In the example of iron ore to sales of utensils made out of it, as mentioned in Chapter 1, only the utensil would be taxed and all the intermediate stage of making pig iron, steel, transporting them, storing them, accounting for it and overheads used would be exempt from indirect taxes. Whatever is collected at each level at present would be finally collected from the utensils. That is what is supposed to happen under GST at present.

Further simplification would arise if the tax is levied as ad valorem rather than VAT. Since no tax is levied on intermediate stages, this tax would be equivalent to VAT. Input tax credit would not be needed since no input would be taxed. So, both ITC and RCM would become redundant. Since ad valorem tax would be simple to calculate, computerization would not be crucial unless the business wishes to computerize for its own accounting purposes. Due to simplification, even small businesses at all levels of production and distribution would be able to cope with this tax. If computerization is required it would be very simple and not require complex accounting.

Administratively, this would simplify the collection of the tax since a large number of units would be freed from the requirement of detailed accounting for indirect tax purpose. In effect, tax would be collected from fewer entities at the retail/wholesale level. Would this lead to greater tax evasion by the producers and dealers at the pre-retail levels? Possibly, but that would have to be checked by other means. In any case, they would not have to pay an indirect tax so question of indirect tax evasion would not arise. Hope lies in the fact that simpler structures are easier to monitor. In any case, all businesses in the taxable brackets file income tax returns and checking for tax evasion can be done there.

The objection could be that presently 5 per cent of the registered units pay 95 per cent of the tax but under the proposal here, the tax would have to be collected from a sub set of the remaining 95 per cent units plus the 5 per cent who are involved in retail/wholesale trade. To overcome this difficulty, tax could be levied on the dealers and wholesalers or the manufacturers on the basis of the entire value addition in the chain, that is, the declared MSP. There would be no tax at the subsequent stages or previous stages so that the issue of cascading would not arise.

Another issue would be that the distinction between final and intermediate goods is often blurred since the same item may be used in either capacity. A car can be a taxi or a personal car. Such cases will be few and can be accepted as a part of a solution that is not entirely perfect. After all huge compromises have been made in the present GST. So why be averse to a few compromises to get a new simpler system? A good or a service can be declared as a final one and taxed, whatever its subsequent use may be. So, a car or a truck or a two-wheeler or an auto rickshaw would be called a final good and taxed. Steel would be an intermediate good and not taxed.

What about services? They are characterized either as consumptive or productive. One can leave out productive services from the net and only tax the consumptive ones. So, a consumptive service like tourism or restaurants could be taxed but productive services like chartered accountant service or transport or finance could be left out of the tax net. If transportation is exempted, the e-way bill requirement and checking would also not be required. Again, there may be some confusion because people may be transported also and that is a final consumption service. What could be called final or intermediate can be defined once and for all, knowing and accepting that this would never be perfect.

The unorganized sector could be spared taxation by exempting their production. Just like at present, a limit can be given for exemption from GST. Say, an average annual turnover of Rs 48 lakh. Since, there would be no reverse charge (RCM) and input tax credit (ITC), the tax would be simple. There could be two tax rates—normal and luxury/sin. Essentials or items of mass consumption could be exempted. Fewer rates would reduce chances of misclassification.

Since basics and intermediates will not be taxed, there will be no cascading effect on this count. Some cascading effect will remain since goods declared final may at times also be used as intermediates. But on the whole, cascading effect will be greatly reduced and the effective tax rate lowered. Thus, prices should be moderate. With the basics and intermediates not required to pay indirect taxes, their prices should decline and that should lead to a decline in prices.

The question, will be, whether businesses will pass on the benefit of no tax on the intermediate and basics to the producer of the final goods and services? Anti-profiteering clause would be required to be in place to keep businesses in check even though it would be difficult to implement. The threat would have to be kept visible even if implemented more in the breach. The large public sector produces much of basics and can be persuaded by the government to take the lead in passing on the benefit to the consumers and other producers.

Distortions created by taxation will be less since the number of stages in production and distribution that will be taxed will be reduced and largely it would be at only one stage, ideally for each final product or service once only. Thus, it should increase market efficiency.

How would the unorganized sector fare under this scheme? It would get the benefit of lower basic and intermediate goods prices. It would also not pay a tax on its output so that it would have a price advantage over the organized sectors and would not become uncompetitive.

The final element of this reform would be collection of more direct taxes. As this fructifies, more items can be taken out of the GST net. The need to depend overwhelmingly on indirect taxes would decline. As the share of direct taxes rises, more and more of basic goods and services can be exempted from indirect taxes. Over time, only final luxury goods and services need be under GST.[8] How to collect more of direct taxes is discussed in various places.[9] If all this can be done, there would be a real win-win situation in the economy with increase in growth rate, less of inequality, increase in public resources and reduction in policy failure.

Conclusion

GST is an indirect tax with all the negative consequences that such taxes have. If more of such taxes are collected, problems will mount as depicted above. If not, then revenues fall short and budget deficit will mount which in the present international situation creates other problems. Further, GST delivered a shock to the economy soon after the shock of demonetization. So, it was not a good time to implement such a complex tax.

One argument can be that GST has not delivered on its promises because the economy was in a shock. Be that as it may, this book shows that the problems are inherent in the design so that it could not have delivered on the promises. While some sections may gain there is a huge chunk that is losing out. So overall, or in the net, the economy is suffering. It is pointed out in this volume that all this is due to the complexity of GST and its adverse impact on the unorganized sectors of the economy.

Further, the black economy is not simply some technical problem but a political one which needs to be tackled politically. Technology can only go thus far and no further. If the human element is not willing, then technology can only play a limited role. The form of black income generation can easily change to adapt to the new technology as has happened repeatedly in the past. Demonetization was implemented with high hopes but failed to deliver since it is only a technical step which does not change the politics or transform the human element. Political will is needed to

---

[8]   See Kumar 1994

[9]   See Kumar (1994) and Kumar (1999b)

curtail the black economy. It is a political choice whether to tackle the black economy and reduce indirect taxes or continue as it is with its negative consequences.

Reform of the GST as it stands is essential even to get limited gains. It needs to be simplified as suggested above. It is time that the political leadership (both the ruling party and the opposition) takes a wider view of the economy and admits its mistakes and gives up the 'Ground Scorching Tax' in favour of a 'Ground Nourishing Tax'. There is still time to retrieve the situation.

APPENDICES

Table 1.1a: Tax Revenue, Centre and States, 1950–51 to 2015–16

Year	Amount in Rs crore		
	Direct Tax Revenue	*Indirect Tax Revenue*	*Total Tax Revenue*
1950–51	231.00	396.00	627.00
1951–52	244.00	495.00	739.00
1952–53	252.00	426.00	678.00
1953–54	242.00	430.00	672.00
1954–55	240.00	480.00	720.00
1955–56	259.00	509.00	768.00
1956–57	288.00	602.00	890.00
1957–58	327.00	718.00	1,045.00
1958–59	344.00	745.00	1,089.00
1959–60	378.00	838.00	1,216.00
1960–61	402.00	948.00	1,350.00
1961–62	449.00	1,094.00	1,543.00
1962–63	560.00	1,305.00	1,865.00
1963–64	693.00	1,632.00	2,325.00
1964–65	743.00	1,856.00	2,599.00
1965–66	734.00	2,188.00	2,922.00
1966–67	767.00	2,494.00	3,261.00
1967–68	780.00	2,676.00	3,456.00
1968–69	840.00	2,919.00	3,759.00
1969–70	963.00	3,237.00	4,200.00
1970–71	1,009.00	3,743.00	4,752.00

Year	Amount in Rs crore		
	Direct Tax Revenue	Indirect Tax Revenue	Total Tax Revenue
1971–72	1,171.00	4,404.00	5,575.00
1972–73	1,346.00	5,090.00	6,436.00
1973–74	1,552.00	5,837.00	7,389.00
1974–75	1,834.00	7,389.00	9,223.00
1975–76	2,493.00	8,689.00	11,182.00
1976–77	2,585.00	9,747.00	12,332.00
1977–78	2,680.00	10,557.00	13,237.00
1978–79	2,851.00	12,677.00	15,528.00
1979–80	3,096.00	14,587.00	17,683.00
1980–81	3,268.00	16,576.00	19,844.00
1981–82	4,133.00	20,009.00	24,142.00
1982–83	4,492.00	22,750.00	27,242.00
1983–84	4,907.00	26,618.00	31,525.00
1984–85	5,330.00	30,484.00	35,814.00
1985–86	6,252.00	37,015.00	43,267.00
1986–87	6,889.00	42,650.00	49,539.00
1987–88	7,483.00	49,493.00	56,976.00
1988–89	9,758.00	57,168.00	66,926.00
1989–90	11,165.00	66,528.00	77,693.00
1990–91	12,260.00	75,462.00	87,722.00
1991–92	16,657.00	86,541.00	1,03,198.00
1992–93	19,387.00	94,779.00	1,14,166.00
1993–94	21,713.00	1,00,248.00	1,21,961.00
1994–95	28,878.00	1,18,971.00	1,47,849.00
1995–96	35,777.00	1,39,482.00	1,75,259.00
1996–97	41,061.00	1,59,995.00	2,01,056.00
1997–98	50,538.00	1,70,121.00	2,20,659.00
1998–99	49,119.00	1,83,898.00	2,33,017.00
1999–2000	60,864.00	2,13,719.00	2,74,583.00

Year	Amount in Rs crore		
	Direct Tax Revenue	Indirect Tax Revenue	Total Tax Revenue
2000–01	71,762.00	2,33,558.00	3,05,322.00
2001–02	73,109.00	2,41,426.00	3,14,535.00
2002–03	87,365.00	2,68,912.00	3,56,277.00
2003–04	1,09,546.00	3,04,538.00	4,14,083.00
2004–05	1,37,093.00	3,57,277.00	4,94,370.00
2005–06	1,67,635.00	4,20,053.00	5,87,688.00
2006–07	2,31,376.00	5,05,331.00	7,36,707.00
2007–08	3,18,839.00	5,51,490.00	8,70,329.00
2008–09	3,27,981.00	5,87,469.00	9,15,450.00
2009–10	3,76,995.00	6,23,849.00	10,00,844.00
2010–11	4,50,822.00	8,20,843.00	12,71,665.00
2011–12	5,01,395.00	9,66,496.00	14,67,891.00
2012–13	5,68,717.00	11,47,400.00	17,16,117.00
2013–14	6,46,907.00	12,93,539.00	19,40,446.00
2014–15(RE)	6,48,966.00	12,30,176.00	18,79,142.00
2015–16(BE)	7,48,643.00	14,89,472.00	22,38,115.00

Source: Indian Public Finance Statistics

Notes: (1) R.E. refers to Revised Estimate; B.E. refers to Budget Estimate
(2) Total Tax Revenue is the sum of Direct Tax Revenue and Indirect Tax Revenue

Table 1.1b: Tax Revenue, Centre and States, % of GDP, 1950–51 to 2015–16

Year	Values are expressed as % of GDP		
	Direct Tax Revenue	Indirect Tax Revenue	Total Tax Revenue
1950–51	2.22	3.81	6.03
1951–52	2.21	4.48	6.69
1952–53	2.32	3.93	6.25
1953–54	2.05	3.64	5.69
1954–55	2.15	4.30	6.45
1955–56	2.28	4.48	6.75
1956–57	2.13	4.44	6.57
1957–58	2.34	5.15	7.49
1958–59	2.21	4.79	7.00
1959–60	2.31	5.11	7.42
1960–61	2.24	5.28	7.52
1961–62	2.36	5.75	8.12
1962–63	2.74	6.39	9.13
1963–64	2.95	6.96	9.91
1964–65	2.71	6.78	9.50
1965–66	2.54	7.58	10.13
1966–67	2.35	7.63	9.98
1967–68	2.04	6.99	9.03
1968–69	2.07	7.21	9.28
1969–70	2.16	7.26	9.42
1970–71	2.12	7.86	9.98
1971–72	2.30	8.64	10.93
1972–73	2.39	9.05	11.45
1973–74	2.27	8.53	10.80

Year	Values are expressed as % of GDP		
	Direct Tax Revenue	*Indirect Tax Revenue*	*Total Tax Revenue*
1974–75	2.27	9.15	11.42
1975–76	2.88	10.02	12.90
1976–77	2.77	10.43	13.20
1977–78	2.53	9.97	12.51
1978–79	2.49	11.06	13.54
1979–80	2.46	11.60	14.06
1980–81	2.18	11.08	13.26
1981–82	2.35	11.38	13.73
1982–83	2.28	11.57	13.85
1983–84	2.14	11.62	13.77
1984–85	2.08	11.88	13.96
1985–86	2.16	12.78	14.94
1986–87	2.13	13.17	15.29
1987–88	2.03	13.44	15.47
1988–89	2.23	13.09	15.32
1989–90	2.22	13.25	15.48
1990–91	2.09	12.87	14.96
1991–92	2.47	12.84	15.31
1992–93	2.50	12.24	14.74
1993–94	2.44	11.25	13.68
1994–95	2.76	11.38	14.14
1995–96	2.92	11.37	14.29
1996–97	2.89	11.27	14.17
1997–98	3.21	10.82	14.03
1998–99	2.72	10.20	12.92

Year	Values are expressed as % of GDP		
	Direct Tax Revenue	Indirect Tax Revenue	Total Tax Revenue
1999–2000	3.02	10.62	13.65
2000–01	3.31	10.77	14.08
2001–02	3.11	10.28	13.39
2002–03	3.45	10.63	14.08
2003–04	3.86	10.73	14.59
2004–05	4.23	11.02	15.25
2005–06	4.54	11.37	15.91
2006–07	5.39	11.77	17.15
2007–08	6.39	11.06	17.45
2008–09	5.83	10.43	16.26
2009–10	5.82	9.63	15.45
2010–11	5.78	10.53	16.31
2011–12	5.57	10.73	16.29
2012–13	5.62	11.35	16.97
2013–14	5.76	10.91	16.67
2014–15(RE)	5.66	10.92	16.58
2015–16(BE)	5.76	11.38	17.15

Source: Indian Public Finance Statistics

Notes: (1) R.E. refers to Revised Estimate; B.E. refers to Budget Estimate
(2) 'GDP' refers to the Gross Domestic Product at Market Prices (at Current Prices) with the base year as 2004–05 (for the new series with the base year as 2011–12, splicing has been done to make the new series comparable with the old series)
(3) *Total Tax Revenue* is the sum of *Direct Tax Revenue* and *Indirect Tax Revenue*

Figure 1.1: Tax Revenue, Centre and States, % of GDP, 1950–51 to 2015–16

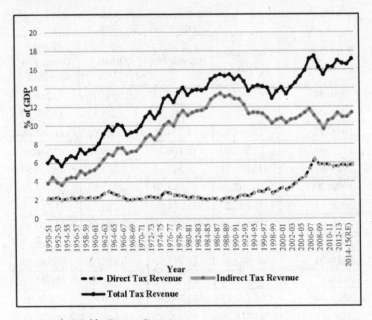

Source: Indian Public Finance Statistics

Notes: (1) R.E. refers to Revised Estimate; B.E. refers to Budget Estimate.
(2) Based on data in Table 1.1b

Table 1.2a: Composition of Direct Tax Revenue, Centre and States, 1990–91 to 2015–16

Year	Amount in Rs. crore			
	Corporation Tax	Income Tax	Others	Total Direct Tax Revenue
1990–91	5,335.26	5,377.10	1,547.75	12,260.11
1995–96	16,487.12	15,591.81	3,699.32	35,778.25
1996–97	18,566.62	18,234.01	4,261.06	41,061.69
1997–98	20,016.00	17,100.60	5,829.46	42,946.06
1998–99	24,529.11	20,240.32	4,351.15	49,120.58
1999–2000	30,692.29	25,654.50	4,517.50	60,864.29
2000–01	35,696.27	31,763.98	4,303.32	71,763.57
2001–02	36,609.14	32,004.09	4,497.64	73,110.87
2002–03	46,172.35	36,865.96	4,054.25	87,092.56
2003–04	63,562.03	41,386.51	4,598.06	1,09,546.60
2004–05	82,679.58	49,268.12	5,145.07	1,37,092.77
2005–06	1,01,277.15	60,756.90	5,600.99	1,67,635.04
2006–07	1,44,318.29	80,408.97	6,649.06	2,31,376.32
2007–08	1,92,910.83	1,11,820.63	14,108.34	3,18,839.80
2008–09	2,13,395.44	1,06,074.90	8,510.96	3,27,981.30
2009–10	2,44,725.07	1,22,417.24	9,852.64	3,76,994.95
2010–11	2,98,687.89	1,39,102.20	13,032.00	4,50,822.09
2011–12	3,22,816.17	1,64,525.33	14,053.42	5,01,394.92
2012–13	3,56,326.00	1,96,844.00	15,548.00	5,68,717.00
2013–14	3,94,678.00	2,37,870.00	16,419.00	6,48,966.00
2014–15 (R.E.)	4,26,079.00	2,72,610.00	18,084.00	7,16,774.00
2015–16 (B.E.)	4,70,628.00	3,20,839.00	21,885.00	8,13,353.00

Source: Indian Public Finance Statistics

Notes: (1) R.E. refers to Revised Estimate; B.E. refers to Budget Estimate

(2) Others include estate duty, interest tax, wealth tax, gift tax, land revenue, agricultural tax, hotel receipts tax, expenditure tax, taxes on professions, trades, employment and non-urban immovable properties, etc.

(3) There is a discontinuity in the series; data for 1990–91 is followed by data for 1995–96

Table 1.2b: Composition of Direct Tax Revenue, Centre and States, Share of Total 1990–91 to 2015–16

Year	Share of total Direct Tax Revenue (in %)		
	Corporation Tax	Income Tax	Others
1990–91	43.52	43.86	12.62
1995–96	46.08	43.58	10.34
1996–97	45.22	44.41	10.38
1997–98	46.61	39.82	13.57
1998–99	49.94	41.21	8.86
1999–2000	50.43	42.15	7.42
2000–01	49.74	44.26	6.00
2001–02	50.07	43.77	6.15
2002–03	53.02	42.33	4.66
2003–04	58.02	37.78	4.20
2004–05	60.31	35.94	3.75
2005–06	60.42	36.24	3.34
2006–07	62.37	34.75	2.87
2007–08	60.50	35.07	4.42
2008–09	65.06	32.34	2.59
2009–10	64.91	32.47	2.61
2010–11	66.25	30.86	2.89
2011–12	64.38	32.81	2.80
2012–13	62.65	34.61	2.73
2013–14	60.82	36.65	2.53
2014–15 (R.E.)	59.44	38.03	2.52
2015–16 (B.E.)	57.86	39.45	2.69

Source: Indian Public Finance Statistics

Notes: (1) R.E. refers to Revised Estimate; B.E. refers to Budget Estimate

(2) *Others* include estate duty, interest tax, wealth tax, gift tax, land revenue, agricultural tax, hotel receipts tax, expenditure tax, taxes on professions, trades, employment and non-urban immovable properties, etc.

(3) There is a discontinuity in the series; data for 1990–91 is followed by data for 1995–96

Figure 1.2: Composition of Direct Tax Revenue, Centre and States, Share of Total 1990–91 to 2015–16

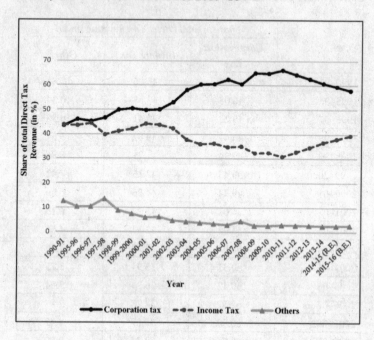

Source: Indian Public Finance Statistics

Notes: (1) R.E. refers to Revised Estimate; B.E. refers to Budget Estimate
(2) *Others* include estate duty, interest tax, wealth tax, gift tax, land revenue, agricultural tax, hotel receipts tax, expenditure tax, taxes on professions, trades, employment and non-urban immovable properties, etc.
(3) Please note there is a discontinuity in the series; data for 1990–91 is followed by data for 1995–96

Table 1.3a: Composition of Indirect Tax Revenue, Centre and States, 1990–91 to 2015–16

Year	Customs	Union excise duties	Service tax	State excise duty	Stamp & registration fees	General sales tax	Others	Total Indirect Tax Revenue
				Amount in Rs crore				
1990–91	20643.75	24,514.36		4,992.48	2,127.89	18,227.98	4,956.71	75,463.17
1995–96	35756.83	40,187.25	862.00	8,659.65	5,923.87	35,692.72	12,398.83	1,39,481.15
1996–97	42850.95	45,007.84	1,059.00	8,930.63	6,294.21	42,226.13	12,625.28	1,58,994.04
1997–98	40192.78	47,961.64	1,586.00	11,482.82	7,176.38	45,539.71	16,179.67	1,70,119.00
1998–99	40068.27	53,246.16	1,957.00	13,532.00	7,458.13	49,438.04	17,597.70	1,83,897.30
1999–00	48419.57	61,901.77	2,128.00	15,187.10	8,589.02	57,811.15	19,682.18	2,13,718.79
2000–01	47542.20	68,526.13	2,613.43	15,928.54	9,365.05	72,874.10	16,707.22	2,33,556.67
2001–02	40268.30	90,157.19	3,301.90	17,248.24	11,184.80	77,308.13	19,557.59	2,59,026.15
2002–03	44851.62	1,00,890.58	4,122.21	18,939.25	13,470.51	83,768.12	22,084.44	2,88,126.73
2003–04	48629.22	90,774.31	7,890.71	19,661.17	15,934.77	98,001.00	23,646.99	3,04,538.17
2004–05	57610.90	99,125.43	14,199.98	22,196.53	19,746.79	1,16,234.31	28,163.39	3,57,277.33
2005–06	65067.14	1,11,225.56	23,055.26	26,359.23	25,758.03	1,36,499.62	32,087.93	4,20,052.77
2006–07	86327.24	1,17,612.76	37,597.82	30,761.68	33,499.69	1,62,297.08	37,235.13	5,05,331.40
2007–08	104118.94	1,23,611.03	51,301.80	35,737.54	36,661.79	1,67,731.27	32,326.92	5,51,489.29

Year	Amount in Rs crore							
	Customs	Union excise duties	Service tax	State excise duty	Stamp & registration fees	General sales tax	Others	Total Indirect Tax Revenue
2008–09	99878.86	1,08,612.78	60,940.99	42,688.27	35,108.01	1,90,816.72	49,423.06	5,87,468.69
2009–10	83323.71	1,02,991.37	58,422.15	50,391.31	40,607.03	2,31,460.92	56,652.29	6,23,848.78
2010–11	135812.51	1,37,700.94	71,015.91	61,697.55	54,239.17	2,93,256.33	67,120.85	8,20,843.26
2011–12	149927.50	1,44,900.97	97,508.96	75,124.94	66,825.67	3,61,332.48	71,474.99	9,66,495.51
2012–13	165346.00	1,75,845.00	1,32,601.00	86,442.00	78,889.00	4,22,578.00	85,699.00	11,47,400.00
2013–14	172085.00	1,69,455.00	1,54,780.00	85,557.00	80,528.00	4,75,131.00	92,640.00	12,30,177.00
2014–15 (R.E.)	188713.00	1,84,731.00	1,68,132.00	98,835.00	92,272.00	5,44,256.00	1,04,462.00	13,81,401.00
2015–16 (B.E.)	208336.00	2,29,054.00	2,09,774.00	1,14,639.00	1,05,171.00	6,22,855.00	1,15,903.00	16,05,732.00

Source: Indian Public Finance Statistics

Notes: (1) R.E. refers to Revised Estimate; B.E. refers to Budget Estimate

(2) *Others* include taxes on vehicles, entertainment tax, taxes on goods and passengers, taxes and duty on electricity, taxes on purchase of sugarcane (including cess on sugarcane), etc.

(3) Please note the presence of a discontinuity in the series; data for 1990–91 is followed by data for 1995–96

Table 1.3b: Composition of Indirect Tax Revenue, Centre and States, 1990–91 to 2015–16

Share of Total Indirect Tax Revenue (in %)

Year	Customs	Union excise duties	Service tax	State excise duty	Stamp & registration fees	General sales tax	Others
1990–91	27.36	32.49	0.00	6.62	2.82	24.15	6.57
1995–96	25.64	28.81	0.62	6.21	4.25	25.59	8.89
1996–97	26.95	28.31	0.67	5.62	3.96	26.56	7.94
1997–98	23.63	28.19	0.93	6.75	4.22	26.77	9.51
1998–99	22.11	28.95	1.06	7.36	4.06	26.88	9.57
1999–2000	22.66	28.96	1.00	7.11	4.02	27.05	9.21
2000–01	20.36	29.34	1.12	6.82	4.01	31.20	7.15
2001–02	15.55	34.81	1.27	6.66	4.32	29.85	7.55
2002–03	15.57	35.02	1.43	6.57	4.68	29.07	7.66
2003–04	15.97	29.81	2.59	6.46	5.23	32.18	7.76
2004–05	16.12	27.74	3.97	6.21	5.53	32.53	7.88
2005–06	15.49	26.48	5.49	6.28	6.13	32.50	7.64
2006–07	17.08	23.27	7.44	6.09	6.63	32.12	7.37
2007–08	18.88	22.41	9.30	6.48	6.65	30.41	5.86

Year	Customs	Union excise duties	Service tax	State excise duty	Stamp & registration fees	General sales tax	Others
						Share of Total Indirect Tax Revenue (in %)	
2008–09	17.00	18.49	10.37	7.27	5.98	32.48	8.41
2009–10	13.36	16.51	9.36	8.08	6.51	37.10	9.08
2010–11	16.55	16.78	8.65	7.52	6.61	35.73	8.18
2011–12	15.45	14.99	10.09	7.77	6.91	37.39	7.40
2012–13	14.41	15.33	11.56	7.53	6.88	36.83	7.47
2013–14	13.99	13.77	12.58	6.95	6.55	38.62	7.53
2014–15 (R.E.)	13.66	13.37	12.17	7.15	6.68	39.40	7.56
2015–16 (B.E.)	12.97	14.26	13.06	7.14	6.55	38.79	7.22

Source: Indian Public Finance Statistics

Notes: (1) R.E. refers to Revised Estimate; B.E. refers to Budget Estimate

(2) *Others* include taxes on vehicles, entertainment tax, taxes on goods and passengers, taxes and duty on electricity, taxes on purchase of sugarcane (including cess on sugarcane), etc.

(3) Please note the presence of a discontinuity in the series; data for 1990–91 is followed by data for 1995–96

Figure 1.3: Composition of Indirect Tax Revenue, Centre and States, 1990–91 to 2015–16

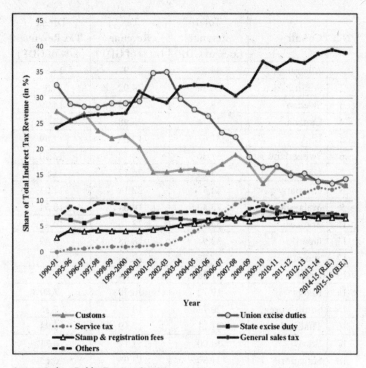

Source: Indian Public Finance Statistics

Notes: (1) R.E. refers to Revised Estimate; B.E. refers to Budget Estimate

(2) *Others* include taxes on vehicles, entertainment tax, taxes on goods and passengers, taxes and duty on electricity, taxes on purchase of sugarcane (including cess on sugarcane), etc.

(3) Please note there is a discontinuity in the series; data for 1990–91 is followed by data for 1995–96

Table 1.4: Total tax revenue of selected countries as a percentage of GDP and share of direct taxes in total revenue, 2014

No.	Country	Total Revenue (as % of GDP)	Tax Revenue (as % of GDP)	Direct Tax Revenue (as % of GDP)
1	Australia*	34.23	27.97	15.98
2	South Africa	28.24	24.02	14.8
3	Sweden	48.53	32.73	14.79
4	Canada	37.74	25.98	14.74
5	USA	31.61	19.85	12.59
6	Switzerland	31.36	20.12	12.40
7	UK	35.74	26.12	11.25
8	Germany	44.57	22.14	11.03
9	Malaysia	23.30	14.84	10.54
10	France	53.54	28.16	10.47
11	Japan*	32.97	18.08	9.89
12	Spain	37.77	22.13	9.80
13	Israel	37.25	25.84	9.66
14	Kenya*	19.72	16.90	7.89
15	South Korea	20.73	18	7.16
16	Thailand	21.21	17.19	6.84
17	Brazil	34.00	31.17	6.71
18	Singapore	21.59	13.93	6.13
19	Egypt	24.98	13.03	6.05
20	India*	19.63	16.63	5.82
21	Indonesia	16.73	11.97	5.18
22	China*	28.54	18.73	4.92
23	Nepal	20.82	15.99	3.89
24	Pakistan	15.30	10.53	3.55
25	Bangladesh*	10.27	8.45	2.71
26	Sri Lanka	11.67	10.73	2.02

Source: World Revenue Longitudinal Data (WoRLD), IMF http://data.imf. org/?sk=77413F1D-1525-450A-A23A-47AEED40FE78

Note: For countries marked with * data is not for the year 2014 but for the year 2013. Direct Tax Revenue includes tax revenue from individual income tax and corporate profits tax.

Annexe 1.1 Cascading effect of different stages of ad valorem tax with input credit

Value of input is V_i and it has a tax rate t_i

Value of ouput is V_o and it has a tax rate t_o

Ad-valorem tax on input is $V_i t_i$

Ad-valorem tax on output is $V_o t_o$

So, the tax to be paid is $V_o t_o - V_i t_i = \underbrace{t_o(V_o - V_i)}_{t_o(\text{Value Added})} + \underbrace{V_i(t_o - t_i)}_{\text{Cascading Effect}}$

The cascading effect depends on $(t_o - t_i)$.

$$\begin{aligned} \text{Cascading effect} &= 0 \text{ if } t_o = t_i \\ &\neq 0 \text{ if } t_o \neq t_i \\ &> 0 \text{ for } t_o > t_i \\ &< 0 \text{ for } t_o < t_i \end{aligned}$$

In the pure VAT case, where $t_o = t_i$, the cascading effect will be zero and the tax paid would be $t_o(V_o - V_i)$.

Table 2.1: Total Public Expenditure of selected countries as a percentage of GDP, 2014

No.	Country	Public Expenditure (as % of GDP)
1	France	56.7
2	Sweden	49.1
3	Spain	44.7
4	Germany	44
5	Brazil	43.8
6	UK	42.4
7	Israel	40.2
8	Japan	39.1
9	South Africa	39
10	Canada	38.4
11	USA	36
12	Australia	35.1
13	Egypt	32.9
14	Switzerland	32.5
15	South Korea	29.8
16	China	28.9
17	India*	27.3
18	Kenya	21
19	Thailand	19.2
20	Indonesia	15.9
21	Singapore	13.4

Source: Government Finance Statistics, IMF http://data.imf.org/?sk=20c2d27c-7969-47ac-91e9-098a70198db4

Note: *Data for India is taken from Indian Public Finance Statistics

Figure 2.1: Expenditure, Centre and States, as % of GDP, 1990–91 to 2015–16

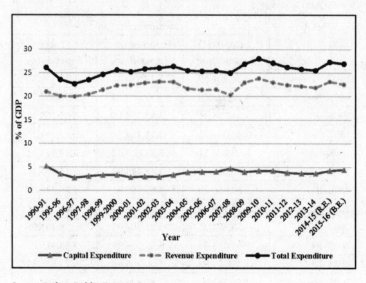

Source: Indian Public Finance Statistics

Notes: (1) R.E. refers to Revised Estimate; B.E. refers to Budget Estimate
(2) 'GDP' refers to the Gross Domestic Product at Market Prices (at Current Prices) with 2004–05 as the base year (for the new series with 2011–12 as the base year, splicing has been done to make the new series comparable with the old series which has 2004–05 as the base year)
(3) *Total Expenditure* is the sum of *Revenue Expenditure* and *Capital Expenditure*
(4) Please note there is a discontinuity in the series; data for 1990–91 is followed by data for 1995–96

Table 2.2a: Expenditure, Centre and States, 1990–91 to 2015–16

Year	Amount in Rs crore		
	Capital Expenditure	Revenue Expenditure	Total Expenditure
1990–91	30,201.59	1,22,950.01	1,53,151.60
1995–96	42,926.69	2,45,635.42	2,88,562.11
1996–97	38,386.31	2,82,779.16	3,21,165.47
1997–98	48,049.91	3,21,144.36	3,69,194.27
1998–99	59,186.11	3,85,325.30	4,44,511.41
1999–2000	66,650.83	4,48,444.93	5,15,095.76
2000–01	60,960.25	4,85,387.82	5,46,348.07
2001–02	70,105.81	5,36,475.92	6,06,581.73
2002–03	73,374.05	5,85,107.03	6,58,481.08
2003–04	94,498.82	6,53,976.95	7,48,475.77
2004–05	1,25,379.98	7,00,306.61	8,25,686.59
2005–06	1,46,311.06	7,89,336.65	9,35,647.71
2006–07	1,70,680.10	9,21,053.44	10,91,733.54
2007–08	2,34,169.67	10,11,221.06	12,45,390.73
2008–09	2,22,854.67	12,90,508.47	15,13,363.14
2009–10	2,72,806.55	15,41,723.66	18,14,530.21
2010–11	3,25,600.72	17,84,314.15	21,09,914.87
2011–12	3,42,109.53	20,17,535.71	23,59,645.24
2012–13	3,74,767.00	22,72,152.00	26,46,919.00
2013–14	4,21,892.00	25,31,370.00	29,53,262.00
2014–15 (R.E.)	5,40,496.00	29,62,919.00	35,03,415.00
2015–16 (B.E.)	6,23,927.00	31,76,210.00	38,00,137.00

Source: Indian Public Finance Statistics

Notes: (1) R.E. refers to Revised Estimate; B.E. refers to Budget Estimate
(2) *Total Expenditure* is the sum of *Revenue Expenditure* and *Capital Expenditure*
(3) Please note the presence of a discontinuity in the series; data for 1990–91 is followed by data for 1995–96

Table 2.2b: Expenditure, Centre and States, % of GDP, 1990–91 to 2015–16

Year	*Values are expressed as a % of GDP*		
	Capital Expenditure	*Revenue Expenditure*	*Total Expenditure*
1990–91	5.15	20.97	26.13
1995–96	3.50	20.02	23.52
1996–97	2.70	19.92	22.63
1997–98	3.06	20.42	23.48
1998–99	3.28	21.37	24.65
1999–2000	3.31	22.29	25.60
2000–01	2.81	22.38	25.19
2001–02	2.99	22.84	25.83
2002–03	2.90	23.12	26.02
2003–04	3.33	23.04	26.37
2004–05	3.87	21.60	25.47
2005–06	3.96	21.37	25.33
2006–07	3.97	21.45	25.42
2007–08	4.70	20.28	24.97
2008–09	3.96	22.92	26.88
2009–10	4.21	23.80	28.01
2010–11	4.18	22.92	27.11
2011–12	3.80	22.39	26.19
2012–13	3.65	22.16	25.81
2013–14	3.64	21.85	25.49
2014–15 (R.E.)	4.21	23.09	27.30
2015–16 (B.E.)	4.42	22.51	26.93

Source: Indian Public Finance Statistics

Notes: (1) R.E. refers to Revised Estimate; B.E. refers to Budget Estimate
(2) 'GDP' refers to the Gross Domestic Product at Market Prices (at Current Prices) with 2004–05 as the base year (for the new series with 2011–12 as the base year, splicing has been done to make the new series comparable with the old series which has 2004–05 as the base year)
(3) *Total Expenditure* is the sum of *Revenue Expenditure* and *Capital Expenditure*
(4) Please note the presence of a discontinuity in the series; data for 1990–91 is followed by data for 1995–96

Figure 2.2: Composition of Revenue Expenditure, Centre and States, Share of Total 1990–91 to 2015–16

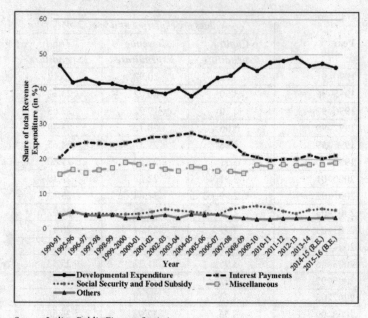

Source: Indian Public Finance Statistics

Notes: (1) R.E. refers to Revised Estimate; B.E. refers to Budget Estimate

(2) *Miscellaneous* refers to the following items summed together: Organs of state, Fiscal services, Administrative services, Pension and other retirement benefits, Relief on account of natural calamities

(3) *Others* include Appropriation for reduction or avoidance of debt, Technical and economic cooperation with other countries, Compensation and assignments to local bodies and Panchayati Raj institutions, etc.

(4) Please note there is a discontinuity in the series; data for 1990–91 is followed by data for 1995–96

Table 2.3a: Composition of Revenue Expenditure, Centre and States, 1990–91 to 2015–16

Amount in Rs crore

| Year | Developmental Expenditure | Non–Developmental Expenditure | | | | Total Revenue Expenditure |
		Interest Payments	Social Security and Food Subsidy	Miscellaneous	Others	
1990–91	57,498.23	25,006.00	4,930.58	19,237.94	4,318.95	1,22,950.01
1995–96	1,02,751.47	58,944.49	11,169.63	41,679.03	12,167.04	2,45,635.42
1996–97	1,21,335.34	69,930.96	11,891.93	45,314.65	11,081.44	2,82,779.16
1997–98	1,33,576.76	78,551.39	14,004.74	54,265.79	11,821.23	3,21,144.36
1998–99	1,59,954.92	92,591.97	16,256.73	67,228.41	15,563.50	3,85,325.30
1999–2000	1,82,194.22	1,10,050.69	18,796.87	85,487.84	13,670.79	4,48,444.93
2000–01	1,94,955.61	1,22,791.75	20,934.47	89,573.79	15,354.56	4,85,387.82
2001–02	2,10,498.41	1,40,889.88	26,247.90	96,685.39	18,445.43	5,36,475.92
2002–03	2,26,329.15	1,54,398.54	33,020.76	1,00,478.50	23,252.93	5,85,107.03
2003–04	2,63,303.68	1,76,372.66	34,541.75	1,08,332.74	20,369.49	6,53,976.95
2004–05	2,65,931.74	1,92,367.33	34,378.94	1,24,793.24	29,322.58	7,00,306.61
2005–06	3,20,495.00	2,06,390.28	36,231.36	1,38,575.11	31,637.30	7,89,336.65
2006–07	3,98,129.14	2,33,019.74	37,862.28	1,52,743.86	39,042.16	9,21,053.44

Year	Developmental Expenditure	Non-Developmental Expenditure				Total Revenue Expenditure
		Interest Payments	Social Security and Food Subsidy	Miscellaneous	Others	
2007–08	4,43,492.35	2,49,195.25	57,417.41	1,66,934.87	34,397.08	10,11,221.06
2008–09	6,07,289.31	2,77,637.55	80,837.78	2,06,151.24	40,369.77	12,90,508.47
2009–10	6,97,543.51	3,17,286.76	1,02,173.58	2,82,801.16	43,299.49	15,41,723.66
2010–11	8,50,770.39	3,51,145.13	1,09,528.51	3,20,330.41	49,696.30	17,84,314.15
2011–12	9,71,885.73	4,03,234.98	1,03,986.14	3,73,180.04	62,237.91	20,17,535.71
2012–13	11,15,865.00	4,57,550.00	1,01,569.00	4,15,445.00	70,444.00	22,72,152.00
2013–14	11,81,750.00	5,37,468.00	1,39,168.00	4,68,605.00	80,004.00	25,31,370.00
2014–15 (R.E.)	14,04,674.00	5,99,570.00	1,73,554.00	5,49,503.00	95,214.00	29,62,919.00
2015–16 (B.E.)	14,68,102.00	6,70,904.00	1,74,084.00	6,05,878.00	1,05,102.00	31,76,210.00

Amount in Rs crore

Source: Indian Public Finance Statistics

Notes: (1) R.E. refers to Revised Estimate; B.E. refers to Budget Estimate

(2) Miscellaneous refers to the following items summed together: Organs of state, Fiscal services, Administrative services, Pension and other retirement benefits, Relief on account of natural calamities

(3) Others include Appropriation for reduction or avoidance of debt, Technical and economic cooperation with other countries, Compensation and assignments to local bodies and Panchayati Raj institutions, etc.

(4) Non-Developmental Expenditure is the sum of Interest Payments, Social Security and Food Subsidy, Miscellaneous, and Others

(5) Total Revenue Expenditure is the sum of Developmental Expenditure and Non-Developmental Expenditure

(6) Please note the presence of a discontinuity in the series; data for 1990–91 is followed by data for 1995–96

Table 2.3b: Composition of Revenue Expenditure, Centre and States, Share of Total 1990–91 to 2015–16

Year	Share of Total Revenue Expenditure (in %)					
	Developmental Expenditure	Non–Developmental Expenditure				
		Interest Payments	Social Security and Food Subsidy	Miscellaneous	Others	
1990–91	46.77	20.34	4.01	15.65	3.51	
1995–96	41.83	24.00	4.55	16.97	4.95	
1996–97	42.91	24.73	4.21	16.02	3.92	
1997–98	41.59	24.46	4.36	16.90	3.68	
1998–99	41.51	24.03	4.22	17.45	4.04	
1999–2000	40.63	24.54	4.19	19.06	3.05	
2000–01	40.16	25.30	4.31	18.45	3.16	
2001–02	39.24	26.26	4.89	18.02	3.44	
2002–03	38.68	26.39	5.64	17.17	3.97	
2003–04	40.26	26.97	5.28	16.57	3.11	
2004–05	37.97	27.47	4.91	17.82	4.19	
2005–06	40.60	26.15	4.59	17.56	4.01	
2006–07	43.23	25.30	4.11	16.58	4.24	
2007–08	43.86	24.64	5.68	16.51	3.40	

| Year | Developmental Expenditure | Non-Developmental Expenditure | | | |
		Interest Payments	Social Security and Food Subsidy	Miscellaneous	Others
2008–09	47.06	21.51	6.26	15.97	3.13
2009–10	45.24	20.58	6.63	18.34	2.81
2010–11	47.68	19.68	6.14	17.95	2.79
2011–12	48.17	19.99	5.15	18.50	3.08
2012–13	49.11	20.14	4.47	18.28	3.10
2013–14	46.68	21.23	5.50	18.51	3.16
2014–15 (R.E.)	47.41	20.24	5.86	18.55	3.21
2015–16 (B.E.)	46.22	21.12	5.48	19.08	3.31

Share of Total Revenue Expenditure (in %)

Source: Indian Public Finance Statistics

Notes: (1) R.E. refers to Revised Estimate; B.E. refers to Budget Estimate

(2) *Miscellaneous* refers to the following items summed together: Organs of state, Fiscal services, Administrative services, Pension and other retirement benefits, Relief on account of natural calamities

(3) *Others* include Appropriation for reduction or avoidance of debt, Technical and economic cooperation with other countries, Compensation and assignments to local bodies and Panchayati Raj institutions, etc.

(4) *Non-Developmental Expenditure* is the sum of *Interest Payments, Social Security and Food Subsidy, Miscellaneous,* and *Others*

(5) Please note the presence of a discontinuity in the series; data for 1990–91 is followed by data for 1995–96

Figure 2.3: Composition of Capital Expenditure, Centre and States, Share of Total 1990–91 to 2015–16

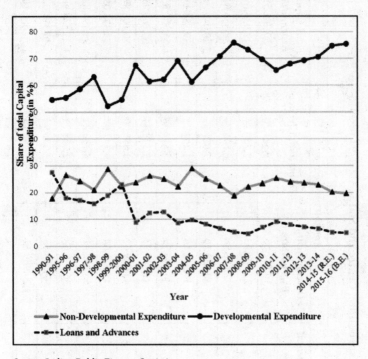

Source: Indian Public Finance Statistics

Notes: (1) R.E. refers to Revised Estimate; B.E. refers to Budget Estimate
(2) Please note there is a discontinuity in the series; data for 1990–91 is followed by data for 1995–96.

Table 2.4a: Composition of Capital Expenditure, Centre and States, 1990–91 to 2015–16

Year		Amount in Rs crore		
	Non-Developmental Expenditure	Developmental Expenditure	Loans and Advances	Total Capital Expenditure
1990–91	5,378.24	16,502.05	8,321.30	30,201.59
1995–96	11,409.50	23,766.95	7,750.24	42,926.69
1996–97	9,322.99	22,498.58	6,564.74	38,386.31
1997–98	10,087.22	30,333.10	7,629.59	48,049.91
1998–99	17,039.74	30,942.16	11,204.21	59,186.11
1999–2000	14,929.36	36,408.99	15,312.48	66,650.83
2000–01	14,471.38	41,140.43	5,348.44	60,960.25
2001–02	18,370.40	43,079.62	8,655.79	70,105.81
2002–03	18,397.44	45,628.64	9,347.97	73,374.05
2003–04	21,004.17	65,362.41	8,132.24	94,498.82
2004–05	36,298.01	76,859.68	12,222.29	1,25,379.98
2005–06	36,809.47	97,565.65	11,935.94	1,46,311.06
2006–07	38,507.34	1,20,980.61	11,192.15	1,70,680.10

Year	Amount in Rs crore			
	Non-Developmental Expenditure	Developmental Expenditure	Loans and Advances	Total Capital Expenditure
2007–08	44,106.16	1,77,839.46	12,224.05	2,34,169.67
2008–09	49,359.48	1,63,319.63	10,175.56	2,22,854.67
2009–10	63,845.64	1,90,086.45	18,874.46	2,72,806.55
2010–11	82,488.21	2,13,661.75	29,450.76	3,25,600.72
2011–12	82,054.45	2,33,034.95	27,020.13	3,42,109.53
2012–13	88,298.00	2,59,757.00	26,711.00	3,74,767.00
2013–14	96,478.00	2,97,989.00	27,425.00	4,21,892.00
2014–15(R.E.)	1,09,061.00	4,03,925.00	27,510.00	5,40,496.00
2015–16 (B.E.)	1,22,677.00	4,70,635.00	30,615.00	6,23,927.00

Source: Indian Public Finance Statistics

Notes: (1) R.E. refers to Revised Estimate; B.E. refers to Budget Estimate
(2) Please note the presence of a discontinuity in the series; data for 1990–91 is followed by data for 1995–96.

Table 2.4b: Composition of Capital Expenditure, Centre and States, % of Total 1990–91 to 2015–16

Year	Share of total Capital Expenditure (in %)		
	Non–Developmental Expenditure	Developmental Expenditure	Loans and Advances
1990–91	17.81	54.64	27.55
1995–96	26.58	55.37	18.05
1996–97	24.29	58.61	17.10
1997–98	20.99	63.13	15.88
1998–99	28.79	52.28	18.93
1999–2000	22.40	54.63	22.97
2000–01	23.74	67.49	8.77
2001–02	26.20	61.45	12.35
2002–03	25.07	62.19	12.74
2003–04	22.23	69.17	8.61
2004–05	28.95	61.30	9.75
2005–06	25.16	66.68	8.16
2006–07	22.56	70.88	6.56
2007–08	18.84	75.94	5.22
2008–09	22.15	73.29	4.57
2009–10	23.40	69.68	6.92
2010–11	25.33	65.62	9.05
2011–12	23.98	68.12	7.90
2012–13	23.56	69.31	7.13
2013–14	22.87	70.63	6.50
2014–15 (R.E.)	20.18	74.73	5.09
2015–16 (B.E.)	19.66	75.43	4.91

Source: Indian Public Finance Statistics

Notes: (1) R.E. refers to Revised Estimate; B.E. refers to Budget Estimate
(2) Please note the presence of a discontinuity in the series; data for 1990–91 is followed by data for 1995–96.

Figure 2.4: Composition of Total Receipts, Centre and States, Share of Total 1990–91 to 2015–16

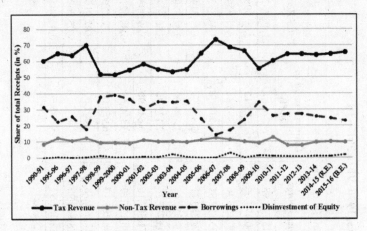

Source: Indian Public Finance Statistics

Notes: (1) R.E. refers to Revised Estimate; B.E. refers to Budget Estimate

(2) *Borrowings* is calculated as the sum of 'Domestic Capital Receipts' net of *Disinvestment of Equity*, and 'External Capital Receipts'.

(3) Please note there is a discontinuity in the series; data for 1990–91 is followed by data for 1995–96.

Table 2.5a: Composition of Total Receipts, Centre and States, 1990–91 to 2015–16

Year	Tax Revenue	Non–Tax Revenue	Borrowings	Disinvestment of Equity	Total Receipts
1990–91	87,723.28	12,286.78	45,741.98	–	1,45,752.04
1995–96	1,75,259.40	32,867.70	60,474.65	1,397.13	2,69,998.88
1996–97	2,00,055.73	33,068.19	80,355.46	455.44	3,13,934.82
1997–98	2,13,065.06	36,999.30	53,857.51	911.78	3,04,833.65
1998–99	2,33,017.88	41,386.43	1,69,236.71	5,873.94	4,49,514.96
1999–2000	2,74,583.08	48,951.09	2,07,512.45	1,724.00	5,32,770.62
2000–01	3,05,320.24	49,361.79	2,03,797.26	2,125.40	5,60,604.69
2001–02	3,32,137.02	62,338.23	1,71,687.16	3,646.00	5,69,808.41
2002–03	3,75,219.29	68,040.14	2,38,117.10	3,150.69	6,84,527.22
2003–04	4,14,084.77	77,927.38	2,68,205.10	16,953.00	7,77,170.25
2004–05	4,94,370.10	86,533.28	3,17,021.78	4,091.00	9,02,016.16
2005–06	5,87,687.81	99,412.27	2,18,868.92	–	9,05,969.00
2006–07	7,36,707.72	1,23,391.71	1,42,352.57	533.54	10,02,985.54

Amount in Rs crore

Year	Tax Revenue	Non–Tax Revenue	Borrowings	Disinvestment of Equity	Total Receipts
			Amount in Rs crore		
2007–08	8,70,329.09	1,40,906.61	2,17,059.90	38,795.57	12,67,091.17
2008–09	9,15,449.99	1,36,971.95	3,26,132.50	565.93	13,79,120.37
2009–10	10,00,843.73	1,63,173.90	6,22,763.34	24,581.43	18,11,362.40
2010–11	12,71,665.35	2,66,926.13	5,47,285.80	22,846.00	21,08,723.28
2011–12	14,67,890.43	1,74,831.76	6,18,309.50	18,088.00	22,79,119.69
2012–13	17,16,117.00	2,06,292.00	7,22,956.00	18,089.00	26,63,454.00
2013–14	18,79,143.00	2,80,377.00	7,52,680.00	29,368.00	29,41,568.00
2014–15 (R.E.)	20,98,175.00	3,24,132.00	7,99,643.00	31,350.00	32,53,300.00
2015–16 (B.E.)	24,19,085.00	3,53,907.00	8,48,075.00	69,500.00	36,90,567.00

Source: Indian Public Finance Statistics

Notes: (1) R.E. refers to Revised Estimate; B.E. refers to Budget Estimate

(2) *Borrowings* is calculated as the sum of 'Domestic Capital Receipts' net of *Disinvestment of Equity*, and 'External Capital Receipts'

(3) *Total Receipts* is the sum of *Tax Revenue, Non–Tax Revenue, Borrowings* and *Disinvestment of Equity*

(4) Please note the presence of a discontinuity in the series; data for 1990–91 is followed by data for 1995–96

Table 2.5b: Composition of Total Receipts, Centre and States, Share of Total 1990–91 to 2015–16

Year	Share of Total Receipts (in %)			
	Tax Revenue	Non–Tax Revenue	Borrowings	Disinvestment of Equity
1990–91	60.19	8.43	31.38	0.00
1995–96	64.91	12.17	22.40	0.52
1996–97	63.73	10.53	25.60	0.15
1997–98	69.90	12.14	17.67	0.30
1998–99	51.84	9.21	37.65	1.31
1999–2000	51.54	9.19	38.95	0.32
2000–01	54.46	8.81	36.35	0.38
2001–02	58.29	10.94	30.13	0.64
2002–03	54.81	9.94	34.79	0.46
2003–04	53.28	10.03	34.51	2.18
2004–05	54.81	9.59	35.15	0.45
2005–06	64.87	10.97	24.16	0.00
2006–07	73.45	12.30	14.19	0.05
2007–08	68.69	11.12	17.13	3.06
2008–09	66.38	9.93	23.65	0.04
2009–10	55.25	9.01	34.38	1.36
2010–11	60.30	12.66	25.95	1.08
2011–12	64.41	7.67	27.13	0.79
2012–13	64.43	7.75	27.14	0.68
2013–14	63.88	9.53	25.59	1.00
2014–15 (R.E.)	64.49	9.96	24.58	0.96
2015–16 (B.E.)	65.55	9.59	22.98	1.88

Source: Indian Public Finance Statistics

Notes: (1) R.E. refers to Revised Estimate; B.E. refers to Budget Estimate

(2) *Borrowings* is calculated as the sum of 'Domestic Capital Receipts' net of *Disinvestment of Equity,* and 'External Capital Receipts'

(3) Please note the presence of a discontinuity in the series; data for 1990–91 is followed by data for 1995–96

Figure 2.5: Overall Budgetary Position, Centre and States, % of GDP 1990–91 to

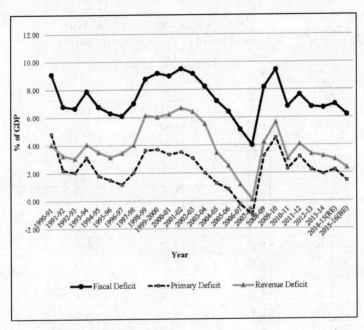

Source: Indian Public Finance Statistics

Notes: (1) R.E. refers to Revised Estimate; B.E. refers to Budget Estimate
(2) 'GDP' refers to the Gross Domestic Product at Market Prices (at Current Prices) with the base year as 2004–05 (for the new series with the base year as 2011–12, splicing has been done to make the new series comparable with the old series)
(3) Note that there was a revenue surplus in 2006–07 and 2007–08, hence the revenue deficit for these two years is plotted below the horizontal axis

Table 2.6: Overall Budgetary Position, Centre and States, % of GDP 1990–91 to 2015–16

Year	Values are expressed as a % of GDP		
	Fiscal Deficit	*Primary Deficit*	*Revenue Deficit*
1990–91	9.10	4.83	4.04
1991–92	6.80	2.20	3.25
1992–93	6.67	2.04	3.05
1993–94	7.89	3.11	4.06
1994–95	6.77	1.80	3.50
1995–96	6.31	1.50	3.14
1996–97	6.11	1.18	3.43
1997–98	7.01	2.02	4.02
1998–99	8.76	3.62	6.13
1999–2000	9.17	3.70	6.03
2000–01	8.99	3.33	6.24
2001–02	9.50	3.50	6.69
2002–03	9.16	3.06	6.41
2003–04	8.23	2.01	5.54
2004–05	7.19	1.25	3.47
2005–06	6.42	0.83	2.52
2006–07	5.14	−0.29	1.18
2007–08	4.00	−1.00	0.08
2008–09	8.17	3.24	4.22
2009–10	9.43	4.53	5.65
2010–11	6.79	2.29	3.03
2011–12	7.64	3.17	4.07
2012–13	6.76	2.23	3.35
2013–14	6.69	1.92	3.21
2014–15 (R.E.)	6.95	2.21	2.96
2015–16 (B.E.)	6.19	1.43	2.36

Source: Indian Public Finance Statistics

Notes: (1) R.E. refers to Revised Estimate; B.E. refers to Budget Estimate
(2) 'GDP' refers to the Gross Domestic Product at Market Prices (at Current Prices) with the base year as 2004–05 (for the new series with the base year as 2011–12, splicing has been done to make the new series comparable with the old series)
(3) (–) sign indicates a surplus

Table 3.1: Year of introduction of VAT/GST in various countries across the world

Country	Year of VAT/GST Implementation
France	1954
Brazil	1964
Germany	1968
Sweden	1969
UK	1973
Israel	1976
South Korea	1977
Mexico	1980
Indonesia	1984
Spain	1986
Japan	1989
Pakistan	1990
Kenya	1990
Bangladesh	1991
Egypt	1991
South Africa	1991
Canada	1991
Thailand	1992
Singapore	1993
China	1994
Switzerland	1995
Nepal	1997
Australia	2000
Sri Lanka	2002
Zimbabwe	2004
India	2005
Iran	2008

Source: Malaysian Customs Department http://gst.customs.gov.my/en/gst/Pages/gst_ci.aspx

Table 3.2: Number of Countries Implementing VAT/GST (as in 2014)

Region	No. of Countries Implementing VAT	Major Countries Not Implementing VAT/GST
ASEAN	7	Malaysia, Brunei, Myanmar
Asia	19	Afghanistan, Bhutan, Iraq, Kuwait, Maldives, North Korea, Oman, Qatar, Saudi Arabia, UAE, Yemen
Europe	53	
Oceania	7	
Africa	44	Liberia, Libya, South Sudan
South America	11	Cuba
Caribbean, Central & North America	19	United States of America
Total	**160**	

Source: Malaysian Customs Department http://gst.customs.gov.my/en/gst/Pages/gst_ci.aspx

Annexure 5.1: Time Line of Roll Out of GST

Chapter 3 presented an outline of the various ideas on VAT and GST as they evolved from the late 1970s. The steps taken towards introduction of GST may be summarized as the follows:

1. VAT suggested in the form of MANVAT in the Indirect Tax Enquiry Report in 1978.
2. Implementation of MODVAT suggested by the Long Term Fiscal Policy Report, 1985.
3. In the Union Budget of 1986–87, implementation of MODVAT proposed for collection of excise duties from select commodities.
4. Taxation Enquiry Committee in 1991 suggests a more comprehensive VAT by bringing in a tax on Services and extension of VAT to sales tax.
5. Implementation of a tax on select Services from 1994.
6. MODVAT converted to CENVAT from 2000 to distinguish it from VAT which term was to be used for sales tax to be implemented by the states.
7. In 2000 an Empowered Committee of State Finance Ministers was set up under the chairpersonship of Dr Ashim Dasgupta, then finance minister of West Bengal, for the implementation of VAT.
8. In 2004, the Task Force Report on Indirect Taxes suggested moving towards a more Comprehensive VAT.
9. GST was proposed by the finance minister Mr P. Chidambaram in the Union Budget 2006–07. He suggested implementation from 1 April 2010. The Empowered Committee was asked to prepare the road map of implementation.
10. In 2008, the Empowered Committee submitted a Report to the Government of India with a blueprint of a GST for India.
11. In 2009, the First Discussion Paper was put out in the public domain for suggestions.
12. In 2009, the then finance minister, Mr Pranab Mukherjee announced that the basic structure of GST set out by the Empowered Committee was acceptable to the government and that it would be implemented from 2010.
13. BJP and especially the then CM of Gujarat opposed the basic structure of GST.

14. Implementation of GST postponed to 1 April 2011 by Mr Pranab Mukherjee.

15. 115th Constitution Amendment Bill for GST implementation presented in Lok Sabha on 22 March 2011.

16. Due to opposition from the Opposition parties, the Bill was referred to the Parliamentary Standing Committee on Finance which was then headed by Mr Yashwant Sinha.

17. In November 2012, Mr Chidambaram held meetings with the state finance ministers to resolve differences on various issues.

18. Mr Chidambaram declared the government's decision to introduce GST soon and allotted funds in the Union Budget to compensate for any losses that the states may suffer due to introduction of GST.

19. The Parliamentary Standing Committee on Finance in its Report to Parliament in August 2013 made recommendations for improvements in GST design.

20. The then CM of Gujarat opposed the GST Bill in October 2013 on the grounds that the state would lose substantially due to the implementation of GST.

21. GST Bill lapsed as the Lok Sabha is dissolved in 2014.

22. NDA government which came to power in May 2014, introduced the Constitution (122nd) Amendment Bill in Lok Sabha in December 2014.

23. The finance minister set the deadline of 1 April 2016 for rollout of GST.

24. Lok Sabha passed the Bill in May 2015 and it was presented in the Rajya Sabha.

25. Congress opposed the Bill in Rajya Sabha and demanded that it be sent to Select Committee. It also demanded that GST be capped at 18 per cent.

26. The Bill was sent to the joint Committee of Lok Sabha and Rajya Sabha in May 2015.

27. Agreement was reached in August 2016 to pass the Bill and it became the Constitution (One Hundred and First Amendment) Act, 2016.

28. The required sixteen states ratified the GST Act by September 2016 and the President gave assent to it.

29. The Act contained a provision for setting up of the GST Council of Finance Ministers of all states. As per the Article 279A (1) of the

amended Constitution, this Council was constituted and it first met in September 2016. It replaced the Empowered Committee.

30. In November 2016, the GST Council proposed four slabs of tax—5 per cent, 12 per cent, 18 per cent and 28 per cent. An additional cess on luxury and sin goods was also proposed.

31. The finance minister announced the GST roll out date of 1 July 2017 on 16 January 2017. Various contentious issues between the states and the Centre were also resolved.

32. A bill for compensating the states for any loss of revenue in the first five years was also approved by the GST Council in February 2017. This was a major worry for the states which got resolved.

33. In March 2017, the Council approved the draft of the CGST and IGST bills.

34. The key bills were passed in the Parliament in March-end 2017 and became Acts.

35. A large number of goods were placed in the four slabs of tax. Items of mass consumption were either placed in the lowest slab of 5 per cent or were exempted. Cess rate was also fixed.

36. In June 2017, all the states passed the State GST Bill, except Jammu and Kashmir.

37. On 30 June, midnight, GST rolled out in a grand ceremony in the Parliament with the Left, Congress and Trinamool Congress skipping the ceremony.

Annexure 5.2: GST Constitution Amendment Act

रजिस्ट्री सं॰ डी॰ एल॰—(एन)04/0007/2003—16   REGISTERED NO. DL—(N)04/0007/2003—16

भारत का राजपत्र
The Gazette of India
असाधारण

EXTRAORDINARY

भाग II — खण्ड 1

PART II — Section 1

प्राधिकार से प्रकाशित

PUBLISHED BY AUTHORITY

सं॰ 55]   नई दिल्ली, बृहस्पतिवार, सितम्बर 8, 2016/ भाद्र 17, 1938 (शक)

No. 55]   NEW DELHI, THURSDAY, SEPTEMBER 8, 2016/ BHADRA 17, 1938 (SAKA)

इस भाग में भिन्न पृष्ठ संख्या दी जाती है जिससे कि यह अलग संकलन के रूप में रखा जा सके।

Separate paging is given to this Part in order that it may be filed as a separate compilation.

MINISTRY OF LAW AND JUSTICE
(Legislative Department)

New Delhi, the 8th September, 2016/*Bhadra* 17, 1938 (*Saka*)

The following Act of Parliament received the assent of the President on the 8th September, 2016, and is hereby published for general information:—

THE CONSTITUTION (ONE HUNDRED AND FIRST AMENDMENT) ACT, 2016

[8th September, 2016.]

An Act further to amend the Constitution of India.

Be it enacted by Parliament in the Sixty-seventh Year of the Republic of India as follows:—

1. (*1*) This Act may be called the Constitution (One Hundred and First Amendment) Act, 2016.

Short title and commencement.

(*2*) It shall come into force on such date as the Central Government may, by notification in the Official Gazette, appoint, and different dates may be appointed for different provisions of this Act and any reference in any such provision to the commencement of this Act shall be construed as a reference to the commencement of that provision.

2. After article 246 of the Constitution, the following article shall be inserted, namely:—

Insertion of new article 246A.

"**246A.** (1) Notwithstanding anything contained in articles 246 and 254, Parliament, and, subject to clause (2), the Legislature of every State, have power to make laws with respect to goods and services tax imposed by the Union or by such State.

Special provision with respect to goods and services tax.

(2) Parliament has exclusive power to make laws with respect to goods and services tax where the supply of goods, or of services, or both takes place in the course of inter-State trade or commerce.

Explanation.—The provisions of this article, shall, in respect of goods and services tax referred to in clause (5) of article 279A, take effect from the date recommended by the Goods and Services Tax Council.".

Amendment of article 248.

3. In article 248 of the Constitution, in clause (1), for the word "Parliament", the words, figures and letter "Subject to article 246A, Parliament" shall be substituted.

Amendment of article 249.

4. In article 249 of the Constitution, in clause (1), after the words "with respect to", the words, figures and letter "goods and services tax provided under article 246A or" shall be inserted.

Amendment of article 250.

5. In article 250 of the Constitution, in clause (1), after the words "with respect to", the words, figures and letter "goods and services tax provided under article 246A or" shall be inserted.

Amendment of article 268.

6. In article 268 of the Constitution, in clause (1), the words "and such duties of excise on medicinal and toilet preparations" shall be omitted.

Omission of article 268A.

7. Article 268A of the Constitution, as inserted by section 2 of the Constitution (Eighty-eighth Amendment) Act, 2003 shall be omitted.

Amendment of article 269.

8. In article 269 of the Constitution, in clause (1), after the words "consignment of goods", the words, figures and letter "except as provided in article 269A" shall be inserted.

Insertion of new article 269A.
Levy and collection of goods and services tax in course of inter-State trade or commerce.

9. After article 269 of the Constitution, the following article shall be inserted, namely:—

"**269A.** (1) Goods and services tax on supplies in the course of inter-State trade or commerce shall be levied and collected by the Government of India and such tax shall be apportioned between the Union and the States in the manner as may be provided by Parliament by law on the recommendations of the Goods and Services Tax Council.

Explanation.—For the purposes of this clause, supply of goods, or of services, or both in the course of import into the territory of India shall be deemed to be supply of goods, or of services, or both in the course of inter-State trade or commerce.

(2) The amount apportioned to a State under clause (1) shall not form part of the Consolidated Fund of India.

(3) Where an amount collected as tax levied under clause (1) has been used for payment of the tax levied by a State under article 246A, such amount shall not form part of the Consolidated Fund of India.

(4) Where an amount collected as tax levied by a State under article 246A has been used for payment of the tax levied under clause (1), such amount shall not form part of the Consolidated Fund of the State.

(5) Parliament may, by law, formulate the principles for determining the place of supply, and when a supply of goods, or of services, or both takes place in the course of inter-State trade or commerce.".

Amendment of article 270.

10. In article 270 of the Constitution,—

(*i*) in clause (1), for the words, figures and letter "articles 268, 268A and 269", the words, figures and letter "articles 268, 269 and 269A" shall be substituted;

(*ii*) after clause (1), the following clauses shall be inserted, namely:—

"(1A) The tax collected by the Union under clause (1) of article 246A shall also be distributed between the Union and the States in the manner provided in clause (2).

(1B) The tax levied and collected by the Union under clause (2) of article 246A and article 269A, which has been used for payment of the tax levied by the Union under clause (1) of article 246A, and the amount apportioned to the Union under clause (1) of article 269A, shall also be distributed between the Union and the States in the manner provided in clause (2).".

Amendment of article 271.

11. In article 271 of the Constitution, after the words "in those articles", the words, figures and letter "except the goods and services tax under article 246A," shall be inserted.

12. After article 279 of the Constitution, the following article shall be inserted, namely:— Insertion of new article 279A.

"279A. (1) The President shall, within sixty days from the date of commencement of the Constitution (One Hundred and First Amendment) Act, 2016, by order, constitute a Council to be called the Goods and Services Tax Council. Goods and Services Tax Council.

(2) The Goods and Services Tax Council shall consist of the following members, namely:—

    (*a*) the Union Finance Minister........................   Chairperson;

    (*b*) the Union Minister of State in charge of Revenue or Finance.................   Member;

    (*c*) the Minister in charge of Finance or Taxation or any other Minister nominated by each State Government...................Members.

(3) The Members of the Goods and Services Tax Council referred to in sub-clause (*c*) of clause (2) shall, as soon as may be, choose one amongst themselves to be the Vice-Chairperson of the Council for such period as they may decide.

(4) The Goods and Services Tax Council shall make recommendations to the Union and the States on—

    (*a*) the taxes, cesses and surcharges levied by the Union, the States and the local bodies which may be subsumed in the goods and services tax;

    (*b*) the goods and services that may be subjected to, or exempted from the goods and services tax;

    (*c*) model Goods and Services Tax Laws, principles of levy, apportionment of Goods and Services Tax levied on supplies in the course of inter-State trade or commerce under article 269A and the principles that govern the place of supply;

    (*d*) the threshold limit of turnover below which goods and services may be exempted from goods and services tax;

    (*e*) the rates including floor rates with bands of goods and services tax;

    (*f*) any special rate or rates for a specified period, to raise additional resources during any natural calamity or disaster;

    (*g*) special provision with respect to the States of Arunachal Pradesh, Assam, Jammu and Kashmir, Manipur, Meghalaya, Mizoram, Nagaland, Sikkim, Tripura, Himachal Pradesh and Uttarakhand; and

    (*h*) any other matter relating to the goods and services tax, as the Council may decide.

(5) The Goods and Services Tax Council shall recommend the date on which the goods and services tax be levied on petroleum crude, high speed diesel, motor spirit (commonly known as petrol), natural gas and aviation turbine fuel.

(6) While discharging the functions conferred by this article, the Goods and Services Tax Council shall be guided by the need for a harmonised structure of goods and services tax and for the development of a harmonised national market for goods and services.

(7) One-half of the total number of Members of the Goods and Services Tax Council shall constitute the quorum at its meetings.

(8) The Goods and Services Tax Council shall determine the procedure in the performance of its functions.

(9) Every decision of the Goods and Services Tax Council shall be taken at a meeting, by a majority of not less than three-fourths of the weighted votes of the members present and voting, in accordance with the following principles, namely:—

    (*a*) the vote of the Central Government shall have a weightage of one-third of the total votes cast, and

    (*b*) the votes of all the State Governments taken together shall have a weightage of two-thirds of the total votes cast,

in that meeting.

(10) No act or proceedings of the Goods and Services Tax Council shall be invalid merely by reason of—

    (*a*) any vacancy in, or any defect in, the constitution of the Council; or

    (*b*) any defect in the appointment of a person as a Member of the Council; or

    (*c*) any procedural irregularity of the Council not affecting the merits of the case.

(11) The Goods and Services Tax Council shall establish a mechanism to adjudicate any dispute—

    (a) between the Government of India and one or more States; or

    (b) between the Government of India and any State or States on one side and one or more other States on the other side; or

    (c) between two or more States,

arising out of the recommendations of the Council or implementation thereof.".

Amendment of article 286.

13. In article 286 of the Constitution,—

    (*i*) in clause (1),—

        (*A*) for the words "the sale or purchase of goods where such sale or purchase takes place", the words "the supply of goods or of services or both, where such supply takes place" shall be substituted;

        (*B*) in sub-clause *(b)*, for the word "goods", at both the places where it occurs, the words "goods or services or both" shall be substituted;

    (*ii*) in clause (2), for the words "sale or purchase of goods takes place", the words "supply of goods or of services or both" shall be substituted;

    (*iii*) clause (3) shall be omitted.

Amendment of article 366.

14. In article 366 of the Constitution,—

    (*i*) after clause (12), the following clause shall be inserted, namely:—

        '(12A) "goods and services tax" means any tax on supply of goods, or services or both except taxes on the supply of the alcoholic liquor for human consumption;';

    (*ii*) after clause (26), the following clauses shall be inserted, namely:—

        '(26A) "Services" means anything other than goods;

        (26B) "State" with reference to articles 246A, 268, 269, 269A and article 279A includes a Union territory with Legislature;'.

Amendment of article 368.

15. In article 368 of the Constitution, in clause (2), in the proviso, in clause (*a*), for the words and figures "article 162 or article 241", the words, figures and letter "article 162, article 241 or article 279A" shall be substituted.

Amendment of Sixth Schedule.

16. In the Sixth Schedule to the Constitution, in paragraph 8, in sub-paragraph (3),—

    (*i*) in clause *(c),* the word "and" occurring at the end shall be omitted;

    (*ii*) in clause *(d)*, the word "and" shall be inserted at the end;

(iii) after clause (d), the following clause shall be inserted, namely:—

"(e) taxes on entertainment and amusements.".

17. In the Seventh Schedule to the Constitution,— Amendment of Seventh Schedule.

(a) in List I—Union List,—

(i) for entry 84, the following entry shall be substituted, namely:—

"84. Duties of excise on the following goods manufactured or produced in India, namely:—

(a) petroleum crude;

(b) high speed diesel;

(c) motor spirit (commonly known as petrol);

(d) natural gas;

(e) aviation turbine fuel; and

(f) tobacco and tobacco products.";

(ii) entries 92 and 92C shall be omitted;

(b) in List II—State List,—

(i) entry 52 shall be omitted;

(ii) for entry 54, the following entry shall be substituted, namely:—

"54. Taxes on the sale of petroleum crude, high speed diesel, motor spirit (commonly known as petrol), natural gas, aviation turbine fuel and alcoholic liquor for human consumption, but not including sale in the course of inter-State trade or commerce or sale in the course of international trade or commerce of such goods.";

(iii) entry 55 shall be omitted;

(iv) for entry 62, the following entry shall be substituted, namely:—

"62. Taxes on entertainments and amusements to the extent levied and collected by a Panchayat or a Municipality or a Regional Council or a District Council.".

18. Parliament shall, by law, on the recommendation of the Goods and Services Tax Council, provide for compensation to the States for loss of revenue arising on account of implementation of the goods and services tax for a period of five years. Compensation to States for loss of revenue on account of introduction of goods and services tax.

19. Notwithstanding anything in this Act, any provision of any law relating to tax on goods or services or on both in force in any State immediately before the commencement of this Act, which is inconsistent with the provisions of the Constitution as amended by this Act shall continue to be in force until amended or repealed by a competent Legislature or other competent authority or until expiration of one year from such commencement, whichever is earlier. Transitional provisions.

20. (1) If any difficulty arises in giving effect to the provisions of the Constitution as amended by this Act (including any difficulty in relation to the transition from the provisions of the Constitution as they stood immediately before the date of assent of the President to this Act to the provisions of the Constitution as amended by this Act), the President may, Power of President to remove difficulties.

by order, make such provisions, including any adaptation or modification of any provision of the Constitution as amended by this Act or law, as appear to the President to be necessary or expedient for the purpose of removing the difficulty:

Provided that no such order shall be made after the expiry of three years from the date of such assent.

(2) Every order made under sub-section (*1*) shall, as soon as may be after it is made, be laid before each House of Parliament.

———

DR. G. NARAYANA RAJU,
Secretary to the Govt. of India.

MANOJ KUMAR

Digitally signed by
MANOJ KUMAR
Date: 2016.09.08
19:53:04 +05'30'

PRINTED BY THE GENERAL MANAGER, GOVERNMENT OF INDIA PRESS, MINTO ROAD, NEW DELHI
AND PUBLISHED BY THE CONTROLLER OF PUBLICATIONS, DELHI—2016.

Annexure 5.3: GST Council Meetings (Up to March 2018)

Meeting Number	Date	Venue
1	22nd & 23rd September, 2016	New Delhi
2	30th September, 2016	New Delhi
3	18th & 19th October, 2016	New Delhi
4	3rd & 4th November, 2016	New Delhi
5	2nd & 3rd December, 2016	New Delhi
6	11th December, 2016	New Delhi
7	22nd & 23rd December, 2016	New Delhi
8	3rd & 4th January, 2017	New Delhi
9	16th January, 2017	New Delhi
10	18th February, 2017	Udaipur
11	4th March, 2017	New Delhi
12	16th March, 2017	New Delhi
13	31st March, 2017	New Delhi
14	18th & 19th May, 2017	Srinagar
15	3rd June, 2017	New Delhi
16	11th June, 2017	New Delhi
17	18th June, 2018	New Delhi
18	30th June, 2018	New Delhi
19	17th July, 2017	Meeting held via videoconferencing
20	5th August, 2017	New Delhi
21	9th September, 2017	Hyderabad
22	6th October, 2017	New Delhi
23	10th November, 2017	Guwahati
24	16th December 2017	Meeting held via videoconferencing
25	18th January, 2018	New Delhi
26	10th March 2018	New Delhi

Source: http://www.gstcouncil.gov.in/meetings

Annexure 5.4: GST Registrations and Returns Filed

S. No.	Details	As on 01st April, 2018
1	No. of transited (migrated) taxpayers	70,42,675
2	Of which, how many did not opt for complete migration	6,36,189
3	No. of completely migrated taxpayers	64,06,486
4	Total No. of new applications received for registration	47,27,074
5	No. of applications approved	41,16,360
6	No. of applications rejected	5,55,826
7	No. of applications which are still in process	54,888
8	**Total No. of taxpayers; new + migrated (3 + 5)**	**1,05,22,846**
9	No. of taxpayers who have opted for composition scheme	17,86,735
10	No. of 3 (B) returns filed for July, 2017	63,62,511
11	No. of 3(B) returns filed for August, 2017	68,06,964
12	No. of 3(B) returns filed for September, 2017	70,50,408

13	No. of 3(B) returns filed for October, 2017	67,01,752
14	No. of 3(B) returns filed for November, 2017	66,80,408
15	No. of 3(B) returns filed for December, 2017	66,37,923
16	No. of 3(B) returns filed for January, 2018	65,27,602
17	No. of 3(B) returns filed for February, 2018	61,65,324
18	No. of GSTR 1 returns filed for July, 2017	59,71,488
19	No. of GSTR 1 returns filed for August, 2017	22,14,857
20	No. of GSTR 1 returns filed for September, 2017	59,71,488
21	No. of GSTR 1 returns filed for October, 2017	22,16,652
22	No. of GSTR 1 returns filed for November, 2017	22,01,501
23	No. of GSTR 1 returns filed for December, 2017	55,65,273
24	No. of GSTR 1 returns filed for January, 2018	18,44,980
25	No. of GSTR 1 returns filed for February, 2018	6,63,351
26	No. of GSTR 2 returns filed for July, 2017	25,72,552
27	No. of GSTR 4 returns filed for quarter July-September, 2017	9,04,815
28	No. of GSTR 4 returns filed for quarter October-December, 2017	12,77,517

Source: GoI (2018a)

Table 5.1: Tax Revenue to All States from Various Products Not Covered by GST, 2016–17

	(Rs Crore)
Product	**Tax Revenue**
Petroleum Products	451424.0
Alcohol and Narcotics Products	108415.7
Electricity	28820.0
Total	588659.6

Source: 1. Petroleum Planning and Analysis Cell, Ministry of Natural Gas, Government of India.
2. State Finances: A Study of Budgets, Reserve Bank of India

Table 5.2 Circulars, Notifications and Orders Issued Up to 31 May 2018

Category	Circulars	Notifications	Other than Rate				Rate Changes				Orders	Grand Total
			CT	UT	IT	Cess	CTR	ITR	UTR	CCR		
Exemption		73	4		4		20	24	20	1		73
Rates		65					20	19	20	6		65
Miscellaneous	5	56	18	19	7	1	3	4	3	1		61
Due Dates and Extension		52	40								12	52
Clarification	36											36
Procedural	9	25	11	1	1		1	1	1			25
Rules		25	19	5	1							25
RCM		24					8	8	8			24
Refund		18					6	6	6			18
Composition		8	3	3							2	8
Exports		4	4									4
Grand Total	50	349	99	28	13	1	58	62	58	8	14	391

Source: Pampapathi, V.G. (2018). https://www.scribd.com/document/378531597/GST-Notification-Summary
Compiled from GST Website

Note: CT is Central Tax   UT is Union Territory   IT is Integrated Tax
CCR is Compensation Cess Rate   CTR is Central Tax Rate   UTR is Union Territory Rate
ITR is Integrated Tax Rate

ACKNOWLEDGEMENTS

The ideas underlying this book have been developed over a long period of time but they crystalized more and more since 2009 when implementation of GST was pushed by the government.

I am grateful to my Public Finance students over the years for keeping me on my toes which enabled me to deepen my understanding of the issues of Public Finance. I would like to acknowledge my PhD students who helped me sharpen my understanding of policy issues which contributed to the development of my ideas.

I would like to acknowledge the research assistance provided for this book by Ms Manisha Jain and Mr Ankur Verma, both of Centre for Economic Studies and Planning, JNU. My discussions with Mr Jogiranjan Panigrahi, my former MPhil student, Mr Vishnu Bhargava who runs an auto parts company and Mr Shailesh of TaxIndiaonline were most helpful. I would be remiss if I do not acknowledge Mr Chitkara, a chartered accountant, for the help he provided in the matter.

I am indebted to Prof. Saumen Chatopadhyay, Dr Astha Ahuja, Dr Sunil Dharan, Dr Prafulla Prushty, Dr Shyam Sunder and Sultan Singh for commenting on parts of the book and giving their valuable suggestions.

I would like to especially thank Mr Lohit Jagwani of Penguin for his constant interest and support in producing this volume. I would also like to thank Ms Paloma Dutta who very skilfully edited this volume.

Through much of the summer of 2018, I worked at the book and made myself scarce from work at home. The burden fell on my wife, Neerja, and my son, Nakul. I must not forget my mother who passed away recently and I regret that due to pressure of work I did not spend as much time with her as I should have. She was ever an inspiration to me.

BIBLIOGRAPHY

Ali, M. (2015). '23 Lakh Apply for 368 Peon Posts in Uttar Pradesh'. *The Hindu*. 17 September. http://www.thehindu.com/news/national/other-states/23-lakh-apply-for-368-peon-posts-in-uttar-pradesh/article7660341.ece. Accessed August 2017.

Banerjee, S. and S. Prasad. (2017). 'Small Businesses in the GST Regime', *Economic and Political Weekly*. Vol. 52, Issue No. 38. 23 September.

Bhaduri, A. (1986). *Macroeconomics: The Dynamics of Commodity Production*. London: Palgrave Macmillan.

Bhushan, P. (2010). 'The Revolving Door of the World Bank: Suborning Policy and Decision-makers by its Pocketbook'. In Kelly, M. and D. D'Souza (Ed.). 2010. *The World Bank in India: Undermining Sovereignty, Distorting Development*. N. Delhi: Orient BlackSwan.

Chattopadhyay, S. (2018). *Macroeconomics of the Black Economy*. Hyderabad: Orient BlackSwan.

Cowell, F.A. (1990). *Cheating the Government*. Cambridge, Massachusetts: MIT Press.

Cullis, J.G. and P.R. Jones. (1987). *Microeconomics and the Public Economy: A Defence of the Leviathan*. Oxford: Basil Blackwell.

Desai, J.P. (2008). *Accountability: Angst, Awareness, Action*. Delhi: Pearson.

ET Bureau. (2017). 'Slowdown in New Investments Post Demonetisation: CMIE'. *Economic Times*. 3 January. https://economictimes.indiatimes.com/news/economy/finance/slowdown-in-new-investments-post-demonetisation-cmie/articleshow/56302642.cms

FE Bureau. (2017). 'GST Rates on Sweets, Garments: CBEC Gives This Clarification'. *Financial Express*. 4 August. https://www.financialexpress.com/economy/gst-rates-on-sweets-garments-cbec-gives-this-clarification/793431/. Accessed 20 July 2018.

FE Bureau. (2018). 'GST Council Meet: GSTN to Now Be 100% Government Owned'. *Financial Express*. 4 May. https://www.financialexpress.

com/industry/gst-council-meet-gstn-to-now-be-100-government-owned/1155871/. Accessed 27 May 2018.

Gandhi, M.K. (1909). *Hind Swaraj*. Navajivan Press.

Ghosh, P. and S.K. Ghosh. (2018). 'Towards a Payroll Reporting in India'. http://www.iimb.ac.in/sites/default/files/Payroll%20in%20India-detailed_0.pdf. Accessed 30 January 2018.

GoI. Department of Economic Affairs, Ministry of Finance. *Economic Survey*. Various Years.

GoI. Union Budget. Various Years.

GoI. Ministry of Finance. Indian Public Finance. Various Years.

GoI. (1956). *Direct Tax Reform: Report of a Survey*. (Chairperson: Kaldor).

GoI. (1978). *Report of the Indirect Taxation Enquiry Committee*. (Chairperson: L.K. Jha).

GoI. Ministry of Finance. (1985). *Long Term Fiscal Policy*.

GoI. Ministry of Finance. (1992). Taxation Reform Committee Report. (Chairperson: R. J. Chelliah).

GoI. (2002). *Report of the Task Force on Indirect Taxes*. (Chairperson: V. Kelkar).

GoI. (2005). *Budget 2005–06, Speech of Minister of Finance, Mr P. Chidambaram*.

GoI, The Empowered Committee of State Finance Ministers. (2009a). *First Discussion Paper on Goods and Services Tax in India*. (Chairperson: Asim Kumar Dasgupta).

GoI. (2009b). *Task Force of the Thirteenth Finance Commission Report*.

GoI, Ministry of Finance, Department of Revenue, Central Board of Direct Taxes. (2012). *Black Money: White Paper*.

GoI, Ministry of Statistics and Programme Implementation. (2013). *Methodology for Estimating Quarterly GDP*. http://mospiold.nic.in/Mospi_New/upload/Methodology_doc_for_compilation_qrt_GDP_14aug13.pdf. Accessed 30 June 2017.

GoI, Ministry of Finance. (2015a). *GST—Concept and Status*.

GoI. (2015b). *Report on the Revenue Neutral Rate and Structure of Rates for the Goods and Services Tax (GST)*. (Chairperson: Arvind Subramanian).

GoI, Ministry of Human Resource Development. (2015c). *Annual Status of Education Report* (ASER). Various Years.

GoI, Ministry of Finance. (2016a). *Economic Survey 2015–16: Statistical Appendix*. New Delhi: Oxford University Press India.

GoI, Ministry of Home Affairs, National Crime Records Bureau. (2016b). *Prison Statistics India, 2015*.

GoI, Ministry of Finance, CBDT (2016c): 'Income Tax Department Time Series Data Financial Year 2000–01 to 2014–15.' http://www.incometaxindia.gov.in/Documents/Time-Series-Data-Final.pdf. Accessed 18 August 2016.

GoI, Ministry of Statistics and Programme Implementation, National Sample Survey Office. (2017a). *Key Indicators of Unincorporated Non-Agricultural Enterprises (Excluding Construction) in India. NSS 73rd Round.* July 2015 to June 2016.

GoI, Ministry of Statistics and Programme Implementation. 2017b. *National Account Statistics.* Various Issues.

GoI, Ministry of Finance, Department of Economic Affairs. (2018a). *Economic Survey 2017–18.*

GoI, CBEC. (2018b). *GST Concept Status.* https://cbec-gst.gov.in/pdf/01052018-GST-Concept-Status.pdf.Accessed 30 May 2018. Also at http://gstcouncil.gov.in/sites/default/files/GST-Concept-Status-01-04-2018.pdf. Accessed 20 July 2018.

GoI, CBEC. (2018c). 'GST E-way Bill. FAQ'. https://cbec-gst.gov.in/pdf/24032018-EwayBill-Faq.pdf. Accessed 3 June 2018.

Goyal, M.K. (2017). *GST Unlocked: Highlights, 2nd Edition.* Delhi: KLH Publishers and Distributors.

IANS. (2017a). 'No GST on "prasadam" but inputs will be taxed: Government'. *Economic Times.* 11 July. https://cfo.economictimes.indiatimes.com/news/no-gst-on-prasadam-but-inputs-will-be-taxed-government/59546316. Accessed 20 July 2018.

IANS. (2017b). 'Single Rate GST Is Not Possible in India, Says Arun Jaitley'. *Financial Express.* 30 November. https://www.financialexpress.com/economy/single-rate-gst-is-not-possible-in-india-says-arun-jaitley/954386/ . Accessed 20 July 2018.

IANS. (2017c). '35% of Businesses Registered in GST Pay No Tax: Arun Jaitley'. *Hindustan Times.* 14 December. https://www.hindustantimes.com/india-news/35-of-businesses-registered-in-gst-pay-no-tax-arun-jaitley/story-JqA2ogbvwValW5LuGopIvK.html. Accessed 18 October 2018.

IMF (2017a). 'World Revenue Longitudinal Data (World)'. http://data.imf.org/?sk=77413F1D-1525-450A-A23A-47AEED40FE78. Accessed 9 September 2018.

———. (2017b). *Government Finance Statistics Yearbook.* http://data.imf.org/?sk=20c2d27c-7969-47ac-91e9-098a70198db4 . Accessed 10 September 2018.

India Today. (2017). '17-year-long Wait Ends; Know from Where the GST Dream Started'. 30 June 2017. https://www.indiatoday.in/fyi/story/congress-gst-modi-congress-17-years-bjp-1021726-2017-06-30. Accessed 22 May 2018.

Kalecki, M. (1971). *Selected Essays on Dynamics of the Capitalist Economy.* Cambridge: Cambridge University Press.

Kasturi, C.S. (2008). 'Shifted Secretary Cries Corruption in UGC'. *Telegraph.* 24 April. https://www.telegraphindia.com/1080424/jsp/nation/story_9180604.jsp. Accessed July 2018.

Kelly, M. and D. D'Souza (Ed.). 2010. *The World Bank in India: Undermining Sovereignty, Distorting Development.* N. Delhi: Orient BlackSwan.

Keynes, J.M. (1936). *The General Theory of Employment, Interest and Money.* (1976 Edition London: Macmillan Press for Royal Economic Society).

Kumar, A. (1985a). 'The Chequered Economy in Black & White' (Review of *The Black Economy in India* by K.N. Kabra). *Economic and Political Weekly.* 30 March.

———. (1985b). 'Sizing up the Black Economy: A Critique of the NIPFP Methodology'. *Economic and Political Weekly.* 31 August.

———. (1985c). 'The Black Economy Report: A Critical Review'. (Review of Aspects of Black Economy in India by Acharya, S.N. & Associates). *Social Scientist.* September.

———. (1986). 'Budget 1986–87: Signs of Growth Pains Without Growth'. *Economic and Political Weekly.* 20 April.

———. (1988). 'Budget 1988–89: Diminishing Returns of Unchanged Fiscal Policy Regime'. *Economic and Political Weekly.* April 2–9.

———. (1991). 'Structural Adjustment Policies: Loss of Sovereignty and Alternatives'. *Lokayan Bulletin.* November–December. 9:6. Pp. 5–23.

———. (1994). 'Proposals for a Citizens Union Budget for the Nation for 1994–95. An Alternative to the FundBank Dictated Union Budget for 1994–95. Presented to the Citizens' Committee on February 12, 1994 at Gandhi Peace Foundation', New Delhi. Prepared for the Preparatory Committee for Alternative Economic Policies.

———. (1995). 'Reinterpreting Retreat of State in Second Best Environment'. *Economic and Political Weekly.* 6–13 May. Pp. 1050–1065.

———. (1999a). 'The Black Economy: Missing Dimension of Macro PolicyMaking in India'. *Economic and Political Weekly.* 20 March. pp. 681–694.

———. (1999b). *The Black Economy in India.* N. Delhi: Penguin (India).

———. (2000a). 'India at the Seattle Meeting: Playing Safe'. *Economic and Political Weekly.* 15 January. Pp. 89–93.

————. (2000b). 'Impact of Globalization'. In Alternative Survey Group (Ed.). *Alternative Economic Survey 1998-2000: Two Years of Market Fundamentalism*. N. Delhi: Rainbow Publishers Limited, Lokayan and Azadi Bachao Andolan.

————. (2002a). 'Globalization of the Indian Economy: Some Current Issues Pertaining to the Health Sector'. Mimeo. Paper presented at a Seminar on AIDS organized by CSMCH, JNU.

————. (2002b). 'Factors Underlying the Economic Slowdown: Growing Disparities, Globalization and the Black Economy'. In the Alternative Economic Survey 2001–02. New Delhi: Rainbow Publishers Limited, Lokayan and Azadi Bachao Andolan.

————. (2004). 'Globalization and India's Food Security: Issues and Challenges'. *Bhartiya Samajik Chintan*. Volume II. No. 4. January.

————. (2005a). 'Factors Underlying Jobless Growth in India and the Need for a New Development Paradigm'. Bhartiya Samajik Chintan. January–March 2005. Vol. III, No. 4 Pp. 215–229.

————. (2005b). 'The Issues Involved in Implementing VAT in India'. Bhartiya Samajik Chintan. Vol. IV. No. 1. April–June.

————. (2005c). 'India's Black Economy: The Macroeconomic Implications'. *South Asia: Journal of South Asian Studies*. Vol. 28, No. 2. August. Pp. 249–263.

————. (2006a). 'Black Economy, Under Estimation of Employment and the Union Budget'. *Economic and Political Weekly*. 29 July 2006. Vol. XLI No 30. Pp. 3315–20.

————. (2006b). 'The Flawed Macro Statistics: Overestimated Growth and Underestimated Inflation'. In *Alternative Economic Survey, 2005–06*. N. Delhi: Daanish Publishers.

————. (2013). *Indian Economy since Independence: Persisting Colonial Disruption*. N. Delhi: Vision Books.

————. (2015). 'Macroeconomic Aspects of Introduction of GST in India'. *Economic and Political Weekly*. 18 July 2015. Vol. L, No 29. Pp. 26–30.

————. (2016a). 'Curbing the Black Economy: Good Intentions Will Not Suffice'. *Economic and Political Weekly*. 3 September. Vol. No. 36.

————. (2016b). 'Estimation of the Size of the Black Economy in India, 1996–2012'. *Economic and Political Weekly*. 27 November. Vol. 51, No. 48. Pp. 36–42.

————. (2017a). *Understanding Black Economy and Black Money in India: An Enquiry into Causes, Consequences and Remedies*. N. Delhi: Aleph.

———. (2017b) 'Unusual Times, Usual Ways: Methods to Use GDP Estimates Cannot Account for the Shock Caused by Demonetisation'. *Indian Express*. 9 March.

———. (2017c). 'With the Post-GST Trend of Rising Prices, Has the Government Taken the Public for a Ride?'. Wire. 20 September. https://thewire.in/179281/gst-and-price-rise-public-taken-for-a-ride/.

———. (2017d). *Demonetization and Black Economy*. Gurugram: Penguin (India).

———. (2018a). 'Job Growth or Number Jugglery'. *Indian Express*. 16 May.

———. (2018b). 'As We Debate GST Collections, Is the New Tax Regime Curbing India's Black Economy?'. 16 August. https://thewire.in/economy/gst-revenue-collections-tax-regime-black-economy. Accessed 17 August 2018.

Kumar, A.S. Chattopadhyay and S. Dharan. (2007). 'Fiscal Policy'. In Alternative Survey Group (Ed.). *Alternative Economic Survey, India, 2006–07: Pampering Corporates, Pauperizing Masses*. New Delhi: DAANISH.

Langa, M. (2017). 'Note Ban, GST Ruined the Nation, Alleges Rahul'. *The Hindu*. 24 October. https://www.thehindu.com/news/national/gst-is-gabbar-singh-tax-says-rahul-gandhi/article19907042.ece. Accessed 8 August 2018.

Lewis, A. (1954). 'Economic Development with Unlimited Supplies of Labour'. *Manchester School*. XXII, May 1954. Pp. 139–91.

Little, I.M.D. (1951). Direct vs. Indirect Taxes. *Economic Journal*. September.

Malay Mail. (2018). 'Market Survey Shows Spending Up as Prices Fell after GST Rollback, Says Minister'. 7 July 2018. https://www.malaymail.com/s/1649829/market-survey-shows-spending-up-as-prices-fell-after-gst-rollback-minister . Accessed 12 October 2018.

Malaysian Customs Department. http://gst.customs.gov.my/en/gst/Pages/gst_ci.aspx.

Mukul, A. (2009). 'CBI Raids on UGC Official over Corruption'. *Times of India*. 5 November. https://timesofindia.indiatimes.com/india/CBI-raids-on-UGC-official-over-corruption/articleshow/5198163.cms. Accessed July 2018.

Musgrave, R.A. and P.B. Musgrave. (1976). *Public Finance in Theory and Practice*. 2nd Edition. New York: McGraw.

NCAER. (2009). 'Moving to Goods and Services Tax in India: Impact on India's Growth and International Trade'. Report for the Thirteenth Finance Commission. Mimeo.

NIPFP. (1985). *Aspects of Black Economy in India*. N. Delhi: NIPFP.

OECD (2015). 'Government at a Glance—2015 Edition: Public Employment'. OECD. Stat. https://stats.oecd.org/Index.aspx? QueryId=66856 Accessed 18 October 2018.

Palan, R., R. Murphy and C. Chavagneux. (2011). *Tax Havens: How Globalization Really Works*. Ithaca and London: Cornell University.

Pampapathi, V.G. (2018). 'GST Notification & Circulars'. Updated as on 31 May 2018. https://www.scribd.com/document/378531597/GST-Notification-Summary. Accessed 10 July 2018.

Panta, K.R. (2015). 'Fiscal Decentralization, Public Service Delivery and Poverty: A Case Study of Nepal'. Mimeo. PhD dissertation submitted to JNU.

Pawlowski, A. (2018). 'Feeling Lonely? How to Stop Social Media from Making You Feel Isolated'. *Today*. 23 April. https://www.today. com/health/how-stop-feeling-lonely-social-media-can-worsen-loneliness-t127466. Accessed 8 August 2018.

PTI. (2010). 'MCI President Ketan Desai Resigns from Post'. *The Hindu*. 13 May. https://www.thehindu.com/news/national/mci-president-ketan-desai-resigns-from-post/article16300457.ece# Accessed July 2018.

Purohit, M.C. (1986). 'National Issues in State's Sales Tax Structure in India'. *Economic and Political Weekly*. 15 February.

———. (1999). *Value Added Tax*. N. Delhi: Gayatri Publications.

Rajya Sabha. 'Unstarred Question 833'. (2014). *Employed Persons in the Country*. 16 July. Ministry of Labour and Employment.

Rastogi, A. (2018). 'E-way bill: All You Need to Know and Experiences of the First Month'. *Economic Times*. 9 May. https://economictimes. indiatimes.com/markets/stocks/news/e-way-bill-all-you-need-to-know-experiences-of-the-first-month/articleshow/64090769.cms. Accessed 3 June 2018.

Ram, N. (2017). *Why Scams Are Here to Stay: Understanding Political Corruption in India*. New Delhi: Aleph.

RBI. (2017). *Quarterly Order Books, Inventories and Capacity Utilisation Survey OBICUS. Various Rounds*. https://www.rbi.org.in/scripts/ QuarterlyPublications.aspx?head=Quarterly%20Order%20Books,%20 Inventories%20and%20Capacity%20Utilisation%20Survey.

Samuelson, P.A. and Crowley, K. (1986). *Collected Scientific Papers of Paul A. Samuelson, Vol. 5*. Cambridge, M.A.: MIT Press.

Singh, M.K. (2018). 'Over 2.8 Crore People Apply for 90,000 Railways Jobs'. *Times of India*. 31 March. https://timesofindia.indiatimes.com/india/

over-2-8-crore-apply-for-90000-railways-jobs/articleshow/63551672. cms. Accessed 19 October 2018.

Singh, S. (2006). 'Revenue Implications of Introduction of VAT in India'. Unpublished MPhil Dissertation Submitted to CESP, SSS, JNU.

Srivastava, S. (2017). 'GSTN to Handle 3.5 Billion Transactions a Month: Chairman Navin Kumar'. *Livemint*. 27 April. https://www.livemint. com/Industry/R5pCrzfCfBzy4mcXMBkInM/GSTN-to-handle-35-billion-transactions-a-month-Chairman-Na.html. Accessed 13 October 2018.

Supreme Court Judgement (1973). *Kesavananda Bharati Sripadagalvaru and Ors versus State of Kerala and Anr, Writ Petition (civil) 135 of 1970*. https://www.sci.gov.in/jonew/judis/29981.pdf

Tax Haven Team. (2014). *Tax Haven, Havala and Swiss Banking*. N. Delhi: CESP, SSS, JNU. Available at, http://www.issin.org/pdf/swissbanking.pdf.

Thakurta, P.G. (2009). 'A Kingly Fiddle'. *Caravan*. 16–30 June.

The Economist. (1992). 'Let Them Eat Pollution. (Excerpt from letter written by chief economist of World Bank)'. *The Economist*. No. 7745. 8 February.

The Hindu Businessline. (2017). 'GSTs 17 year time line'. https:// www.thehindubusinessline.com/economy/gsts-17year-timeline/ article9743284.ece. Accessed 4 April 2018.

The Wire Staff. CMIE. (2017). '1.5 Million Jobs Lost During First Four Months of 2017, Says CMIE'. The Wire. 13 July. https://thewire.in/ business/1-5-million-jobs-lost-2017-demonetisation. Accessed 8 August 2018.

Tresch, R.W. (1981). *Public Finance: A Normative Theory*. Texas: Business Publications. 2nd edition 2002.

Vaishnav, M. (2017). *When Crime Pays: Money and Muscle in Indian Politics*. Noida, India: Harper Collins Publisher.

Vyas, M. (2018). 'Improving Employment Data: Task Force Suggestion Will Take Years to Execute'. *Business Standard*. 23 January. https:// www.business-standard.com/article/opinion/payrolls-database-ahoy-118012200627_1.html. Accessed 8 August 2018.

Williamson, J. (1989). 'What Washington Means by Policy Reform'. In Williamson, J. (Ed.). *Latin American Readjustment: How Much has Happened?*. Washington: Institute for International Economics.

INDEX